Praise for *The Lynching*

"America's unaddressed history of lynching [...] has left this nation vulnerable [...] devastating than what is docu[...] We ignore Laurence Leamer's [...] —Bryan Stevenson, author of the [...]

"Leamer does a truly remarkable job of humanizing Donald and his family, and of depicting the Mobile of the era. . . . The author welds it all into lean, clear storytelling. Leamer cuts straight to the heart of Mobile's unique racial history." —*Alabama Today*

"Morris Dees walks tall in American history. For decades, he has fearlessly demolished white supremacist hate groups with his legal cunning. Laurence Leamer does a wonderful job in *The Lynching* describing how Dees put the KKK out of business. This legal thriller is destined to become a major motion picture. Highly recommended."

—Douglas Brinkley, author of *The Great Deluge*

"Today, the Klan still exists. *The Lynching* reminds us why that matters." —*BookPage*

"Leamer's compelling and unsparing portraits of all the historical actors in this drama—Dees included—create a narrative as powerful as any novelist could imagine."

—Dan T. Carter, author of *The Politics of Rage*

"Former journalist and *New York Times* bestselling author Laurence Leamer brilliantly illustrates not only the cruel murder of a young black man and the aftermath, but also the circumstances in Alabama that led to the death." —*The Trial Lawyer* magazine

"Powerful. . . . Engrossing . . . and a pertinent reminder of the consequences of organized hatred." —*Kirkus Reviews*

The Lynching

Also by Laurence Leamer

The Paper Revolutionaries: The Rise of the Underground Press

Playing for Keeps in Washington

Assignment

Ascent: The Spiritual and Physical Quest of Willi Unsoeld

Make-Believe: The Story of Nancy and Ronald Reagan

As Time Goes By: The Life of Ingrid Bergman

King of the Night: The Life of Johnny Carson

The Kennedy Women: The Saga of an American Family

Three Chords and the Truth: Hope, Heartbreak, and Changing Fortunes in Nashville

The Kennedy Men: 1901–1963

Sons of Camelot: The Fate of an American Dynasty

Fantastic: The Life of Arnold Schwarzenegger

Madness Under the Royal Palms: Love and Death Behind the Gates of Palm Beach

The Price of Justice: A True Story of Corruption and Greed in Coal Country

The Lynching

The Epic Courtroom Battle That
Brought Down the Klan

Laurence Leamer

WILLIAM MORROW
An Imprint of HarperCollins*Publishers*

Dedicated to the memory of Julian Bond (1940–2015)

HarperCollins books may be purchased for educational, business, or sales promotional use. For information please e-mail the Special Markets Department at SPsales@harpercollins.com.

A hardcover edition of this book was published in 2016 by William Morrow, an imprint of HarperCollins Publishers.

FIRST WILLIAM MORROW PAPERBACK EDITION PUBLISHED 2017.

Designed by William Ruoto

Library of Congress Cataloging-in-Publication Data has been applied for.

ISBN 978-0-06-245836-0

HB 10.05.2020

Contents

PART TWO | A TIME OF JUDGMENT

PART THREE | ROLL CALL OF JUSTICE

Prologue: Fists Against the Earth

EARLY SATURDAY MORNING on March 21, 1981, a young woman was out riding her bicycle with her dog along Herndon Avenue in Mobile, Alabama, a modest residential street no more than three hundred yards long. It was the first day of spring, and in the predawn light, the woman saw what she assumed was a dummy hanging from a camphor tree and continued down the road. A few minutes later, an elderly man went out to buy the morning paper and saw what he figured was a black man breaking into a house. Once he got back to his own home, he called the police. Other passersby saw what they thought was a man strung up by a noose, his feet barely off the ground, and they too phoned the police.

When the officers arrived there shortly after dawn, they found the body of a black man hanging from a tree. They cordoned off the vacant lot at 112 Herndon Avenue but left the body there and waited for the coroner to do the job of taking it down and removing it. When one black person heard about the murder, he called a friend, and that person called someone else, and soon scores of black spectators arrived.

There had not been a lynching in America in a quarter century, and no one standing looking at the body had ever seen such a crime, but they had heard about it from family members and read about it in social science books in school. And they believed they knew what had occurred. White men had lynched a black man, and they had done it to send a message of intimidation and terror. This was something they thought would never happen again, and many of the black onlookers wept, others fell to the ground beating their fists against the earth.

PART ONE

Night of the Burning Cross

Klan Business

AT THE WEEKLY meeting of Klavern 900 of the United Klans of America (UKA) in Theodore, Alabama, on March 18, 1981, Bennie Jack Hays stood before the dozen Klansmen and raged against the rise of black people. Bennie was the Great Titan, the highest-ranking officer of the UKA in the southern half of Alabama. The bespectacled, white-haired sixty-four-year-old might have spent his last years rocking his grandchildren on the porch, but he had risen quickly in the Klan despite being Catholic in an overwhelmingly Protestant organization that had once considered Catholics no better than infidels.

The Klan leader lived in a house on seven acres in Theodore, which was fifteen miles southwest of Mobile. Theodore was a poor white man's redoubt, small homes and trailers spread out among the jungle-like foliage. It was as close to paradise as Bennie was likely to get, especially because he had a cabin for Klan meetings on his property.

The Klansmen attending the evening assembly sat in several rows of chairs. An altar-like shrine stood in the front of the room. There set a candle, a container of water, an open Bible, and an American flag with a cross laid across it. A Confederate flag stood in the corner.

"Your Excellency, the Sacred Altar of the Klan is prepared, the Fiery Cross illumines the Klavern," said Thaddeus "Red" Betancourt, the Klokard or teacher, pointing to the lit candle.

"Klansmen, what means the Fiery Cross?" asked Bennie's son-in-law Frank Cox, the Exalted Cyclops or Klavern president.

"We serve and sacrifice for the right," said all the Klansmen.

No one in the Klavern spoke the sacred language with more passion than did Teddy Lamar Kyzar. He was a plump, expressionless young man with an enormous head and pink, baby-like skin. Kyzar stood just barely over five feet and looked like a boy among grown men. A few years before, a group of black men had stolen Kyzar's watch. From then on, he had hated the whole race, and the Klan gave him the chance to strike back.

Some of his fellow Klansmen dismissed Kyzar because of his height, but that just compelled him to do almost anything to be accepted as their equal. He placed himself at the head of the line volunteering for what the UKA called "missionary work," and his favorite involved beating up black men.

When the Klansmen had their victim bloodied, bruised, and spread-eagled on the ground, the last thing they did before walking away was to tell the man straight-out: "The cops are Klan, and you go to the cops, and we'll come back and kill you."

Kyzar lived in Mobile on Herndon Avenue in one of the four houses Bennie owned and had broken up into apartments. A few weeks earlier, the Klan leader had come to the street and thundered about whites watching black Mardi Gras parades.

For the next black parade, Bennie commanded that Kyzar and some other Klavern members slash tires all around the area and ordered that the tires be cut on the sides so they could not be patched and that at least two tires of each car be punctured. The Klansmen waited until the sounds of music and cheers wafted out across the streets and then started slashing and puncturing away. Kyzar bragged that he had damaged tires on sixty-five cars in one parking lot alone.

That had been a great day for Kyzar, but since then, he had gotten in trouble. He had taken a recruit's application money and spent it at a bar. The Klavern could have decided he was not proper Klan material and thrown him out. But he was liked by a number of Klan members, and the group decided instead that they would whip him.

Kyzar shuffled to the front of the room. If he had walked out of the meeting, no one would have stopped him, but these were his friends and he was part of what he considered a marvelous kinship, and he knew he had to take his punishment.

Per protocol, the sacred items were taken off the altar, and Kyzar knelt down with his hands on the wooden surface. After a few words justifying and ennobling what was about to take place, the Exalted Cyclops hit him with a leather belt. Kyzar tried not to flinch or to show any pain, but he was close to crying. After the Exalted Cyclops struck him the last of the required fifty lashes, Kyzar limped back to his seat.

The men deferred to Bennie not only because he was the Great Titan, but also because they saw him as a man of a substance far beyond theirs. Bennie also had all kinds of properties and business interests to which they could hardly dare aspire.

He was born Herman Otto Houston in rural Missouri in 1916. His own father was a drunk, and for a time, the family was so poor they lived in a tent on the riverbank. At age sixteen, the illiterate teenager left home for good.

Bennie loved to spin tales of how he had ridden the outlaw roads with the infamous Bonnie Parker and Clyde Barrow of criminal legend. It seemed an unlikely story, but Bennie had such vivid details that his family thought it was probably true. He talked too about what it was like jumping into some of the worst hellholes on the European front as a paratrooper in World War II. After the war, he was twice sent to prison, once for cattle rustling and then for check forging. In 1952, he saddled a horse and fled from the prison farm.

The escaped convict was able to build a new life for himself with a new name, Bennie Jack Hays. By the time the police tracked him down, he was married to Opal Grace Frazier and had two young sons, Raymond and Henry. While he served out his remaining time in prison, Opal picked cotton and had a daughter, Gail, by another man.

When Bennie was released, he moved with his wife and

three children to Charleston, South Carolina. He worked tearing up old rail tracks from Texas to New York and was gone weeks at a time. That wasn't getting him anywhere, and one day in 1969, he put the family's meager belongings in a car and drove to Mobile for a new start.

He got together enough money to put a down payment on a Texaco gas station and later on another gas station and a house on Herndon Avenue and then several other rental houses along the block-long street. Forever a country boy, he moved the family out to Theodore once he had enough money from his growing businesses.

When Bennie's three children were young, he struck them so hard with his belt it was as if he thought he could beat righteousness into them. Sometimes Bennie's wrath grew to the point where he could not control it. When Opal saw him get that familiar look of glazed intensity, she stayed away from him. There was no telling what he would do, how he would strike out, and whom he would hurt. And then the fury would be gone, as suddenly and inexplicably as it began.

No one was more afraid of Bennie than his youngest son, Henry, and no one did more to upset the old man. His father even nicknamed him "half-assed Henry." The scrawny, five-foot-eight-inch teenager had earned that title for among other things being caught in a hotel with two underage girls, and for having one grunt-level job after another, including parking cars in downtown Mobile with a bunch of black men.

In his late teens, Henry served in the U.S. Army, and once when he came home on leave, he owed his father some money. When the son didn't pay, Bennie started chasing him around the yard with a hammer, threatening that he was going to kill him. A police siren sounded in the distance, and Bennie charged into the kitchen where his daughter-in-law Denise Hays was standing, holding her nine-month-old in her arms.

"You called the cops!" Bennie screamed, and reached to punch Denise in the face with his fist.

"No, I did," said his fourteen-year-old daughter, Gail, lying to protect Denise.

He loved his adopted daughter more than anyone else in the family, but he knocked her to the ground and was kicking her when the police entered the kitchen and stopped him. His friends in the police force protected him from punishment, but Henry was terrified. He left that day and did not come back for several years.

When Henry was thrown out of the army after he was caught in the barracks with an officer's daughter, he returned to Mobile. He was pulled toward his father, who controlled all their lives, dominating them, pushing them where he wanted them to go.

Henry's older brother, Raymond, had been married to Denise from 1972 to 1975, and the couple had two children. Bennie asked Henry to marry his brother's ex-wife to keep his grandchildren close and so Raymond could avoid paying alimony. Those were pathetic reasons to marry, but to please his father, Henry went along.

There may have been another reason Bennie wanted to keep Denise close to him. She claimed that her father-in-law struck her when she refused to sleep with him. "We used to get in run-ins with him all the time, mostly because I wouldn't go to bed with him," Denise said.

Bennie felt his biggest problem was trying to help his youngest son shape up. At one point, Bennie told Henry he would find him a job in construction. He would even give him a free apartment in one of the houses he owned on Herndon Avenue in exchange for collecting rents and watching over his interests. All Henry had to do was to join his father in the Klan.

Bennie hoped the Klan would give Henry discipline and purpose. "You've got to join the Klan," Bennie told his youngest son. "You've got to be respectable." On the cold day in November 1977 when Henry was initiated, he felt like an "altar boy" as the black-hooded Nighthawk led Henry and five other recruits into the ceremony.

Henry believed that joining the Klan would bring him closer to his father, something he had sought all his life. And he would be somebody. Bennie even made Henry the Exalted Cyclops, the highest position in Klavern 900, but when he did not handle the position well, Bennie gave the honor to Gail's husband, Frank Cox, and made Henry the Kligrapp, or secretary.

Even when Henry was a grown man, Bennie kept trying to teach his youngest son how he thought he should behave. Bennie had a white German shepherd named White Hope who kept trying to dig a hole under the fence that kept him in the yard. One day Bennie told his son to get the dog and hold it tightly. Then he took a knife and cut off the toes on White Hope's front paws before dipping the bloody stumps in hot tar. That's how the dog learned its lesson. Bennie felt Henry couldn't face it. He was a grown man, but he ran in the house crying.

Bennie thought more highly of Frank Cox than he did of his own son. Cox was a brawny, self-confident young man who appeared unlikely to spend his whole life working as a truck driver. He was wildly in love with his young wife, Gail, and joined the Klan primarily to ingratiate himself with his father-in-law. He and his wife had gone off to North Carolina where they had a happy life. But they had returned. Frank was willing to go far to please his father-in-law. That was something almost no outsider understood: the almost hypnotic power this rude man had over those who came within his shadow.

Bennie's favorite Klansman was James "Tiger" Knowles, a seventeen-year-old with a take-charge manner that made him seem half a dozen years older. The husky, five-foot-eleven-inch-tall teenager was nicknamed "Tiger" because he weighed a whopping thirteen pounds when he was born. When Tiger was in the ninth grade, the Feds charged his father, a Klansman, with tax evasion, and he lost his construction company. Tiger dropped out of school for good and made good money as a plumber. For a while he ran a small business renovating kitchens and laying tile while overseeing half a dozen or so employees, including Henry.

In 1978, Knowles attended the annual UKA Klanvocation with his parents. At the convention, the teenager was given the first Klan youth charter in the state. At sixteen, Knowles took the oath to become a full-fledged adult member of the UKA. A few months later, Imperial Wizard Robert Marvin Shelton named the teenager Klaliff, which put him in charge of "military activities" in the southern half of Alabama and made him one of the top Klansmen in the entire state. Although Knowles was a member of the Klavern in Grand Bay, fifteen miles away, he frequently attended the Theodore Klavern.

Often Knowles drove with Bennie to the UKA national headquarters, a 7,200-square-foot building in Northport, outside Tuscaloosa, for Imperial Wizard Shelton's monthly meeting with the leaders of the Alabama Klaverns. The teenager believed that one day he would wear the resplendent robes of the Imperial Wizard, the greatest Klansman in America.

Knowles despised anyone who seemed weird to him. Once, he and another Klavern member, Johnny Matthew Jones, were driving in Knowles's truck when they spotted a long-haired hitchhiker. They picked him up, cut off his hair with their pocketknives, and left him on the side of the road.

On the night before the weekly Klavern meeting on March 17, 1981, Henry and Knowles had gone out for a little missionary work of their own. The Klan had no more use for homosexuals than it did for black and Jewish Americans. The two young Klansmen convinced a gay man to go off in their car to a nightclub. Instead they put a knife to his neck and drove him out the causeway into the wilderness. There they made him strip, and while they debated what to do with him, he ran off into the woods, and the two friends sped off in Henry's Buick Wildcat sedan. In the atavistic excitement of the moment, they might have killed him if he had not gotten away.

A Public Display

NEAR THE END of the March 18 Klavern meeting in Bennie's run-down, tin-roofed cabin, Red Betancourt walked in front of the dozen Klavern members and stood before the altar. He was a genial, accommodating man who had joined the Klavern after a group of four Klansmen showed up at his house in Mobile one night. One of the men was his next-door neighbor; he said Betancourt was beating his children far beyond necessity. Betancourt convinced them that was not true. And in the course of this exchange, the men impressed him, and he asked to join the Klan.

Betancourt had served time for burglary, and he, like so many others, had found in the Klan a purpose and kinship he hadn't found anywhere else. He had no special animus toward black people. His father had worked in the Mobile shipyards as a skilled laborer, earning enough money so the family had a full-time black maid paid five dollars a week. Almost everyone in the Betancourts' apartment complex had a black maid and paid her the standard wage. This was one of the perks of being a white person of even modest means. When Red went with his family to downtown Mobile, they rarely saw a black person, and Betancourt grew up thinking of African Americans as a race of housemaids and servants who otherwise stayed out of view.

Betancourt yearned to be one of the trusted Klan insiders. He saw early on that you got there much faster through deeds than you did merely with words, and that led him to go out burning crosses and beating up black people. He believed that if he continued doing that and keeping his mouth shut, one day he probably would be privy to the Klan's most intimate secrets and plans.

One of Betancourt's official duties for Klan meetings was to bring in news articles or other important information. He took that job so seriously he even made a plywood-covered scrapbook in which he neatly placed relevant material. This evening he read a clipping about Josephus Anderson, a black man charged with killing Birmingham Police sergeant Gene Ballard during a bank robbery. The case had been so widely publicized and controversial that the trial had been moved down to Mobile, where it was being heard before a jury of eleven black citizens and one white.

The Klansmen were constantly warned that betrayers were everywhere and that a white man could not even speak his piece openly any longer. At these meetings rarely was any possible action discussed except in veiled terms. But the anger over the possibility that this bank robber might get away with murder because African American jurors would not convict him was so powerful that Bennie could not keep quiet, and he blurted out words that set off a torrent of threats from the other Klansmen.

"If a nigger can get away with killing a white man, a white man should be able to get away with killing a nigger," Bennie shouted out in a screeching, taunting voice, his words reverberating through the cabin.

"Ought to be a damn nigger hung, if this guy is found not guilty," said William A. O'Connor Jr., the Klokan, a Klan state officer.

"A nigger ought to be hung by the neck until dead to put them in their place," Henry Hays said.

"We're gonna kill ourselves a nigger," another Klansman shouted.

"One ain't enough," yelled out another man.

Most of the Klansmen had brought pistols to the meeting. In the old days, they might not have even waited for a verdict. They would have gone down to the jail, pulled Anderson out of there, and lynched him in front of the courthouse. Klan justice would have been done, and it would send a message that black men had better stay in their place.

After the meeting Bennie got together outside the Klan cabin with Knowles and Henry to talk about the accused killer from Birmingham and what they should do if he were acquitted. Nobody said anything directly. They spoke in half sentences, knowing nods, and mumbled assertions. At one point Bennie suggested that if the black bank robber got off, they should go out and kill a black man.

The two young Klansmen leaped at the idea and even spoke of leaving the body strung up on Herndon Avenue. "Well, we don't want to do anything until after Friday when I close the deal on the houses," said Bennie. He was selling a number of his properties on the street and did not want to risk the buyer backing out.

They could have planned to dump the body in the bay or deposit it out in the woods to be devoured by coyotes and vultures. But that would not do. It was important to leave the body hanging from a tree where people could see it.

Lynching had historically been the Klan's emblematic act. But there had not been a hanging since 1955; the end of the era of lynching and the birth of the civil rights movement had coincided. By resurrecting it, the Klansmen were attempting to bring back the old times when hooded night riders roamed the southern night, meting out what they called justice to frightened, intimidated black people.

The Klan's other strong symbol was the burning cross, and Bennie, Henry, and Knowles agreed that on the evening of the lynching, a fiery cross would illuminate the nighttime sky. They wanted black people to know that wherever they went, whatever they did, they too might feel a rope around their neck, and they should fear Klan justice.

Henry and Knowles were convinced that no overwhelmingly black jury would convict a man of their own race. And so when they departed the Klan meeting that evening, they believed that in a few days they would be killing a black man and leaving his body hanging from a tree on Herndon Avenue.

Herndon Avenue was an obscure little road, but it was known as a home of the Klan. Bennie had lived there with his family for years before moving out to the country. Henry and his family still lived on Herndon Avenue, as did other Klansmen including Kyzar.

Knowles thought it was a shrewd idea to leave the body on the Mobile street. He argued, "Would the Klan be so stupid to put the body right across the street from where they own property and live?"

Thirteen Knots

ON THAT FRIDAY evening, Knowles and Henry sat in Hays's apartment on Herndon Avenue with Henry's wife, Denise, and several of their friends. Bennie had closed escrow on his houses, and earlier in the evening the two best friends had driven out to Theodore with Cox and borrowed a rope from Cox's mother. Knowles had tied the thirteen knots of a hanging noose, and it looked almost professional when they placed it in Henry's trunk. Executioners use this special noose because when the condemned drops, the rope slides up around his neck, breaking it, and killing him instantly. They also borrowed a small-caliber pistol from another Klansman.

Knowles was a boastful youth, but he did not want to kill

anybody. He often bragged about what he would like to do to black people, but he never imagined it would come to this. Yet every time Knowles thought about refusing to go along, he came up with the same answer. When Bennie found out that Henry had done the job alone, Knowles's days as the bright young hope of the Klan would be over. The whole center of his life and most of his friends would be gone. Bennie would consider him a traitor to the cause, and Knowles's life might be in danger.

Henry's motivations were even stronger. As he saw it, he had done nothing of value in his life. Here was a chance to do something special that would set him apart. His father would accept and honor him. If Henry did not do what he was supposed to do this evening, he would stand exposed as the cowardly slacker his father took him to be.

At 10:00 P.M., Henry turned on the television to watch the local news.

"Josephus Anderson is accused of killing Policeman Albert Eugene Ballard on November 29, 1979, this while the officer sat in his police cruiser," said newscaster Mel Showers. "The twelve jurors couldn't reach agreement, according to the foreman. And Judge Joseph Hockerlander said he was forced to declare a mistrial. Josephus Anderson said he should have been declared not guilty."

"The goddamn nigger got off," Henry said.

"The niggers are going to be up all night over this," Knowles said.

That was the signal the two young men needed to leave the apartment and head out in Henry's decade-old Buick Wildcat, searching for a black man to lynch. Knowles and Henry did not seem like hateful men. They were two guys out on a Friday night to have a good time. Knowles was nine years younger than Henry, but in some respects, he was the leader. Knowles believed he could do what he wanted to do whenever he wanted to do it, and nobody could stop him. If he got caught, he could always talk his way out of trouble. That was yet another of his gifts. "I thought I was invincible," Knowles says. "I could pretty much do anything I wanted without any serious consequences. And I figured I could bullshit my way out of anything if I needed to."

In January, Henry had broken three fingers on his right hand when a cement mixer at work fell on him. He could still drive, but the hand wasn't of much use. Even though he had the grown-up responsibilities of a wife and three children at home, his family car told how little regard he had for the common niceties of life. It was a squalid mess full of crumpled cardboard drinking cups, a crushed beer can, a rag, paper towels, a transmission fluid bottle that might have been useful if it hadn't been empty, various auto belts, and a scattering of nuts and bolts.

As the two young men prowled through the black neighborhood, they were not looking for any black man in particular. Their victim could be young, old, fat, skinny, weak, strong. They didn't care. They weren't afraid. They had a gun. All that mattered was that he was the right color.

It was after 11:00 P.M., and they headed out to a foreboding area near the Mobile River, little but warehouses and industrial plants. It was not that easy finding someone walking these streets alone at this time of night. They slowed when they saw an old black man talking on a pay phone, but to get him they would have had to get out of the car, and they decided to pass.

It was easy for them to be blasé about killing a black man when they were tying the hanging knot or sitting in the living room on Herndon Avenue with family and friends, but Henry and Knowles were just as dispassionate as the moment drew near. They had beaten up black and gay men in the past, their actions escalating over time, and it seemed only natural for them to kill a black man to prove their Klan manhood.

They had been trolling for about twenty minutes when they saw five-foot-ten-inch-tall, lean Michael Donald walking along Davis Avenue. Pulling up beside him, Knowles leaned out the window from the backseat and asked Donald for directions to the Powell Social Club, a black nightclub. He figured most black residents of Mobile would have heard of it. Donald told them how to get there, but Knowles asked him to come closer. Then the Klansman pulled a gun and told the teenager to get in beside him in the backseat of the two-door car. Donald said nothing but got into the auto.

Henry drove the jet-black Buick over the causeway, taking the old truck route past a series of paper mills to the same stretch of scruffy trees and wilderness in Baldwin County where they had taken a gay man three nights earlier. The area stretched on seemingly forever and was full of dirt roads and waterways.

"Empty your pockets," Knowles ordered, worried that their victim might have a gun or a knife.

All Donald had in his pockets was a wallet that he pulled out, and Knowles took and placed on the floorboard.

"Oh, God, I can't believe this is happening," said Donald.

"You know all about those little nigger kids that's been getting killed up in Atlanta?" Henry said referring to the wave of child kidnapping occurring in the Georgia capital. "Well, a lot of people think the Klan is behind it. But we are not. You know, the same thing could happen to you."

"No, please don't kill me," Donald begged. "You know you can do whatever you want to, beat me or anything else. But just don't kill me."

"Nah, you're not gonna be killed," Henry said, seeking to calm him down. "How old are you?"

"Nineteen."

When they reached the secluded, wooded destination adjacent to a garbage dump, Henry stopped the car, got out, and stood in the clearing. Knowles pointed his pistol at Donald and ordered him out of the car. A brilliant full moon spotlighted the scene.

"Please don't kill me," Donald pleaded, shaking his head. "Let me go."

"Calm down," Knowles said. "Nothin' gonna happen to you."

At that instant, Donald threw himself upon Knowles, knocking them both to the ground. In the scuffle, Knowles's gun went off in the air and skittered away.

Donald yanked Knowles's silver St. Christopher's medal from around his neck.

"I'll kill you for that," Knowles shouted.

Henry joined in the melee immediately. He had a razor knife he used when he worked laying linoleum. In the fight, it fell to the earth, and he and Donald grappled for the weapon. The two Klansmen pried Donald's fingers off the knife and with their fists beat him until he could fight no more and lay there looking to them like a beaten animal.

They were relieved they had finally gotten the best of this enraged black man, and that he lay there vulnerable to whatever they chose to do to him. Then, out of a strength and resolution that seemed superhuman, Donald rose up, grabbed a tree limb, and started flailing away at his tormenters.

Henry and Knowles had been brought up thinking that African Americans were a timid, superstitious lot who were terrified half to death of men riding through the night wearing white robes. It was unthinkable that this lean, black youth could stand yet again to confront them. Henry and Knowles were frightened by his tenacity, but they managed to take the limb from Donald and used it to hammer him to the ground.

Henry went to the trunk of his car and took out the rope tied with a hangman's noose. While Knowles pressed Donald's arms to his side, Henry placed the rope around his neck. Henry put his foot on Donald's head, leaving its imprint on his face. It was a gesture savage in its malevolence. Then Henry started pulling the rope as tightly as he could, hoping to snuff out Donald's life in an instant. But yet again Donald rose to his knees and then to his feet.

This was beyond maddening. Their victim was rising up again and again to haunt them, and no matter what they did, they couldn't keep him down. Knowles grabbed a tree limb and struck Donald with all his might while Henry kept pulling at the rope. And still Michael Donald did not fall.

Finally, Henry and Knowles began working together, saying nothing, the only sound their hurried, anxious breathing. With only one good hand, Henry had difficulty pulling hard enough on the rope so that Michael would stop breathing. After a while Knowles took over and, with both hands grasping the rope, pulled while Henry took on the easier task of trying to beat Donald to death with the branch. Eventually the young black man fell limp to the ground.

Henry kept on pounding on Donald's head and chest with the limb. Knowles's years in construction work had made him unusually strong. He drew the rope so tight that he broke a bone in Donald's neck and cut through the skin, causing him to bleed before finally strangling him to death.

"Do you think he's dead?" Knowles asked as they dragged the body over to the Buick and loaded it into the trunk. To make sure, one of the two killers took the razor knife and slit Michael Donald's throat the way you would slaughter a chicken.

"Good Job, Tiger"

BEFORE THEY LEFT the murder scene, Henry and Knowles brushed the dirt off each other and covered over the Buick's tracks. Henry was so overwrought that Knowles was worried his partner might drive the car off the causeway or weave so erratically the cops would stop them. So Knowles drove back to town as Henry sat beside him.

Back on Herndon Avenue, Knowles parked the car behind

some bushes. Henry grabbed the noose and hauled the body out of the trunk while Knowles hoisted it by the feet. The two men set the body on the ground waiting until there were no cars taking the shortcut along Herndon Avenue. Then they carried it across the street, where they planned to hang it from a tree in a vacant lot between two houses.

Henry and Knowles knew the body had to hang high up so everyone could see it, and they were disappointed that the vacant lot didn't have a tree with a branch high enough to hang the body properly. The best they could come up with was a camphor tree with a thick trunk that didn't have even one appropriate branch. But that would have to do, and they couldn't dally either. They didn't want to be there and have a car catch them in its headlights. So they improvised hurriedly strapping the body to the tree with the rope sagging and Donald's feet barely off the ground. It didn't look the way it was supposed to look, and this was the evening's first disappointing moment.

They had no time to fiddle around any longer and walked back across the street and sat on the porch at 115 Herndon Avenue no more than twenty-five yards away. With the full moon, they could see the outline of the body.

Henry's apartment was at 117 Herndon Avenue, and when they got there, a card game and party was going on full blast including Henry's wife Denise, Klansmen Kyzar and Cox, and several neighbors. People were drinking beer. Kyzar knew something was going on when he saw Knowles coming into the living room. Kyzar jumped up and pushed Knowles out into the hallway.

"I don't know what you've been doing, but your shirt is soaked in blood," said Kyzar.

Knowles looked down at his denim shirt. He had not even realized he was drenched in blood, from the cuffs of his long-sleeved shirt to his chest and stomach.

"Had a nosebleed," Knowles said.

Out in the hallway, he ripped off the shirt so quickly the buttons popped off. Then Bennie's son-in-law, Frank Cox, said he had an extra shirt in his car, and they left to get it.

"What was y'all doin' to have blood on your clothes?" Kyzar asked with annoying persistence.

"We beat up a faggot," Knowles said matter-of-factly.

"Next thing y'all do, I want in on it," Kyzar said.

Knowles, Cox, and Kyzar walked over to the carport to Cox's truck, which had a three-foot-tall cross wrapped with rags inside. The crosses that Klansmen usually lit were often twenty-five feet tall; by comparison, this one was almost pathetic. Cox told Kyzar to put it in the back of his vehicle, where Knowles also placed a gallon of diesel fuel.

Cox got in the driver's seat, and Kyzar entered the passenger's side. Cox drove downtown, and after riding around the Mobile County Courthouse three times, he stopped beside the building.

"That's where I want it," Cox said, pointing to a spot on the lawn.

Kyzar got out and, carrying both the cross and the fuel, trudged up the lawn where he poured fuel over the cross. Then he pushed the cross into the grass as best he could, set the rags on fire, and hurried back to the truck, carrying the fuel can.

Cox drove out over the causeway into the countryside to a Waffle House where he was supposed to call Henry to tell him the job was done. But neither Cox nor Kyzar had even a dime for the pay phone, so they drove back into Mobile, past the courthouse. The cross was still blazing, and police and firefighters had surrounded the building.

When Cox and Kyzar arrived back at Henry's apartment, they joined their fellow Klansmen on the porch. "Good job, Tiger," Kyzar said, punching Knowles gently in the side. Knowles found it unsettling that Kyzar had already figured out what had happened.

A little later, Henry called his father and said, "There's a nigger hanging across the street." Then he phoned the newsroom at WKRG-TV, a local TV station, and WUNI, a country music radio station, and without giving his name told them a body was hanging on Herndon Avenue.

A Precious Enclave

MICHAEL DONALD'S BODY was still hanging from a tree when State Senator Michael Anthony Figures arrived on Herndon Avenue. A crowd stood across the street whispering anxiously about the horror. Most of them were black, and as their numbers kept growing, the Mobile police had blocked off the street and put up barriers to keep them back from the murder scene. The African Americans believed they were witnessing the archetypal crime against the black man. The assembly kept growing as people brought their children and their grandparents.

Figures knew there hadn't been a racial lynching in many years, but he believed that he was at the scene of such a death. The thirty-three-year-old black politician and lawyer feared what might happen when black people across the Alabama city came to the same conclusion.

Mobile's torpid climate and the heavy air blowing in from the Gulf Coast gave the port city a Caribbean feeling. It had a complex mixture of cultures and peoples. There were whites of all sorts and classes, from good ole boys to Louisiana Cajuns. The black residents were the descendants not just of slaves, but also of free men and women who had lived here in large numbers since the early years of the nineteenth century. And then there were Creoles of biracial ancestry, a substantial group that had always considered themselves socially superior to other black residents. Many of the elite whites lived in mansions, some of which had been in their families since before the Civil War. The homes sat on vast grounds among oak trees and legions of azaleas. In these neighborhoods, the Spanish and French roots of the city stayed alive, and on moonlight nights, one could feel transported back a hundred years.

Mobile's white establishment saw their city as a precious enclave apart from the rest of the South. They were proud that Mobile had avoided the racial violence that had plagued its sister cities, Birmingham and Montgomery, and had made them pariahs in the national media.

There was, however, another Mobile that for the most part the elite studiously ignored, and another history as well. At the beginning of the twentieth century, 181,000 African Americans across the state were registered to vote, and black and white residents sat next to one another on public transportation. The rise of the black race threatened the conservative business and political leaders, and they rushed through a series of measures that created an American apartheid.

The state's 1901 constitution stated that voters had to have at least forty acres of land or $300 in property, which disenfranchised all but 3,000 black Alabamans as well as poor whites. New Jim Crow laws and local initiatives mandated that African Americans drink from colored water fountains and eat only at restaurants that catered to their race. This did not all go down without a struggle. In 1902 black citizens in Mobile boycotted the newly segregated trolley system, but they eventually gave in to sitting in the backseats.

In the early years of the century, whites lynched at least a dozen black men in Mobile. In 1906, a mob took two black men accused of raping white women off a train outside Mobile and hanged them from a tree. When people in the city heard the news, 3,000 of them took the short train ride to enjoy the spectacle. They took pictures to send to northern friends as evidence of southern justice, and they cut swatches off the victims' clothing as souvenirs.

In 1909, in a crime similar to the murder that led to the death of Michael Donald, a black carpenter purportedly shot and killed a white police officer who was trying to arrest him. A mob grabbed the accused out of jail and hanged him from an old oak tree beneath Christ Episcopal Church. The *Mobile Daily Item* was impressed by how well the lynching had been carried out: "So noiseless was the hanging that people in the immediate vicinity were not aware that impromptu justice was being meted out to a guilty human who had put himself beyond the pale of pity."

The elite was not happy that the lynching had been carried out on the property of Mobile's oldest Protestant church. "If the mob had the common sense and basic decency to conduct their bloody business outside the city limits, Mobile leaders simply could blame it on the rural 'lawless element,'" writes Mobile historian David E. Alsobrook.

During World War II thousands of workers descended on the port city to work in the shipyards. The 7,000 black workers held only menial jobs. When President Franklin Roosevelt's Committee on Fair Employment Practice ordered that African Americans be given better opportunities, a dozen were promoted to welders. That led to a riot by white workers yelling "get every one of them niggers off this island." The threat was so menacing that the promotions were rescinded, and no other black workers were advanced.

Despite the systematic attempt to hold down black Alabamans, World War II was an economic bonanza. Many black people had cars or other property easily worth $300. That led to the 1946 Boswell Amendment to the Alabama constitution, stating that in order to register to vote, an applicant must be able to discuss a section of the U.S. Constitution. If he could not answer satisfactorily whatever question was put to him, he would not be registered. In much of Alabama, this gave racist clerks at registration offices the opportunity to dismiss potential black applicants, no matter how much they studied the Constitution.

In the postwar era, Mobile's black population advanced in a glacially slow manner, much of it orchestrated by two public-spirited citizens, a black postman, John L. Leflore, the long-time secretary of the Mobile NAACP, and a white lawyer and politician, Joseph N. Langan. Leflore worked to get black citizens registered to vote. Then he orchestrated black bloc voting, passing out "pink sheets," guides that listed the names of the more racially moderate candidate. No black man could win in a citywide election, but thanks to an overwhelming black vote, in 1953 Langan was elected one of Mobile's five commissioners and three times won reelection.

In the 1950s and 1960s, Mobile had an image as one of the most progressive cities in the South. When Reverend Martin Luther King Jr. led a boycott of the Montgomery buses in 1955 and 1956, the goal was not integration so much as it was for blacks there to have what their brothers and sisters in Mobile already had. There, African Americans did have to sit in the back of the bus, but if they were seated, they did not have to get up to give their seat to a white person who boarded later. It was the white Montgomery leadership's dismissal of that modest reform that led to the boycott demanding that African Americans be allowed to enter the bus from the front door and sit wherever they chose.

By the mid-1960s, a new generation of black activists in Mobile despised what it took as the hat-in-hand obsequiousness of their seniors. Many of them were black separatists who mocked Reverend King's vision that "one day right there in Alabama little black boys and black girls will be able to join hands with little white boys and white girls as sisters and brothers." They were repelled at Leflore working in tandem with the white Langan to institute such tepid reforms as a few black police officers who patrolled only black neighborhoods.

In 1967 Leflore's Mobile home was bombed. The FBI's most likely suspects were not Klansmen but black militants fed up with what they considered the Uncle Tom who thought he could still lead them. Four months later, black youths shouted down Leflore at a rally, chanting the slogan "Black Power."

A new activist organization, Neighborhood Organized Workers, went on to show its disdain for the Leflore strategy of using the ballot box as the primary engine of black advancement. They were for black candidates or no candidates at all. Without a large number of black votes, Langan lost his 1969 reelection campaign for a seat on the city commission to a segregationist candidate.

In an era of increasing racial confrontation, white people stood overwhelmingly with their race and black people with theirs, and the Klan had what appeared to many white people to be a legitimate place in Mobile life. Only five years before the Michael Donald lynching, the Klan had been sufficiently accepted that the *Mobile Register* listed its rallies the way the paper did high school football games.

One of the events noted took place in February 1975 in Theodore. The Klan might have been diminished in other parts of the South, but about 1,500 people attended the rally, including forty-two rows of Klansmen.

The main speaker was Robert Shelton, the Imperial Wizard of the United Klans of America (UKA), and the most powerful Klan leader in the second half of the twentieth century. The five-foot-ten-inch-tall Shelton had tiny, blue eyes set deep beneath his high forehead; he also had thin, pursed lips, and a narrow peaked nose that ran down half his face. Standing there in his scarlet robe and peaked scarlet hat, the rail-thin Klan leader was a grandly intimidating figure. After Shelton finished condemning the FBI and the press for calling the Klan violent, a twenty-five-foot-high cross was lit, and it illuminated the Alabama night.

Two years later Shelton led a march through the downtown streets of Mobile to a rally in Bienville Square, a historic gem of the old city. When the Mobile commissioners had given permission for such a rally, they must have known what a provocation it was to the city's black population, but this was not the African American community of old. "Black people no longer fear the Klan," said the Mobile NAACP. "Their feeling toward it is contempt."

On the day of the rally, the Klansmen carried a Confederate flag and a large banner emblazoned with THE UNITED KLANS OF AMERICA in Gothic script. The Klan had boasted about the time and place of their march, and when they reached Bienville Square, a line of young black men was there to confront them with their fists.

After the police stopped the fighting and Shelton tried to speak, he could not be heard above the boos and taunts. The next morning, the *Mobile Press Register* ran a photo of a black man at the rally standing over a Klansman, who was staring up in abject fear. That was the image of the new black man in Mobile, and it had nothing to do with John Leflore's genteel approach.

Despite what his youthful opponents charged, Leflore understood perfectly well his people's abuse by the police, and he had fought it in his own way most of his life. "Mobile cannot continue to 'write off' as justified all charges of alleged police brutality against those in the custody of police officers, including the several incidents involving the taking of lives by minions of the law during the past three or four years," Leflore wrote the Mobile City Commission in April 1975, the year before his death. But his entreaties led to nothing.

Most Mobile's black citizens may have given off a veneer of tranquility and courteous accommodation, but they were seething with discontent, and Figures knew that from the ground level up. His father had been a porter at the International Paper Company, and his mother in her young years worked as a maid—positions that the white world considered among the lowest of the low, but that were decent jobs for black people in Mobile.

But on Sundays, when Mr. Figures donned his black robe as a minister of the Mount Zion Missionary Baptist Church, he was the most honored of men. In preaching that all God's children were the same, Reverend Figures was preaching equality and justice, messages his two sons, Michael and Thomas, would remember.

ON HERNDON AVENUE, Michael Figures watched as more and more African Americans arrived on the street. In Mobile the more racially mixed a neighborhood was, the poorer it was. Although only one or two African Americans resided on Herndon Avenue, many lived in the surrounding neighborhood.

Part of Michael Figures wanted to walk across the street and join his black constituents in their angry laments, but he knew that if this tragic matter were not handled correctly, it would turn against his people and become an even greater disaster. He understood that this lynching was not an isolated incident, but that, in the words of Mobile historian Scotty E. Kirkland, it represented "the culmination of decades of anger within the local white supremacist community of the late 1960s and 1970s."

If something did not slow the momentum, the two races were headed for a dreadful confrontation. Although African American residents made up nearly a third of the population, the city didn't have a single black city commissioner, thanks to the jerry-rigged system. Figures and other black leaders were involved in a number of difficult legal and political negotiations with the local government in seeking greater representation. The politician knew that if this crime was not solved, black rage might explode in riots and that could set back their cause many years.

Figures took out his camera to take some pictures. He photographed the victim and the police, and then he shot three white men leaning on a car across the street. He didn't know who they were, but he had just photographed three Klansmen, Bennie and Henry Hays and James Knowles.

The Klan's Signature

MOBILE COUNTY DISTRICT attorney Chris Galanos was the next official to arrive at the scene, and he gently pushed his way through the growing crowd of African Americans who had gathered there. A classic lynching would have had the body higher in a tree and a group of white people would be beneath it, celebrating the death of a black man. Here an overwhelmingly black crowd was mourning the death of one of their own. Most of them had been brought up in the traditions of their church, and they did not grieve in the self-contained way of many white people.

Galanos saw that those in front of him were "hysterical, weeping, wailing, people falling to the ground." The thirty-two-year-old D.A. had been elected in 1979 with overwhelming black support, and he understood immediately that he had a profound obligation to solve this crime, and that if he failed, he might not be reelected.

Galanos had served as a second lieutenant in Vietnam and had seen his full share of corpses—but he'd never seen anything like this in his hometown. As he looked at the corpse, he saw the moment of death frozen onto the young victim's battered face.

Michael Donald's body was not really hanging from the tree, as in a typical lynching, but was strapped onto it. His feet in their high-topped Converse sneakers touched the ground, and though he had a hangman's noose around his neck, the rope was tied around the tree perpendicular to his head. It was clear that his throat had been slashed, and his left arm was bent ninety degrees, as if he were about to make some gesture. His blue jeans and blue jeans jacket were covered in dirt and dried blood.

Galanos stood back a few feet while Coroner Dr. Leroy Riddick gingerly laid out the body on a rubber sheet on the grass. The coroner observed that rigor mortis had set in, and that the victim had been tied to—not hung from—the tree. Riddick immediately concluded that the young man had died somewhere else and had been transported here. Police looked in the deceased's pants for a wallet, which they would use to identify him, but they found nothing.

Once the body was on the ground, Chief of Detectives Sam McLarty examined the rope. "See these thirteen knots, the way it's tied," McLarty said as Galanos looked down at the rope. "That's what they call a hangman's noose, and it's the Klan signature."

The police officers at the scene did not want to speculate that Klansmen had lynched the deceased. One of the young black men standing across the street knew all about the racial attitudes of the Mobile police. Five years earlier Glenn Diamond and a friend had been standing not far from Herndon Avenue when a police squad stopped them, suspecting they were robbers. Diamond was so startled that he ran. When eight officers caught him, they put a noose around his neck, threw the rope around a tree branch, and hoisted him up, lifting his feet just off the ground like the body on the camphor tree. At that moment, a plainclothes officer arrived and told the police to cut him down. Because of their actions, several of the policemen faced indictment.

The squad was notorious in Mobile's black community. Just the day before Diamond was attacked, one of the same policemen had shot an unarmed black man seven times when he caught him trying to steal a CB radio from a truck.

After the incident with Glenn Diamond, Robert Shelton drove down to Mobile and met with the police commissioner to defend the officers who had been indicted. The Imperial Wizard offered to bring in thousands of his Klansmen to "restore order." The next day the *Mobile Press Register* ran a front-page photo of Shelton standing beside the commissioner, the paper treating the Imperial Wizard as a public-spirited activist worthy of respect. The city's black residents saw this as an insult beyond measure and direct evidence of the police department's racist nature. In the end, one of the cops was fired and several supervisors were temporarily suspended, but the other policemen involved faced no serious consequences, and things on the Mobile police force continued pretty much as before.

Michael Figures was stunned when he realized that the lead detective at the Herndon Avenue murder scene was Wilbur Williams, who had been indicted and then reinstated for his alleged role in the false lynching. Figures was not someone who backed off around white people. He went up to Williams and expressed his doubts that the detective could possibly do a fair job.

Williams tried to assure Figures that he was wrong. "I told him if he would give me time and the benefit of the doubt, I would prove him wrong," says Williams.

Galanos was still wandering around the crime scene at around 7:00 A.M., when two men walked across Herndon Avenue and approached the officers. "My name's Bennie Jack Hays, and I own all of this," said the elderly man, pointing to the houses across the street.

"My son, Henry, lives here," Bennie went on, nodding toward the young man who stood slightly behind him. Henry was twenty-six years old, but with his slight frame, slouching manner, and anxious glances, he looked more like a troubled teenager. "I want to know what's going on."

Bennie was well known to the police, some of whom were members or admirers of the Klan, and he quickly admitted his affiliation.

"I just sold most of my houses on the street," Bennie said, pointing to three of the houses. "I don't know nothin' about this lynchin', nothin' at all." With that settled, the father and son walked back across Herndon Avenue.

Upon close inspection, the police found a single drop of blood in the bushes across the street, in front of one of the houses Bennie had owned until a few hours earlier and where Henry lived. Later that morning the officers talked to several witnesses, including a former Klansman, who from a window in his apartment had seen the hanging body, but knew nothing about how it had gotten there. When the police returned to do a formal interview, he told them that after they left earlier, Bennie had come over and asked what he had told the police.

"He told me if I am telling the cops anything, that I would be sorry," the neighbor said.

The next day the police interviewed yet another person on Herndon Avenue who had things to say about Bennie and Henry that should have made the police scrutinize them with greater attention. The neighbor described Bennie as a proudly intolerant man who boasted how he hated "niggers, Jews, Spicks [sic], Cubans, and others." Bennie and Henry were "very violent people. Mr. Hays can change in a second. One minute he will be very quiet, and the next he will go crazy."

That evening, when the police interviewed the father and son, Bennie took charge. He told the officer there were good black people and bad black people, and he had nothing against them as a race. He said he was a proud member of the Klan, but his unit would never lynch a black man. Through all of this, his youngest son kept silent.

"Would you take a lie detector test, Mr. Hays?" the police officer asked.

"I'm not going to take a test to satisfy some *blacks!*"

"What about you, Henry, would you take the test?"

"I'll just have to go along with my daddy," Henry said, speaking for the first time.

"I've got a bad heart," Bennie avowed. "I don't think my doctor would allow me to take one."

"What about your son?" the officer asked. "Henry doesn't have a bad heart."

Bennie wasn't going to let this officer think he controlled his son's every action. "Do you want to take one, Henry?" he asked.

"I'll do what you say, Daddy." The young man did not understand he was supposed to pretend he was making the decision on his own.

"We'll just have to sleep on it," Bennie said, although he knew neither he nor his son would ever take the test. "We'll let you know tomorrow."

The Value of Things

WHEN BEULAH MAE Donald went to bed in her apartment on the night of the murder, she had a strange dream. A steel gray casket sat in the middle of the living room. When she moved forward to see the face of the deceased, somebody came up to her and said, "You don't need to see this." That's when she woke up, at about two in the morning, and realized that her nineteen-year-old youngest son, Michael, had not come home.

Michael was a gentle, unassuming young man who rarely strayed far from his home in his mother's cinder-block apartment in the projects. The development was called Orange Grove, and the best thing about it was the name.

Michael had grown up staying away from trouble as best he could. He avoided the drug dealers, the gangs, and the fights. Like his mother, Michael had a broad, expressive face that telegraphed even the hint of an emotion. He worked part-time stuffing inserts into the *Mobile Register*. It earned him the respectable sum of $125 a week, on top of which he was training to become a brick mason at Carver State Technical College.

Donald boasted about his girlfriends, but no one had ever seen one, and his sisters figured their shy brother was spinning a dream. As long as he had a fresh comic book to read and a pickup game of basketball to play, he appeared content. He also liked to go dancing at the Busby Recreation Center. Sometimes he'd come home and do a dance called the "popcorn" in front of his family, moving as if he were James Brown.

The teenager had spent the Friday evening of March 20, 1981, at the Orange Grove apartment of his sister, Betty Wyatt. He liked to think of himself as a sharp dresser. He had spent his tax refund on the clothes he wore that night: Converse sneakers, blue jeans, and a belt with a Led Zeppelin buckle. While he watched the NIT basketball tournament on television in the next room, his mother, who was also visiting her daughter, played Pitty Pat, a rummy-like card game, with family members.

When the ball game ended, the news came on, and Michael watched the newscaster talking about how a jury had failed to arrive at a verdict in the murder trial of a black bank robber. He watched a bit and then walked out into the other room to be with his relatives.

At about 11:00 P.M. his niece Vanessa Wyatt asked him to go out and get her cigarettes. Some teenagers would have growled that they were not errand boys, but Michael was always willing to help. His aunt gave him a dollar bill that he put in his wallet, more than enough money for a pack of Marlboros.

When Michael did not return, everyone figured he probably had stopped in at the dance at The Rec. But when hours passed and Michael had still not returned, Mrs. Donald naturally began to worry. He was the youngest of her seven children, and he held a special, even exalted place, in her heart. She simply could not understand where her always reliable son might be.

. . .

MRS. DONALD HAD become pregnant for the first time when she was in the tenth grade in Mobile in 1936. In the next quarter century, she had four daughters—Mary, Cecelia, Cynthia, and Betty—and three sons—Stanley, Leo, and Michael. Her "sorry husband" left her soon after Michael's birth in 1961, and she moved with her brood into public housing. She knew how dangerous the streets could be, particularly at nighttime—her own sister had been murdered in them—and had made it her mission to help her children avoid trouble.

"I wasn't able to get everything for them," Mrs. Donald recalled, "but I let them know the value of things." Instead of the streets, Mrs. Donald emphasized church. She took her children to services Sunday morning, and they would stay all day. She showered them with love, but she had strict rules, which they respected. Principally, they did not talk back to her.

Of all her children, Michael was the most solicitous of his mother. "If he came home and I was lying down, he'd know something was wrong, and he'd do little things to help, that's the kind of boy he was," Mrs. Donald reflected. She lived largely on Social Security, and he gave her most of his wages and did whatever task she might have for him, big or small.

Even when the grown-up children were living with her, such as Michael or twenty-six-year-old Cynthia, they had to be back home by 11:00 P.M. But as she prayed for her son's return, she worried the discipline she had instilled had been for naught. Mrs. Donald's concerns were exacerbated by news reports that a black man had been found hanging from a tree on Herndon Avenue. But the police did not know the victim's name, and as much as this news upset her, she kept hoping her son would come popping in the door smiling sheepishly.

And yet she knew. Of course, she knew. Mrs. Donald had been born in 1919, at a time when black men were sometimes dumped into a river or the bay or buried in the woods, and never heard of again. Things were better now, but that fear was always there.

And then the phone rang. A woman said her husband had spotted a wallet in a Dumpster near Herndon Avenue, and when he fished it out, he found identification for a Michael Donald.

"That's my son," Mrs. Donald said.

"I believe he might have met foul play," the woman responded.

When the police called later in the morning, they told her nothing she did not already know. Her soul had gone out to Michael the day he had been born. All of her life she had protected Michael and her six other children. She had brought them the blessings of God and the protective shield of faith.

She felt terrible despair. Without her faith, she would hardly have been able to rise from her knees.

Bloody Nails

CHRIS GALANOS KNEW he needed help, and he needed it right away. Given the circumstances of the death, the D.A. believed he was likely dealing with a hate crime, and that meant he did not have to rely exclusively on the Mobile police. He could call in not only state investigators but also the FBI, and by the afternoon after the discovery of the body, he had put together a multiagency task force.

He brought in Bob Eddy, one of the top state criminal investigators, to head the local team. Eddy had grown up in Walker County, an almost entirely white section of the state. He was just a kid when his uncle took him on a little ferry across the Warrior River to Cullman County. There at the dock stood a billboard bigger than life that said: NIGGER DON'T LET THE SUN GO DOWN ON YOU IN CULLMAN COUNTY.

Those words had so troubled young Eddy that they had stayed with him. As a young deputy sheriff in Huntsville in the late 1960s, Eddy was driving his squad car at 2:00 A.M., when he came upon a black man walking along the road. The police officer stopped and offered the man a ride. He refused but Eddy insisted, and the man got in the car. Eddy drove him two miles down the road and let him out outside his home in the projects.

The next morning Eddy told another cop the strange story. "You fucked him up," the cop said. "He was afraid because he thought you were bringing him in, and when you let him out there, everyone's gonna figure he's a snitch, and his life will be ruined."

Eddy never made that mistake again. He was a genial sort with a good sense of humor and a ready laugh at life's endless ironies. He almost never got upset. He did not even get angry with suspects. No matter what they had done, or how horrendous their crimes, he treated them in the same easy way, and he got things other investigators rarely got.

Eddy had been a cop, a sheriff, and an investigator all across the state, and he had a deep understanding of the Klan and racial matters. In 1977, Eddy had done much of the investigation that led to the conviction of UKA stalwart Robert Chambliss, who was one of a group that bombed and killed four black girls at Birmingham's 16th Street Baptist Church in 1963.

Mobile fancied itself better on racial matters than the rest of Alabama, but from what Eddy was learning, that was not the case. When he first got to town, Eddy went into the Mobile police headquarters to meet with the detectives investigating the Donald murder. They threw the *n* word back and forth across the room like a Ping-Pong ball. That did not happen any longer among the cops Eddy knew, and as they were using this language, a black detective was sitting at his desk within earshot.

Eddy believed that four of the five main white detectives were probably racists. He was convinced that these men thought their primary task was to protect good, decent white people against a violent underclass of black drug dealers, pimps, robbers, welfare cheaters, and other hustlers. These officers, he feared, would be disinclined to indict Klan members for killing a young black man.

Galanos's recruitment of Bob Eddy to head the state team was a strong indication that the D.A. was serious about finding the killers. The D.A. also thought that having the FBI involved was another plus, but Mobile's top FBI agent was in the process of being transferred to New Jersey, and Galanos wasn't sure the new man would know enough to be of much help.

In his last significant act before leaving, the departing agent wrote a memo noting the coincidence of three seemingly disparate events. In Birmingham, a black career criminal, Josephus Anderson, had been charged with killing Police Sergeant Gene Ballard during a bank robbery. The trial had been moved down to Mobile, where it was heard before a jury of eleven black jurors and one white. On the evening of the lynching, the jury had announced that it was unable to reach a unanimous verdict. Later that night, a cross was burned at the Mobile County Courthouse, an action that was usually the work of Klansmen. A few hours later, Donald's body was found hanging from a tree. "It is unknown if any of these events are connected," the report concluded.

MICHAEL FIGURES TRIED to tamp down the black community's rage so it would not explode into the streets while he was pushing the Mobile authorities to pursue the investigation with seriousness and purpose.

"There is a feeling of tenseness in the black community here which recalls so vividly the lynch attempt on Glenn Diamond almost exactly five years ago and other acts of brutality against and civil rights violations of black citizens in this area," Figures wrote in a press release two days after the body was found. "We are calling upon Mobile's black community to be as cool as possible. We are not definitely saying at this point that race was involved but we can not take any chances and allow a situation to develop, if race is involved, like the ones that have developed in other cities throughout this country."

Figures said he could feel a palpable tension whenever he went out to the city's streets. He told reporters that the murder had created "the most volatile situation that has ever come to Mobile." When he drove across the city, he saw nooses hanging from highway overpasses and schools in apparent support of the lynching.

The local authorities should not have needed Figures's urgent pleas to convince them to make the Klan a prime target of their investigation. But the Mobile police force was determined to focus on other theories, including one that Donald was having an affair with a white coworker at the *Register*, and he had been murdered in retaliation. There was no evidence to support this story, but the idea of black men sleeping with white women was still an underlying fear of much of the white South.

The police ditched that idea when they heard a very different story told by an ex-con named Johnny Lee Kelly. The twenty-seven-year-old white man had two convictions and three other charges pending in circuit court. If he were found guilty of any of those, Alabama's three-strikes-and-you're-out law would send him to prison for the rest of his life. His uncle was a cop, and he knew things about the lynching most people did not yet know. He also knew that if he provided testimony leading to the conviction of the murderer or murderers, he would be given a keep-out-of-prison pass.

Kelly told police he had been cruising around with a buddy in his cab on the evening of the lynching when they came upon three young Cajuns, Ralph Hayes and two brothers, Jimmy and Johnny Edgar. Kelly said Hayes had blood on his shirt and that Jimmy Edgar cleaned his bloody nails with his pocketknife, while the men boasted about "jumping on" a black man who had stiffed them on drug money.

Police Sergeant Wilbur Williams spoke with the friend in the car with Kelly, and the man said none of this was true. Yet in the eyes of the Mobile police, Kelly was credible enough to be their crucial witness.

Four days after finding Donald's body, the police arrested the three men for the murder. In exchange for his promise to testify against the three young Cajuns, Kelly no longer faced life in prison.

From what the police told the *Mobile Register*, a drug deal had gone bad; three junkies had killed this lowlife black man who thought he could take drugs from them and not pay. The murder had nothing to do with race. It was a tale of bad people killing bad people on the darkest streets of the city and then depositing the body on Herndon Avenue.

Every speck of real evidence the police had gathered suggested that the Klan murdered Michael Donald, but it was untenable that such a crime could have taken place in Mobile in 1981. A few racist cops may have conspired to indict three innocent men. It is also possible that the police may not have known they were arresting three innocent young men, but they had not done their due diligence and instead went with a quick pleasing solution. Once the police had the three Cajuns in jail, the officers went out and tried to find anything to justify what they had done. The Mobile authorities knew that no one would look twice if these marginal men, these ill-fated Cajuns, were sent to the electric chair or spent years in prison.

The police tried to gather evidence that Donald had led a secret criminal life, but they came up with nothing but vague, unsubstantiated rumors. A white transvestite prostitute volunteered that he had slept with Donald and that the teenager was a "hustler." When the prostitute saw Donald's photo in the paper, he admitted it did not look like the man he knew, but the police, nonetheless, tried to validate his story. They found someone else who said that Donald was a drug dealer.

The police went to Mrs. Donald and asked her about these

reports. As gently as the officers tried to pose their questions, she felt the police were impugning the honor and integrity of her murdered son. To the elderly mother, it was almost unbearable to have her beloved son maligned so shamelessly.

An Open Casket

MICHAEL'S FACE WAS so beaten and broken that the Christian Benevolent Funeral Home could not possibly make him whole and unblemished, presentable for viewing. But as Emmett Till's mother had insisted when her fourteen-year-old was brutally murdered in Mississippi in 1955 for supposedly whistling at a white woman, Mrs. Donald wanted her son's silver casket open "so the world could know."

The Revelation Missionary Baptist Church was a second home to the Donald family, and the pews were overflowing with more than a thousand mourners. Senator Michael Figures was there, as were his brother Thomas, an assistant U.S. attorney, and many of the most prominent black citizens in the city. No one knew for sure who had killed Michael, and this was not a day to place the teenager in the company of civil rights heroes. This was a traditional funeral.

The black church was a place of solace and sanctuary and hope, and so it was on this day. Mrs. Donald had heard these words and sung these songs many times, but on this day, the familiar hymns and biblical passages spoke to her in a way they never had before. "No more sorrow will be mine, no more burdens must I bear," the mourners sang. "I will go to that city, where God's holy angels sing!"

As they filled the church with their voices, Michael Donald's family and friends feared the Klan would show up to disrupt the event. It was extraordinary that at this solemn moment, they would have such a worry, and it showed how profoundly the Klan had made its way into their souls. That did not happen, but even at this moment the organization filled them with trepidation and dread.

But that weekend the UKA was busy with another activity. Dressed in their new robes, the Klansmen drove around looking for places where black mourners had placed ribbons on trees in memory of Michael Donald. After Iranian militants took more than fifty Americans hostage at the embassy in Teheran in 1979, people had started placing yellow ribbons around trees to symbolize that they had not forgotten. The custom had been picked up for other occasions. Now everywhere the Klansmen spotted the ribbons, they stopped and ripped them off the trees.

IN APRIL 1981, Reverend Jesse Jackson came to Mobile to lead a protest march of about 8,000 black citizens. "Don't let them break your spirit," Jackson told the massive crowd. After revving the assembled into a frenzy of raw grief and anger, the civil rights leader led them through the streets to Herndon Avenue where, in a dramatic, provocative gesture, they chopped down the tree from which they believed Donald had been hung. But they chopped down the wrong tree because on the morning of the murder, after the body had been removed, the *Mobile Register* had photographed another tree. When the black protesters learned the truth, it was just another reason not to trust the white establishment.

After the three Cajuns had spent two and a half months in jail without bond, Chris Galanos brought them before a state grand jury. These citizen panels were part of the machinery of the criminal justice system. Their members generally had no sophisticated knowledge of the law, and for the most part rubber-stamped whatever the prosecutors asked them to do. But here the evidence was so weak and there were so many "conflicts in statements," the grand jury bravely refused to give the D.A. an indictment. The police freed the three suspects and arrested Kelly. He was charged with felony perjury, found guilty at trial, and sentenced to life in prison.

Still, Sam McLarty, chief of detectives, continued to insist that the crime had nothing to do with race and said that the Klan would not lynch somebody practically on their own front lawn. Lead detective Wilbur Williams wasn't so sure. He would have liked to have chalked up the false arrests to bad police work, but he felt there was a chance that some of the detectives had decided "we need to give this to somebody else. This doesn't need to fall on the Klan."

The false arrest had enormous costs. The FBI walked away from the investigation when they were told the murderers had been arrested in a drug deal gone bad. This left the investigation solely to the Mobile police, who were doing so in a halfhearted way.

If justice was not done, the black people of Mobile might rise in the streets and burn the city, as their northern brothers had done from Newark to Los Angeles to the detriment of themselves and their cities. After the three Cajuns were released, young African American militants demonstrated at the courthouse and passed out crude, provocative flyers that called for a race war: "Any black man with a gun should target and shoot at any white Klansman. The first shot is the signal for every black man to shoot and burn," one of them said.

Another was meant to set off a tinder of hate with a cartoon of a white man raping a black woman as he says, "I rape nigger women too." The cartoon character also claimed incorrectly "they cut Donald's penis off and stuck it in his mouth too." That custom was once common and suggested how the realities of lynching were still very much part of the consciousness of black southerners.

Even though their anger at justice denied was real, the black citizens of Mobile did not riot or flame up in acts of racial reprisal. Most of them added Donald's unsolved murder to the list of abuses they believed they had endured, and they kept their anger largely to themselves. Mrs. Donald was still so upset at the aspersions she felt the police had made about her son that nothing they could say or do would make her feel positive about the Mobile authorities.

Michael's murder and the lack of effort to find his killers were horrible enough for the Donald family, but it was made infinitely worse because he had been lynched, a crime that historically was almost never punished. After the Civil War, lynching became a preferred method to control the former slaves. The idea was not simply to penalize supposed malefactors, but also to strike terror into all black men, making them subservient and impotent in the process. According to a 2015 study by the Equal Justice Initiative, "racial terror lynchings" in the twelve southern states occurred on average more than once a week from 1877 to 1950. That totaled 3,959 deaths across the South in seventy-three years. The lynch mobs were not merely idle riffraff, but often included everyone from the sheriff and local ministers to parents, with their children in tow.

Key to the southern mythology about the Civil War's aftermath was *The Birth of a Nation,* one of the most socially significant films in American history. D. W. Griffith's 1915 epic tells the story of the birth of the Ku Klux Klan. In it, several hundred thousand Klansmen ride forth in gowns and masks through the southern night, petrifying the former slaves, and ultimately saving the region from a vulgar black tyranny and the mongrelizing of America.

It was not just the presence of the white-robed riders that so terrified black people—there was also the reality that these hooded men might lynch, beat, or burn them in their homes. Long before Donald's murder, his cousin Monica Jackson recalled dreaming about her and Michael being chased through a field by men in sheets. Few black people in the South had seen *The Birth of a Nation*, but those images of the night riders inhabited and shaped even the nightmares of black southerners.

The Donalds had always been a close family, but after Michael's death there was a seamless bond between Mrs. Donald and her four daughters and two surviving sons. No one was stronger in his resolve than Stanley, her eldest son, who along with Cynthia and Cecelia led the Donalds' determined efforts to bring a measure of justice.

The family could not let their fear overcome them. They knew almost nothing about the legal system and its lawyers, but they figured that was the only way that they could seek justice. One day a group of about twelve family members, including Mrs. Donald, went downtown and knocked on one lawyer's office after another. The attorneys hemmed and hawed, making one excuse after another as to why they couldn't help, and after a long day talking to an endless array of attorneys, the Donalds trudged back home.

Mrs. Donald's third daughter, Cynthia, knew a lawyer who had handled her divorce, and she called him. "I'm just going to tell you, Cynthia, nobody's going to touch this," the lawyer said.

"I figure it this way," says Cynthia Donald. "Nobody wanted to put a taint on the city is what I'm thinking. A lynching in Mobile? They didn't want it to be said."

Next the Donald family set up a meeting with Chris Galanos. It was difficult for Mrs. Donald to sit listening to the D.A. making one excuse after the next. Finally after an hour and a half, Galanos began to speak openly about what he suspected.

"It's a lynching," he said, with a hint of tears in his eyes. "It's a lynching by the Klan. But can we prove it? No."

"Well, you all need to get to work," said Cynthia Donald.

A Major Injustice

A NUMBER OF people in Mobile were determined to push the federal government to take the case. Leading them was thirty-six-year-old Mobile assistant U.S. attorney Thomas H. Figures, who was working closely with his younger brother, State Senator Michael Figures.

Thomas Figures had gone north to graduate school and had received both an M.B.A. from Indiana University and a law degree from the University of Illinois. For several years, Figures worked in New York as a corporate lawyer for Exxon and then joined the office of the Westchester County district attorney.

He was a success by any measure, but his father had a dream that one day his two lawyer sons would work together, and Mobile had its own pull on its native son. With his brother helping to drive the U-Haul truck, he returned home to become the first black assistant district attorney in Mobile County.

Figures went on to become the first and only black assistant U.S. attorney in southern Alabama. He was taciturn and highly suspicious of white people, and he lacked his younger brother's glad-handing political skill. But he shared with his brother a sophisticated awareness of race in the city on the bay. As a government attorney, he had to be judicious in what he concluded, as well as circumspect in what he said. He was perfectly aware that he risked being set in a corner where he might handle only cases dealing primarily with racial matters. He didn't care. He thought of himself as the surrogate for his people.

Figures had studied and worked in the North, and he had

traveled all over the South. With that breadth of experience, he didn't see Mobile as the progressive city its leaders thought it was. He admired the role the *Atlanta Constitution* was playing in advancing civil rights in its city, and it appalled him how the *Mobile Register* wrote so disparagingly about the advance of African Americans in theirs. He believed the city on the bay could have become another Atlanta, but Mobile was held back by what he called the "two *R*s, racism and redneckism."

Thomas Figures had come into the Justice Department soon after former Georgia governor Jimmy Carter became president in 1977. Reagan's election four years later gave him an ominous feeling about where government was headed, and he wanted to leave and go into private practice with his brother. But Figures was convinced that if he left, the Justice Department would never enter the Michael Donald case, and it would end up as just another in the long list of unsolved and unpunished lynchings.

Figures believed that bringing the power and integrity of the federal government into the pursuit of Michael Donald's killer or killers was the most important thing that could be done in the struggle of Mobile's African Americans for justice. Everywhere he looked, he saw what he privately called "rabbit trails," leading away from seeing Klansmen as the most likely suspects in the murder. He had watched the investigations with dismay and anger. "They went down these rabbit trails designed to appease the establishment by going through the motions," he says.

The assistant U.S. attorney was convinced that the Mobile police and the Mobile County district attorney did not have the will, intention, or even the ability to find whoever had lynched Michael Donald. As he saw it, the original FBI investigation had not been much better than the local investigation and had ended before it even began.

Figures considered his new boss, Jefferson "Jeff" Beauregard Sessions III, the U.S. attorney for the Southern District of Alabama and a future United States senator, as a closet racist. Figures said that Sessions called him "boy," the most demeaning of terms for a southern black man. And the Reagan appointee also said that he figured the Klan was okay until he learned some of its members smoked pot. Sessions said later he was only joking, but such comments made Figures even more suspicious of what even the most elevated of white people truly thought about his race. Yet Sessions believed almost as strongly as Figures that the Civil Rights Division should enter the case, and by his actions in that matter hardly seemed a racist.

Figures lobbied Daniel Rinzel, chief of the division's Criminal Section, to have the federal government take on the case. Figures was endlessly persistent. He never preached. He never blustered. And he never went away.

A YEAR AFTER the murder, a thousand miles away, in his tiny office at the U.S. Department of Justice's Civil Rights Division in Washington, D.C., attorney Barry Kowalski opened a filing cabinet, pulled out a file of documents dealing with the murder of Michael Donald, and tried to decide what he should do.

Kowalski's father was a West Point graduate and a career military man who served two terms in Congress in a Connecticut seat that in the 1950s went to a Polish-American. Representative Frank Kowalski was a liberal Democrat who was opposed to the war in Vietnam. His son was antiwar too, and the retired congressman was concerned when Barry decided to enlist in the Marine Corps. He told his father he did not think it was fair to sit it out while other less advantaged young men of his generation were drafted and dying.

Kowalski led a rifle platoon in combat. His experience in Vietnam only deepened his opposition to the war. When the short, intense veteran got back to the United States, he studied for his law degree at Catholic University and ended up teaching at Antioch Law School in the District of Columbia.

The innovative institution mixed classroom learning with

real legal work and was the most liberal law school in America. The young law professor led students fighting any number of criminal cases. After Kowalski's seventh year teaching there, the school folded, throttled by the excesses of its egalitarian ideals, leaving the thirty-seven-year-old attorney without a job.

Kowalski joined the Civil Rights Division of the United States Justice Department in January 1981, the day before the inauguration of President Ronald Reagan. He worried that the new president might throttle the actions of the activist agency and that he had arrived at the worst possible time. After all, Reagan had denounced the 1965 Voting Rights Act—central to the activities of the Civil Rights Division—as "humiliating to the South." The lawyer had learned a full measure of political acumen from his politician father, and Kowalski did not parade his liberalism before his new colleagues.

The country was experiencing a backlash to the federal government's involvement in civil rights, and Reagan had used that to help him to win the election. He opened his 1980 campaign for the Republican nomination in Philadelphia, Mississippi, where three civil rights workers were murdered in the bloody summer of 1964. The candidate had come neither to commemorate the three activists nor even to mention the names of James Chaney, Andrew Goodman, and Michael Schwerner. Instead he was there to condemn the federal government's intrusion into the life of the South.

"I believe in states' rights, and I believe we have distorted the balance of our government today by giving powers that were never intended to be given in the Constitution to that federal establishment," Reagan told the great crowd at the Neshoba County fairgrounds.

As he sought to become the fortieth president, Reagan may have been trying to stake out a legitimate political position, but he was also mouthing one of the most pernicious code words in modern American politics. When Alabama governor George Corley Wallace made his quadrennial journey north to run for president from 1964 to 1976, he too had spoken of "states' rights," and Reagan was merely picking up where the flamboyant segregationist had left off. These so-called states' rights were, among few other things, a cover for a continuation of segregationist policies. They gave southerners the wildly erroneous idea that their ancestors had fought the Civil War primarily for other reasons than to maintain what President Barack Obama would later call "this nation's original sin of slavery."

In Kowalski's first few months at the division, he was surprised that there was no backing off in the enforcement of criminal civil rights law. When he was a fiery liberal professor, he might have speculated that pursuing criminal actions was the Republican administration's way of providing a cover for also backing off on political and civil issues such as affirmative action and fair employment practices, but he was just glad he could pursue his new job forcefully.

Kowalski saw immediately just how bureaucratic the federal government's decisions were about what cases would be investigated, and how careful he had to be in those he sought to advance. Each year the division received more than a thousand requests for assistance from all across America. The department took on fewer than a hundred of these cases, all of which involved serious charges of civil rights violations. Kowalski vetted a good share of these applications and made recommendations to his superiors.

The lawyer led the prosecution of Joseph Paul Franklin, a UKA member and Nazi, for violating the civil rights of Vernon Jordan Jr., the president of the National Urban League, by shooting him down in a parking lot in Fort Wayne, Indiana. Franklin was found not guilty in August 1982. It was hardly an auspicious beginning for Kowalski's career in the federal government and would have made many lawyers extremely careful about what cases they took next.

The lynching of a black man might seem to cry out to be investigated by the Justice Department. But in 1981, killing a black man because of his race was by itself not a federal crime; it would have to be proven that the killer or killers also intended to violate the victim's constitutional rights.

Nobody in the Mobile Police Department was saying that the murder was racially motivated and that Michael Donald's civil rights had been abused. As things stood, the Justice Department had no identifiable legal authority to stick its nose into the business. That's why Kowalski kept shoving the file back in his drawer. But he was also so appalled by the lynching that he never did the paperwork to close it out.

When Figures called the first time, trying to enlist Kowalski's help, the Justice Department lawyer was impressed with the assistant U.S. attorney's passionate desire to bring justice to this case. It was just another marker along the road that led him to lobby his superiors that the case had enough merit to be worth pursuing. Kowalski was taking a big chance here. The department would first have to find the killers and then show that a federal law had been violated.

Once the Justice Department opened the case, Kowalski worked with Figures and Sessions to get the FBI to reopen the investigation. The FBI jealously protected its authority and did not like having its parent agency, the Justice Department, tell it what to do. The FBI worked regularly with state and city police agencies and was therefore reluctant to elbow its way into local cases, because doing so suggested that the local authorities were not doing a good enough job.

Late in 1982, when the FBI reluctantly agreed to open the case, shrewd bureaucrats within the agency simply packaged up the old Mobile police files and sent them over to the Justice Department. Kowalski and Figures were able to read police interviews with Bennie and Henry Hays and other Klavern members that cried out for further questioning. It was obvious the Klan should have been a prime suspect, and there was still plenty of investigating to do.

Kowalski was convinced that a major injustice had been

committed. He saw a chance to right a wrong—or at least to clear the mystery over the unsolved case. They might have to upset some people and damage a few egos, but he vowed to go back to the FBI with specific requests. Kowalski and Figures prepared a detailed entreaty to the FBI—including a list of potential subjects to interview.

IN JANUARY 1983, FBI Special Agent James Bodman was sitting in the FBI office in downtown Mobile trying to look busy when his boss, Special Agent in Charge Morris Stacks, came over to his desk and said, "The United States Attorney's Office here in Mobile wants the FBI to stay on the Michael Donald case. You're being assigned to the case."

"What do you expect me to do?" Bodman asked. The case was almost two years old and was considered dead. "We've already interviewed everybody in town two times."

"You take it, and you work it," Stack said. "Just do it. Whatever you have to do, you do it."

Bodman had only a few years left before retirement, and he wanted to go out as a desk jockey without any more big cases. He had grown up in the Mississippi countryside. His father, a rural mail carrier, had the one radio in the area, and when the great black heavyweight Joe Louis was boxing, black sharecroppers came from all around in their mule-driven carts and sat outside the house, listening to the fight on that radio, which Bodman's father set on the porch.

In the early 1960s, the FBI sent Bodman home to Mississippi where he made his reputation fighting the Klan. Well-suited for investigative work, he had an engaging nonjudgmental manner, which lulled people into confiding in him. When he sniffed a false note, however, he could be intimidating, letting it be known what would happen if they didn't tell the truth.

The self-styled "Mississippi redneck" was assigned to work with Assistant U.S. Attorney Thomas Figures. The first time they met, Bodman looked Figures in the eyes and said, "Why the hell do you want to reopen this can of worms?" That was Bodman. He didn't care if Figures was black, white, or chartreuse; he was going to say precisely what he thought.

Figures was used to dealing with white people who displayed their uncertainty around him either through an exaggerated politeness or a backslapping congeniality that reeked of falseness. But Bodman treated Figures pretty much the way he treated everybody else.

Bodman could tell immediately that Figures was a serious man who was consumed with finding Michael Donald's murderer. These two southern men had this in common. They started meeting almost every day to share information and to boost each other's morale. The investigation soon focused on the dozen or so members of Klavern 900 who met weekly in Theodore.

Missionary Work

JAMES BODMAN WAS finding it tedious, thankless work running around reinterviewing subjects who had no intention of telling him anything new. He was largely convinced the case was going nowhere until he talked to Teddy Kyzar, a member of Klavern 900, on February 10, 1983.

"I'm not really interested in you and Frank Cox burning a cross against the courthouse building the same night as the lynching," Bodman said.

Kyzar didn't think anyone knew that he and Cox had done it, and if the FBI agent intended to scare Kyzar, it worked. An effusive sort, Kyzar was capable of talking his way into a jam, out of a jam, and then back into a jam before he stopped speaking. And on this night, he did a little of both.

Bodman took out a still photo pulled from a local television station's footage on the morning Michael Donald's body was found. It showed Bennie, Henry, and Knowles leaning on a car on Herndon Avenue. Kyzar had no idea such a photo existed.

"You were there that night, Teddy," Bodman said. "Don't lie to me now. That's the one way you're gonna get in trouble. You were there. Don't lie."

"I seed nothin' a what anyone did," Kyzar said carefully. "I was up there in Henry's apartment. All I seed was when they come in, Knowles had blood all over his shirt, and I told him I seed it."

The hairs on the back of Bodman's neck tingled at the mention of the blood-soaked shirt. He knew he was hearing crucial information that could turn this into a real case. Even so he acted as if Kyzar had said nothing important and continued questioning him.

"I kept staying in that apartment there on Herndon," Kyzar said. "Weren't more 'an two three days later, Henry's wife Denise said she'd talk before she'd go to jail for anyone. Henry said she would die if she talked. Must a said that two three times if he said it once."

Bodman hurried back to the office to type up a FD-302 report that he, like all FBI agents, filed on everyone they interviewed. He had survived in the trenches of the federal government by giving his superiors what they wanted the way they wanted it. He laid out the bare facts, giving his bosses the idea that they were the only ones who could understand the meaning of the agent's grunt work.

None of this would likely have happened without Figures's efforts, and Saturday morning Bodman called him with the news. The FD-302 had invigorated Bodman's superiors, as he had known it would. The Washington office sent a copy of the report over to the Justice Department, where Barry Kowalski was even more excited.

Prayers in the Night

DURING THE LAST week of April 1983, Kowalski and another Civil Rights Division lawyer, Burt Glenn, flew down to Mobile. Bodman's memo had given Kowalski what he needed to take the case to a federal grand jury.

Kowalski intended to use the sixteen citizens on the grand jury as an investigative panel. He would call witness after witness, sometimes bringing a person back several times. His goal in the end was for him and Thomas Figures to seek the indictment of the accused killer or killers. It was an exhaustive, expensive procedure, and only the federal government had the long-term grand juries and the resources to make it work.

Before calling the witnesses into the grand jury room, Kowalski first interviewed them privately. As often as possible, he borrowed the U.S. attorney's large, elegantly outfitted office, hoping its dark wood and stately marble, combined with city views out of the large windows, would intimidate people into telling the truth.

When witnesses walked into the impressive office, it wasn't just this little Washington lawyer sitting there behind a huge desk, but Figures, a tall, stern black man with fierce, relentless eyes, and James Bodman, a short white son of the South, and often Burt Glenn as well. Figures stared down at the witness and asked questions in a stern voice while oftentimes Kowalski played the understanding friend.

Kowalski prepared by going over the FBI interviews and other case material, but he did not have the voluminous state investigative files, and he believed they were crucial. To get the state documents, he had to go through Chris Galanos, but he had been warned to stay away from the D.A. His superior in Washington, Daniel Rinzel, had heard wrongly that Galanos had a drinking problem and was probably unreliable.

It took several weeks for Kowalski to get permission to go down into the basement of the Mobile County Courthouse to look for the records. The basement was a damp, dark repository. The Justice Department attorney labored through scores of scrambled boxes before he finally found several marked MICHAEL DONALD CASE.

The police had scooped up anything that might be evidence, including candy from the Dumpster near Herndon Avenue where Donald's wallet had been found and had thrown it all unceremoniously into these boxes. The rats had long since discovered the sweets, and while there, they had chewed away at much else in the boxes, leaving their droppings throughout.

Kowalski plowed through the mess as best he could. He came across a jacket that had been found in the Dumpster. He kept staring at it, thinking that the killer may have worn it. He was making a point of not touching the filthy, stinking garment, but he remembered he was almost precisely Henry Hays's size, so he held his breath and tried it on. The jacket fit Kowalski perfectly.

Of all the suspects who had come before the grand jury, Henry was the only one small and thin enough to have worn the coat. When the garment was tested, it had Donald's blood type on it. This was another glaring example of the shoddy job the Mobile police had done investigating the crime.

Justice Department prosecutors often consider their local counterparts less competent than the Feds, while their local counterparts frequently have the same low opinion of the visitors in suits from Washington. But there was such mistrust here it risked hurting the case. Galanos believed rightfully that the

Feds were holding information back from him. He was outraged by what he considered their disingenuous posturing. "It was the typical federal bullshit," Galanos wrote in a memo on May 25, 1983. "And I made it known that I'm well aware of the game being played." What Galanos did not know was that the federal authorities believed he had personal problems, which made them steer warily around him.

Kowalski didn't worry about Galanos. With the Mobile police interviews in his hand and other investigative materials, he had more than enough witnesses to bring in front of the grand jury. He subpoenaed not just members of Klavern 900 but also their wives, kin, and friends. He drew his net as wide as he could, calling a steady stream of people into the United States District Courthouse.

Day after day, meanwhile, Bennie Hays went over to the federal courthouse and sat outside in the corridor, watching witnesses proceed into the grand jury. He carried a cane that he held like a weapon and sat with cold, glaring eyes, looking at everyone who passed down the corridor.

One day Teddy Kyzar came walking down the hall on his way to testify and sat next to Bennie. The Klan leader listened to the nervous, small talk pouring out of his former tenant and Klan colleague. Then he threatened, "All these people that's testifying against Henry, in the long run it's gonna hurt 'em more 'an it will hurt Henry."

Kyzar and the other Klansmen also had others pressuring them to keep quiet. Robert Shelton, who suspected the Feds wanted to indict one or more members of his organization for the lynching, subtly suggested that they deny, deny, deny. That was his tactic whenever a member of the UKA was accused of a violent crime. Even though the Imperial Wizard wanted to stay far away from the Donald murder, he also needed to learn enough to protect himself and the Klan.

So Shelton sent a polygraph expert down to Mobile and ordered the Klansmen and their wives to hook up to the machine and answer any questions. That was intimidating by itself, but when one of them started talking about what Henry had told him about the murder, the man hurriedly shut off the device.

Bennie wasn't noticeably worried about the polygraph tests—he just wanted to protect himself and his family from the Feds. He was sitting in his usual spot when truck driver Jackie Lange walked up the corridor toward the grand jury room and sat down next to Bennie. Lange had joined the Klavern only three days before the lynching, but he knew Henry well. Lange told Henry's father all of the people to whom his son had confessed. The truck driver said that Henry had even told his wife, Phyllis, what he had done. And he had laughed about it.

Bennie listened and said, "You go in there and tell 'em the truth." There was an epidemic of suspicion among the Klansmen, and it was unlikely the Klan leader wanted Lange to do any such thing.

After testifying, Lange drove back to Eight Mile on the bay where he was selling shrimp from the back of a truck. When he drove home at dusk, a car tried to run him off the road. A few days later, he was driving his camper when someone hit it with rifle shots. Almost anyone else would have called the cops, but Lange knew too much about the Klan's connection to the police to consider doing such a foolish thing.

Bennie kept up his vigil in the corridor, day after day, until one afternoon when he was making his way out of the building, he collapsed on the courthouse steps of an apparent heart attack. Kowalski could look down to the precise spot where the Klan leader fell and was taken away by ambulance. He was glad Bennie could no longer intimidate witnesses by his presence in the hallway, but he was a resilient man and was soon back up on his feet.

The day after Bennie's supposed heart attack Kowalski called in former Klansman William O'Connor for a chat in the U.S. attorney's palatial office. O'Connor had already appeared before the grand jury where he, like most of his Klan mates, had been uptight and evasive. Kowalski still had no convincing evidence that someone in the Klan had strangled Donald and slit his throat. The Klan had an oath of secrecy that was as formidable as the Mafia's, and no matter how hard he pushed, he was getting nowhere with most of these men.

"The assistant attorney general for civil rights, Mr. William Bradford Reynolds, sent me down here," Kowalski said. "I'm his best man, and I'm here because I'm gonna find out what happened. I know you're the killer or you know who the killer is. If you're the killer, you ought not to talk to me. If you aren't the killer, you better be honest with me. That's the best thing for you. It's the only thing."

"What if I lied in the grand jury?" O'Connor asked.

Kowalski took out a large volume of federal codes and showed O'Connor that if he recanted and told the truth while the same grand jury was still in session, he would suffer no legal consequences for his lies.

"I was up all night praying with a friend about what I should do," O'Connor said.

Kowalski had rarely been to church in his life, but in this moment, he decided that faith had its benefits. "Bill, I was up all night too, thinking how Bennie Hays had a heart attack right down *there* yesterday," he said, looking down at the spot far below, where Bennie had fallen the previous afternoon. "I couldn't figure if it was a coincidence or if it was the Lord who struck down Henry's father."

That was all it took to get O'Connor talking. Before he started speaking in detail, Kowalski walked him into the grand jury. Although that testimony is confidential, O'Connor almost certainly told the jurors what he admitted to James Bodman in later interviews. The Klansman said he had been at Henry's home when Henry admitted that he "and Tiger Knowles had picked him [Donald] up, took him to the woods, put a rope around him, dragged him, and as Donald was fighting, they cut his throat."

Kowalski was convinced that Henry had played a major role in the murder, but he knew Henry was unlikely to crack, because he had his father's backing. Kowalski figured he might do better by pressuring Knowles, even though he had no direct evidence linking him to the murder. Knowles has already faced the federal grand jury twice and had given nothing. But Kowalski was ready to do it again.

On May 26, 1983, Kowalski called Knowles into the U.S. courthouse for an interview. The suspect's attorney, A. Holmes Whiddon, accompanied him. Kowalski began by talking about another legal matter. In May 1981 when Knowles still owed $6,300 on his tired pickup truck, he and Frank Cox had set it on fire. To stop further payments, Knowles reported that the vehicle had been stolen.

Most federal prosecutors would ignore this kind of charge when far more serious matters were at stake, but Kowalski decided to bludgeon Knowles with it to try to get him to confess to the murder. Knowles had used the U.S. mails to write the insurance company, so he could be charged with a federal crime and sent away for as long as ten years.

A few days later, the Feds brought Knowles in again and charged him with wire fraud for having collected on his burned-out truck. He made bail and left thinking he would have some time before his next judicial appearance. But on June 2, 1983, Mobile authorities arrived at his father's company in Grand Bay, Alabama, twenty-five miles southwest of Mobile, to arrest Knowles again. The reason, he was told, was that his bail had been reset.

Knowles was embarrassed and humiliated that the police arrested him in front of his distraught parents. His father flared out in anger. Mrs. Knowles was even more distressed. "I know this is about that murder," she said. "I know it is. You people just won't let my son alone."

"Be quiet, Mother, calm down," Knowles said.

His mother had already been brought before the grand jury,

and that had troubled him more than anything else. It was no longer just about him. It was about his family. He posted the new, higher bail, but he knew that did not make any of his problems go away.

A Lesser Crime

JAMES KNOWLES NEEDED money. Bennie Hays had bailed him out on the wire charge, promising to put up his one remaining house on Herndon Avenue as security. But now with the Feds climbing up his back, Knowles needed Bennie to come through again. That's why in early June 1983, Knowles drove out to the Hays house in Theodore.

Raymond Hays, the Klan leader's eldest son, had returned from the army to help out in this time of crisis, and he was there that day. Knowles was a swaggering fellow, but Raymond could see fear in his eyes. Bennie and Knowles went off to talk privately. Raymond couldn't hear what the two men said, but he could tell they were arguing. Knowles then jumped into his truck and gunned it, spinning off in a cloud of dust and gravel.

A few days later at about 8:00 P.M. on Friday, June 10, 1983, Knowles received a call from Roger Brown at the Apple Bonding Company. The bail bondsman asked the young man to come into the office. The matter seemed urgent enough that Knowles drove immediately into Mobile from Grand Bay, arriving before 9:00 P.M. Brown told him that Bennie had changed his mind about putting up one of his houses for bail.

The bondsman made it clear to Knowles that he was in big trouble. He faced a federal indictment for wire fraud, and if he could not raise increased bail money, he would be spending his days in a cell. He could conceivably end up spending years in prison, and that had nothing to do with the Donald murder.

By now, Knowles was fed up. The Feds had dragged his family before the grand jury. Bennie had double-crossed him. And the grand jury was getting closer and closer.

At a little after ten o'clock that evening, FBI agent Bodman's telephone rang. Knowles was on the other end of the phone. "I want to meet with you," he said. "I want to put you straight. You're leaning on the wrong people."

Bodman was growing weary of these games. "Tiger, listen, I know better than that," he said. "But, yeah, I'll meet with you."

Knowles asked that they convene later in a parking lot in downtown Mobile next to the Admiral Semmes Hotel. Bodman was nervous about getting together with a possible killer in the middle of the night, so he called John Lewoczko, a special agent who had recently been transferred to the Mobile office, and asked him to come along.

The two FBI agents got there early and surveyed the area. Then Bodman drove into the parking lot. At around 11:30 P.M., just as the federal agents got out of their car, Knowles and his attorney, Whiddon, appeared out of the darkness.

Knowles shook hands with the FBI agents. Then he said again that the Feds were going after the wrong people.

"I'm not going to spend half the night hearing your lies," Bodman told him. "No way. I'll tell you what. You take your attorney, and you guys step around the corner there and figure this out and then come back, and we'll resolve this."

Bodman thought Knowles and his lawyer might not be back. But after a few minutes, they returned.

"Tiger, now don't lie to me," Bodman said. "Look, I don't believe you and Henry meant to kill him. You two decided you were going to have a little fun with him. But he was scared to death, and he jumped you and was about to whip you, and you couldn't handle him."

Out of nowhere, Bodman had presented Knowles with a story that just might be the escape he'd been seeking. It would mean some time in prison, but it would be a lot better for him than it would be for Henry. And with his ability to finesse his way out of just about anything, who knew how lightly he might be punished and how few days he would spend in a cell?

"Cool," Knowles said. "Honest, Mr. Bodman, we didn't mean to do it."

Knowles said that he and Henry had told the victim they were not going to kill him. But then Donald had done what Bodman said he had done. He had picked up a limb and started flailing away at Henry and Knowles. That's when a "scuffle" broke out, and though Knowles tried to calm the man down, he just kept on scuffling. The way Knowles described it, Donald was complicit in his own death. If only he had the good sense not to do anything, they would have beaten him up and gone on their way.

In dramatic detail, Knowles said that after Michael Donald stopped fighting and lay there, he and Henry were concerned with their victim's deteriorating condition. They put him in the trunk—the trunk, not the backseat—with the intention of taking him to the hospital. Instead, they drove down to Herndon Avenue, where Knowles held the body while Henry used a rope to tie it to a tree. Knowles then noticed that Donald's throat had been cut. He said he hadn't done that, and he didn't think Henry had done it either.

Bodman now had what he needed, and he was not going to risk upsetting Knowles by pushing him to say even more. "Look, Tiger," he said, "you got one choice here. The Feds can save your life. But you gotta move fast."

Bodman did not even consider arresting Knowles. Whiddon watched his client leave and said he wanted to talk to the FBI agent. They drove over to the twenty-four-hour Waffle House out on the peninsula.

"Tiger never told me he killed anybody," Whiddon said. "This is the first time I'm hearing this."

Whiddon was not a criminal defense lawyer. He specialized in divorces and other civil matters. "I'm afraid," Whiddon said, "I need protection. With Knowles turning, there's no telling what the Klan might do."

Bodman thought Whiddon seemed more concerned with his own future than with his client's, and he tried his best to calm down Whiddon.

The next Tuesday, Knowles sat down with Bodman, Kowalski, and Thomas Figures at a Mobile hotel. The federal attorneys were afraid Knowles might back out, so they pushed him to sign a plea agreement. But first he signed a Miranda statement waiving his right to have a lawyer present. That made it perfectly legal to go ahead, but it was questionable if the federal attorneys should have proceeded when this legally naïve young man had no lawyer beside him.

"Just tell 'em what you told me the other night," said Bodman.

It was a horrific tale, but nobody in the room flinched. Knowles had hardly begun when Kowalski began interrupting with questions. Bodman admired Kowalski's dogged intensity, but he had been doing this far longer, and he knew a confession is like a song. You have to give the person the chance to sing it.

"Let the man tell his story," Bodman insisted. "Then you can ask your questions, Barry."

Knowles told how Henry had placed his foot on Donald's forehead and pulled the noose. Previously Knowles had said he had no idea how Donald's throat had been slashed, but that was the most transparent of lies, and he placed the blame on his friend.

Kowalski kept trying to steer Knowles's confession. He did so because there was no law that made it a federal crime to commit a racist murder. Unless the Justice Department attorney came up with a plausible factual scenario in which Knowles had committed some other federal crime, he might leave the room without ever facing federal indictment.

Kowalski's colleague Burt Glenn had pored over statutes, trying to find something that could send Knowles away for life. He had also read in the various testimony that during the weekly Klavern meeting, the Klansmen had discussed the Mobile trial of a black bank robber for the murder of a white police officer, before a nearly all-black jury. Several Klansmen said in their depositions that their colleagues had asserted that if the murderer was not convicted, a black man deserved to die. Just as significantly, Knowles and Henry had followed the jury deliberations of the alleged killer on television news. When the trial ended in a mistrial, they not only sought out a black man to murder, but they also sent other Klansmen to burn a cross in front of the Mobile Courthouse, where the jurors had deliberated.

From this, the federal lawyers came up with a charge that a death had resulted because of a conspiracy to intimidate jurors and "thereby to deny present and future black defendants the equal protection of the law." Kowalski and his team believed this was a sound legal theory. But the convoluted, bizarre charge had never been used before and has not been used since.

To justify this federal charge, Kowalski had to get Knowles to say his motive in killing Michael Donald was more nuanced, beyond simple revenge for a jury failing to convict a black man for murdering a white cop. He nervously pushed Knowles to talk about how the hung jury in the bank robber's trial set off the murder and that in murdering Donald, he and Henry were trying to influence future juries not to free a black man charged with a crime.

The teenager had been out there that night to kill a black man because of the jury's decision, but he was not thinking about affecting the future of jurisprudence. Despite his ninth-grade education, Knowles was an intelligent, perceptive young man, and he quickly grasped what Kowalski wanted—and he also figured that if he went along with Kowalski, he might get a reduced sentence.

The prosecutors still had a major problem: the law was clear that Knowles's confession could not be used to convict Henry.

Unless Knowles agreed to testify against his former friend, Henry might not spend a day in prison.

"Tiger, I've got from the Justice Department an offer of life imprisonment," Kowalski said, "but you would have to testify against Henry."

Kowalski could see that Knowles was frightened.

"Look, Tiger, here's something else we'll do for you," Kowalski continued. "We'll put you in the federal witness protection program. You'll be kept apart in prison, and you'll be safe. You let the folks here indict you, and you'll be in the Alabama prison system where nobody will be there for you. And you'll be staring down the road at the electric chair."

Kowalski figured it was highly unlikely the state would execute a man who had committed murder when he was only seventeen years old, but scaring Knowles might do the trick.

"What about life imprisonment?" Knowles asked. "How long is that?"

"Listen to me closely," Kowalski said. "Look. We got you on a federal charge for burning that truck for insurance fraud. Okay? That carries a ten-year sentence, and that's what we're going for. Okay? Take our deal, and we'll forget the truck. And you know what, Tiger, you'll be eligible for parole after ten years. I'm a little over thirty-five. You could be out when you're my age with most of your life ahead of you."

Kowalski knew the fury over this crime meant Knowles would be in prison for far longer than a decade, but this gambit was worth it, and it worked. When Knowles agreed to the federal plea, Kowalski rushed to push it through and get him in front of a judge. Kowalski called his superior, chief of the division's Criminal Section, Daniel Rinzel, to get down to Mobile as quickly as he could to present the plea to a judge.

FOR THE HEARING on June 16, 1983, Federal District Court judge W. B. Hand presided. Kowalski kept everything as simple as possible. Knowles would receive his negotiated sentence only if he testified against Henry and told the full truth. At this juncture, Kowalski did not press Knowles to admit to anything more than what was necessary to justify the federal charge.

"I would like to say that the death of Michael Donald was not intentional," Knowles said with his lawyer Whiddon beside him.

"You took and prepared a noose intending to use it?" Judge Hand asked.

"The intent was not to use it," Knowles said. "It was just to tie a hangman's noose."

Knowles wanted the judge to believe that on the evening of the lynching, the two killers had laboriously prepared a hangman's knot with no more purpose than Boy Scouts tying knots for merit badges. Kowalski suspected rightfully that Knowles was saying less than the full truth, but he did not know for sure, and he did not want to risk losing the case's best witness—and a guilty plea with a federal life sentence—in an effort to find out.

In a courtroom, what was called justice and what was the truth did not always coincide, and Kowalski had no interest in confronting Knowles with his apparent lies. He counted the minutes until Knowles was handcuffed, taken into custody, and led away for what he hoped was a life spent in prison.

Black Sheep

ON THE DAY that Knowles pled guilty in federal court, Henry drove to the Hudson Oil gas station and convenience store out on the causeway on Mobile Bay. He was in training to run the station, and for the first time in his adult life, he would be someone of importance.

When his father sold his houses on Herndon Avenue, Henry had moved to a house trailer down the road from his father's place, where Bennie cast a shadow over everything his son did or said. But now Henry was no longer there. He had left his wife, Denise, a few days before and had moved in with Janet Deem, an older woman who managed the five Hudson stations in Mobile.

That morning a line of police cars descended on the gas station. FBI agents shackled Henry in handcuffs behind his back, read him his rights, and drove him downtown. Wearing jeans, a T-shirt, dark glasses, and slicked-back hair, he looked like a punk who had been arrested for shoplifting. The Feds remanded him to the Mobile authorities, who charged him with murder. This was happening to him at the best moment in his life, and he stumbled ahead in handcuffs as if in a dream.

Bennie understood full well what might be in store for his youngest son. Recovered from his apparent heart attack, he shouted that Henry was innocent and that this was all a conspiracy. Bennie was not just signaling to his son that they were a united front and should stand together. He was also protecting himself, his son-in-law, the rest of the Klavern, and even the United Klans of America.

Bennie believed that because he was one of the state leaders of the UKA and his son was an officer of the Klavern, they deserved the UKA's full financial backing as well as Robert Shelton's moral support. However, this was not the 1960s, when a Klansman who murdered a black man could be celebrated. These days it wasn't good to be too closely associated with the possible killer of a young black man.

As soon as Shelton realized the consequences this indictment might have for the UKA, he decided to back off. He was not going to spend the UKA's resources on an expensive defense.

Nor would he vouch for Henry's innocence, as he had for other Klansmen accused of murder in the past.

Henry stood alone facing a possible death sentence. Only Bennie and Henry knew what the father had said to his son before the lynching and how much he had pushed Henry to fulfill his pledge to kill a black man. Whatever it was, Bennie was worried what would happen if Henry opened his mouth and brought his father beside him at the tribunal of justice. And that was enough of a reason for why Bennie was doing whatever he could to help his son.

Henry needed a top defense lawyer, and one of the best, and most expensive, in Mobile was M. A. "Bubba" Marsal. Two years earlier when Bennie had sold four of his houses on Herndon Avenue, he was a man of some means. But much of that money was gone, and he did not have anywhere near the $50,000 Marsal wanted up front to defend Henry.

Desperate to get the money, in July 1983, Bennie decided to set his house on fire and collect the insurance money. He and a fellow Klansman removed a prized new television before torching the place. He then pushed to have the insurance money expedited, so he could give it to Marsal. Both the local fire investigator and the Allstate Insurance Company thought the fire was suspicious and began investigations. And so while his son faced a murder trial, Bennie risked joining Henry in the county jail.

As Henry sat in his tiny cell, he knew the testimony of his closest friend might cause him to be found guilty and be sentenced to die in the electric chair at Holman Prison. That possibility was so horrendous that in his love letters to Janet Deem he did not discuss it even once.

Henry felt sorry for himself. He might have railed out at Bennie and blamed him on any number of levels for bringing him to such a terrible place. Instead he moaned about the sheer unfairness of his plight. He had not killed Donald, and it was wrong that the prosecutor was trying to make him take the rap for someone else. He was just now getting his act together and had met the woman he planned to spend the rest of his life with, and then this terrible misfortune had happened to him.

When Henry talked to Deem, he cried and told her how weak and sad he felt. To his father, he had to play the man, and as he wrote Deem, "I'm learning I'm not that much of a man." He hated talking to Bennie, and he vowed "lots of things are going to be different between us when this is finally over." But these were not words he could speak to his father or even insinuate. He was more dependent on him than ever, perhaps for his very life. His father said he had already spent $63,000 on the defense. That was a fortune, and they had not even come to trial yet.

It was bad enough sitting in a tiny jail cell, but it was far worse because Henry felt he had no control over his case. Bubba Marsal and his father oversaw everything. "I'm nobody, never have been," he wrote his love. "My mother thinks I'm a doper, my father thinks I'm a doper, a liar, a good for nothing, a black sheep, my sister thinks I'm cold, unfeeling, selfish."

Henry woke up screaming in the middle of the night in a cold sweat.

A Capital Offense

D.A. CHRIS GALANOS was a meticulous man who kept notes in tiny, spider-like handwriting and liked to do everything with precision. He had incredible bursts of energy, fueled by the prescription diet pills he was popping like smoked almonds. He didn't think he had a drug problem. He was working all these cases, kicking butt right and left. He had a young family he loved. As far as he was concerned, everything was fine.

But Galanos knew he had a problem with the upcoming trial. His capital murder case against Henry Hays was largely based on James Knowles saying in court that he and Henry had set out that evening to lynch a black man. But Knowles kept repeating the original story he had told FBI agent James Bodman in a Mobile parking lot: they hadn't intended to kill Donald; it had gotten tragically out of hand. If Knowles told that story in the courtroom, Henry might be convicted, but it wouldn't be for premeditated murder, which could send him to the electric chair.

Knowles knew his words could get Henry killed, and he did not want to speak them. "I was afraid he'd go to the electric chair," says Knowles. He was trying to walk the narrowest of pathways, saying enough to keep his plea deal, but not so much that his words could be used to convict Henry of premeditated murder. And he was doing this without the advice of a lawyer or anyone with whom he could discuss what he was attempting.

The trial was scheduled for December 1983, and in late October Galanos and Bodman flew to San Diego, where Knowles had been moved to protective custody within the federal Metropolitan Correctional Center. The night before their meeting, Bodman heard Galanos pacing all night long in their adjoining hotel rooms. As far as the special agent could tell, the D.A. did not sleep all night.

In the morning, Knowles stuck to his story that Michael Donald's death was all a big mistake. Galanos was livid that his best shot at convicting Henry for premeditated murder was falling apart. He asked Bodman if he could interview Knowles alone in the afternoon. Knowles was supposed to be interviewed only with federal officials present, but Bodman worked it out with his bosses and the interview went ahead.

Galanos considered the convicted killer a sociopath who had landed a sweet deal he did not deserve. The D.A. spoke so slowly that he could have been dictating, his words charged with anger. "This is what you signed, Tiger," Galanos said, showing the plea bargain. "You promised to tell the truth, all of it, and you haven't done it. Keep it up, Tiger, and you're going to the electric chair. I'll put you there, and I'll be there the day they strap you in Yellow Mama, and I'll watch you burn. And I'll enjoy it. You hear me, Tiger."

Knowles didn't realize there was almost no way he would be sent to the electric chair. He was horrified by the idea of taking that final walk. "What do you want?" Knowles asked.

"I want the truth," Galanos said. "I don't want any more bullshit."

"Henry and I made plans to kill a black man a few days before it happened," Knowles said. "Henry's father knew about it, and so did Frank Cox."

"Here's what we're gonna do, Tiger," Galanos said, standing up. "I'm Michael Donald. Okay? And you're going to do to me just like you did to him. Understand?"

And so Knowles told Galanos how he and Henry murdered Donald, detailing every last bloody blow.

WHEN CHRIS GALANOS returned from California and marched back into his Mobile office, he boasted in his bold, almost manic way that he had gotten Knowles to talk, and he had the case under control. The same was not true of his life. For months he had been ingesting prescribed Dexedrine diet pills in such numbers that they had changed almost everything in his public conduct. He thought he could manage his problem, but he had been pulled over by the police, who wrote him up for a charge of driving under the influence of drugs.

In early December, the week before the most important trial of his life, Galanos spent much of his time trying to get the misdemeanor dismissed. He was able to have the charges thrown out, but the whole matter had become public.

Galanos had overseen the attempt to indict three innocent young Cajuns for the Donald murder, and in presiding over

Henry's murder trial, he would redeem himself and his reputation on any number of levels. But finally he realized that a D.A. with an acknowledged drug problem could not prosecute Henry Hays.

Three days before the beginning of the trial, Galanos told Chief Assistant District Attorney Thomas E. Harrison that he would be handling it. A few days later, the D.A. got in his car and drove to Atlanta to turn himself in for twenty-eight days of drug rehabilitation.

For months, Harrison and everyone else around the D.A. had been dealing with Galanos's increasing irritability and quirkiness, known side effects from the use of prescription amphetamines. The D.A. would erupt over the most trivial matters and show up at 3:00 A.M. to go to work. But Galanos's colleagues had no idea that he had a drug problem and figured he was under too much stress.

Harrison was tall, handsome, elegantly presented, articulate, forceful, and well connected. He had kept up with the documents and filings passing across his desk, but that did not mean he was prepared to prosecute Henry Hays at trial. On such short notice, even a more typical murder case would have been difficult, but this trial would be unlike any in decades.

As Harrison worked frantically preparing for the trial, Knowles had already been transferred to the jail in town, sitting in a cell, waiting to be called as the trial's star witness. Harrison figured the best and quickest way to learn about the case was to spend a few hours with Knowles at the murder scene, recreating as much as possible what had gone on. He arranged to do so over the weekend accompanied by state investigator Bob Eddy and an FBI agent.

As the four men drove out to Baldwin County, Knowles told the story of the murder once again. He said things had gotten out of hand, and they had not intended to kill Donald. Knowles was again trying to walk the tightrope between saving both himself and his friend. Although Harrison kept his composure, the prosecutor was livid, knowing that if Knowles told that tale on the witness stand, Henry would likely not be convicted of capital murder.

The chief assistant D.A. was under extreme pressure to walk out of the Mobile courtroom with a death sentence. The last time a white man had been executed for killing a black man was in 1913. If Henry were given life imprisonment, many in the black community, including members of the Donald family, would consider it just another example of white man's justice.

Back in his office, as Harrison worked his way through the piles of documents, he discovered that in seeking to execute Henry, D.A. Galanos had overlooked one major problem. The indictment charged that Henry had killed Donald by strangling him with a rope during a kidnapping. To the layman that would seem sufficient to ask for the death penalty. But Alabama law put forth highly specific criteria for any jury considering "capital murder."

To send Henry to the electric chair, Harrison would have to show that the accused had set out to commit a felony. That was defined as using either force or fear and, once the victim was dead, robbing him of personal property.

Harrison had learned that in the months since the indictment, Knowles had given several more confessions to various investigators, during which he mentioned having held a pistol on Donald. In one interview, he said that in the car on the way to the murder site, he ordered Donald to empty his pockets, and when he did, to set his wallet on the floorboard.

As Harrison continued going through the police reports, he read that Donald had left his home that evening with one dollar in his wallet. That money was no longer in the wallet found in a Dumpster the morning after the murder. The police had no evidence that the dollar had been in the wallet when Donald got in the car or that Henry had anything to do with the wallet. Harrison, nonetheless, decided that Henry had committed armed robbery, and with that, he could charge him with capital murder.

Chris Galanos had known all of this for months and had done nothing about it. Now, as the trial was beginning, Harrison hoped he could get a new indictment including the armed robbery charge, and Knowles would tell the full truth. Harrison feared that if these things didn't happen, he might end up overseeing a legal debacle for which he would receive much of the blame. It did not make for a weekend of easy sleeping.

Harrison had another reason he wasn't sleeping well. He had heard rumors that if he obtained a conviction the Klan planned to go after him—and that if he failed to convict, there would be race riots in the streets of Mobile. The threats were serious enough that Harrison decided to drive a different car to the courthouse each day and to take different routes while constantly watching behind him.

WHEN HARRISON CAME into the state courthouse for the first day of trial, instead of going to the courtroom, he walked upstairs and successfully asked a recently impaneled county grand jury for a new indictment that would raise this case to capital murder.

The indictment charged that Henry Hays had used a pistol to steal one dollar from Michael Donald's wallet and of the wallet itself, which was valued at two dollars. If Henry ended up dying in the electric chair, it would be because he had stolen a wallet containing a single dollar while he was committing the murder.

As Harrison walked into the courtroom carrying the new indictment, he was happy to see M. A. "Bubba" Marsal, a man he respected. Everyone called the fifty-nine-year-old lawyer "Bubba," even the judges in court. It was a nickname that in the South was an honored term of endearment.

But Marsal was furious when Harrison handed him the enlarged indictment. "I attack the indictment on grounds of misconduct," Marsal told Judge Braxton L. Kittrell Jr., not even trying to contain his rage. "This indictment now charges an aspect that has never been charged. Now is the first time we see the element of robbery. Why weren't we told back then that a gun was involved and the money was taken? I have a right to find out all about the weapon."

Harrison kept responding that it was the same case, but that now Henry Hays was being charged under the proper statute. Judge Kittrell was not about to throw out the indictment, but he did everything he could to placate Marsal. It would be a public relations disaster to delay the trial any longer, but the judge also couldn't have the defense attorney staging a revolt in the courtroom.

The Second-Most-Hated Man

MORRIS SELIGMAN DEES Jr. showed up at the Mobile Courthouse for the first day of the trial the moment the outer doors were opened. The cofounder of the Southern Poverty Law Center (SPLC) sensed that this lynching was not just about Henry and Knowles. There had to be others involved in the Mobile Klavern who must feel the lash of justice, and beyond them loomed Robert Shelton, the Imperial Wizard of the United Klans of America.

There was no telling what the lawyer might learn roaming the corridors chatting with folks. Even if nothing panned out and the SPLC was unable to file a civil lawsuit, he was happy just to be there. He loved the old courthouse, the hangers-on and the riffraff, the savvy old bailiffs, the hustling attorneys.

The coat and tie he wore suggested that he cared about courtroom decorum, even if the quality of its cut said he didn't care as much about style. The forty-six-year-old lawyer had a mane of curly dark blond hair, intense blue eyes, and such sculptured good looks he might have been a member of the old elite. But he was not a gentleman in the way the blue bloods of Alabama defined the term. The lean, six-foot-tall lawyer was the son of a tenant farmer. In high school in Montgomery, when his well-born classmates were driving off to cotillion classes, Dees was slopping hogs.

Fresh out of the University of Alabama Law School in September 1960, Dees proved himself not just a good attorney, but along with his law partner, Millard Fuller, a successful entrepreneur. The two men made a fortune in direct mail. They knew what to sell and how to sell it, from birthday cakes to tractor cushions to cookbooks.

In 1969, when the lawyer-businessman sold his company for $6 million—about $30 million in today's money—he decided to form a pro bono law firm that would focus entirely on the civil rights work he was already doing part-time. Dees and another young Montgomery attorney, Joseph J. Levin Jr., founded the SPLC in 1971. It worked just as Dees hoped it would, and with its five lawyers and small support staff, and his extraordinary marketing skills, the SPLC did an outsized job.

In 1975 *Time* called Dees "the second most hated man in Alabama," outranked only by federal judge Frank Johnson. He knew a lot of people would not be happy that he was becoming involved in the Michael Donald murder case. His conservative critics considered Dees a turncoat, a former segregationist who now hobnobbed with people he would have once shunned. It wasn't just those on the right who had no use for him. Even Montgomery's small liberal community had its problems with Dees. He was flamboyant and self-aggrandizing. He was nothing but a provocateur. He stole their light. He worked without their counsel. He never knew when enough was enough. And worst of all, and this was indisputably true, he didn't give a damn what they thought about him.

In June 1983, when he read about the arrests of Klansmen

Henry Hays and Tiger Knowles for the Donald murder, he sensed immediately that the SPLC should become involved. He knew he would need a local attorney sitting beside him, one who knew Mobile's black community. He remembered hearing a speech delivered by State Senator Michael Figures. The youthful politician was powerfully eloquent, and Dees thought Figures could bring those same abilities into a courtroom.

Dees called Figures and learned that he had visited the Donald home after the murder to pay his respects to the family. Mrs. Donald had not forgotten that gesture, and Figures was one of the few people she trusted. Dees asked Figures if Mrs. Donald would consider having the SPLC file a civil lawsuit on her behalf against those who had murdered her son.

Mrs. Donald never asked Figures how much money she might get if they won. She was fine living in her ninety-eight-dollar-a-month apartment with Michael's bedroom just as it had been. What she wanted was meaning for her son's life. She did not want her Michael to be "just another colored man, as they say, gone on and forgotten."

She told Figures that yes, the civil lawsuit against the Klan could be filed in her name. But she was still suspicious. She had learned long ago that the bigger a promise the less likely it would ever happen, and in her experience that was doubly true when white men made the promise.

A Matter of Justice

ALTHOUGH ALABAMA NO longer had the segregated courtrooms so vividly portrayed in Harper Lee's *To Kill a Mockingbird*, black observers and white observers of the murder trial still took places apart from one another.

On one side of the courtroom sat African Americans, including representatives from the NAACP and other activist organizations. Defense attorney Marsal had used his challenges against potential black jurors and there was only one black member on the twelve-person jury. That enraged many of the African American spectators, who doubted if a just verdict would be found before what they considered a racist jury. Dees too would spend most of his time on this side of the courtroom.

Mrs. Donald would like to have been there sitting with members of her race hoping to see some measure of justice for Michael's death. But the memory of the questions the police had asked about her son made her fear what the defense attorney might say about Michael. She just could not bring herself to come to the courtroom, but numerous other members of the Donald family attended.

In the middle sat white members of the general public and lawyers intrigued by the case. The other side was filled primarily with Klan members. Bennie Hays, his wife, other Hays family members and friends sat among their Klan colleagues. Most of the men wore jeans with enormous brass belt buckles that set off the metal detectors that were being used for the first time in the Mobile County Courthouse.

With them sat Bill Stanton, who in his blue jeans and work shirt looked to be what he said he was, a truck driver who hated what was being done to Henry. But Stanton was actually head of KlanWatch, a new program the SPLC had formed to keep tabs on the various Klan organizations and other white-supremacist activity. Knowing that there would be all kinds of Klans people in the courtroom, Dees had asked Stanton to sit with them in the courtroom and to pretend to be a sympathizer. This was over-the-top dangerous, and if Dees had not been so recognizable, he might have done it himself.

When James Knowles was sworn in as a prosecution witness,

he had federal marshals both inside and outside the courtroom to protect him. Dressed in blue jeans and a sports jacket, the chunky, twenty-year-old confessed murderer had grown long sideburns and a mustache while he was in prison.

He pronounced his name in such a quiet voice that Judge Braxton Kittrell admonished him to speak more loudly. He continued to speak softly throughout the proceedings, but the words rocketed out of him at a fast clip, as if he couldn't wait to be finished.

"Would you look about the courtroom and see if you see the individual you know as Henry Hays?" Harrison asked.

"The man sitting right there," Knowles said, pointing to Henry, who sat twenty-five feet away at the end of the defense table. Henry wore pink slacks and a multicolored vest and did not look like a man on trial for his life. Henry kept smiling at his girlfriend, Janet Deem, to whom he passed handwritten letters every morning.

Knowles knew that this day he could either save himself from trial in Alabama or save Henry from possible execution, but he couldn't do both. He had decided he would tell the whole story of the premeditated murder so he could save himself and guarantee his sentence in a federal prison.

No one was making a sound in the courtroom as Knowles explained how he and Henry headed out into the nighttime streets, looking for a black man they could lynch. He told how their victim huddled in the backseat of the car as Knowles periodically poked the gun toward him. "I asked Donald to empty his pockets out," the young killer said, in his bloodless retelling of the tale. "I didn't know what kind of instruments or anything he might have in his pockets. As far as I recall, all he had was a wallet. I laid it on the floorboard of the car."

When they reached the secluded wooded destination beside a garbage dump, Henry got out and stood in the clearing. "Michael Donald kept shaking his head and saying 'Please don't kill me' and 'Let me go,'" Knowles testified. "And the defendant and myself kept saying, 'Calm down, nothing's going to happen to you.' And then Donald, it was like he was a crazed madman all of a sudden. I had the gun in my hand, and Donald jumped me."

Harrison's questions became shorter and shorter, and Knowles was soon speaking without interruption about the final moments of Donald's life.

"I fell to the ground, and we were all three piled up," he said, with no emotion. "The pistol went off. No one was hit. Donald broke loose and he got ahold of a limb off of a tree. And somehow or another, it got knocked out of his hand, and we started struggling again. And he was just like he'd give out, like he was a mad animal, and he just laid there on the ground breathing real heavily like a madman.

"Henry went to the automobile and got the hangman's noose, and the both of us managed to get it around Donald's neck. Henry started pulling on the rope, and I got this limb that Donald had, and I started hitting Donald with it. Donald would get up to his knees, and then he would almost fall back. Something prompted us to just switch places. I got the rope, and Hays got the limb and started hitting Donald. And just moments later Donald just fell face flat on the ground.

"Henry Hays and myself put the body in the trunk. I asked Hays, 'Do you think he's dead?' And he said, 'I don't know, but I'm going to make sure,' and he cut Donald's throat three times.'"

Knowles spoke with such clinical detachment he sounded at times as if he were speaking about an event he had observed from a cautious distance. Mrs. Knowles had come to the courtroom to hear her son's testimony. She could not believe he was talking about these horrendous events in such a disengaged manner.

Henry Hays appeared to be as emotionally detached. While Knowles was describing the murder, the accused kept fidgeting, looking back at Janet Deem and smiling, as if he too were a spectator to the trial.

There was nothing distanced in the way Michael Donald's family and friends and most of the other African Americans in the courtroom listened to Knowles's testimony. They whispered to each other nervously and shook their heads in disbelief at the horrifying things they were hearing.

BUBBA MARSAL COULD see that this trial was turning out to be a battle of two stories, and that the person whose story was more compelling would win. The way Knowles delivered his may have sounded like he was distanced from the horrifying event, but everyone could tell that his story was mesmerizing the jury. He was speaking the most riveting, gut-wrenching detail, creating a tale that would surely burn its way into the consciousness of the jury. Marsal couldn't jump and complain about how unfair it was that Knowles was such a compelling witness, but even so he was looking for some way to stymie the prosecutor.

"Just a moment, please, Judge," Marsal said, interrupting the testimony. Judge Kittrell called a break in the trial and sent the jury back to their room.

"I ask the court to take view of the two parcels in transparent plastic bags that appear to be rope," Marsal said after the jury had left. "They now sit approximately four to five feet immediately in front of the jury box, and I submit to the court that such is contradictory of a fair trial afforded to the defendant."

Judge Kittrell did not think it a problem that the jury had seen the rope that Knowles said the two men had pulled tightly around Donald's neck, strangling him. Marsal lost that challenge, but nevertheless he had successfully broken the rhythm of the testimony.

Harrison's questions throughout his examination of Knowles had been simple and straightforward. When the jury returned he ended with the simplest questions of all.

"What were you looking for on that particular evening?"

"A black man off by hisself secluded from anyone else."

"And what did you intend to do with that black man off secluded by himself?"

"We intended to hang him on Herndon Avenue."

"Did you intend to kill him at the time you picked him up?"

"Yes, we did."

"Simply because he was a black man isolated?"

"Yes, sir."

"That's all we have at this time, Your Honor."

"The Forces of Evil"

WHEN BUBBA MARSAL got up for the cross-examination, it was obvious from the murmurs in the courtroom, especially from black members of the audience, that many thought Knowles had been a successful witness. That irritated Marsal. "I don't think I have to tolerate those remarks that's coming from my back," Marsal said.

"If I hear any further remarks, I'm going to have them removed from the courtroom," the judge said, reprimanding the spectators.

Marsal pointed out that Knowles had changed his testimony many times. He read from his original June 1983 confession and got the convicted murderer to admit that much of it was untrue or half true. Whether or not that did some damage to Knowles's credibility, it gave the jury yet another recounting of the disturbing tale.

Marsal next attempted to discredit the witness by showing that he had cut a deal with the Feds to testify. As Marsal described the agreement, it suggested that Knowles might exaggerate or even lie to get a lesser sentence. At minimum, it was grossly unfair. He had agreed to testify against his closest friend in exchange for going to federal, instead of state, prison. Meanwhile his hapless partner, whose life was one miscue after another, faced the possibility of death in Alabama's electric chair.

It enraged Marsal that the slippery Knowles would not even admit what he had done. He had cut his deal with the Feds six months ago, but he had not yet been sentenced. It was clear the federal government was waiting to see what Knowles said in this courtroom, but there was nothing a defense attorney could do but live with this and move on.

Marsal needed a plausible scenario for the murder that did not involve his client. He said Knowles had committed the crime by himself.

"During that night, is it not a fact that while this young man was in that house playing cards or having a party that you left in that pickup truck and you came back with the body of Michael Donald?"

"That is not true," Knowles said.

"And isn't it a fact that you went over there and pulled up a canvas to be sure that Michael Donald was still under there?"

"No, it's not true."

Marsal had nothing to support this scenario. If Harrison had thought this account gained any traction with the jury, he could have refuted it by calling any number of witnesses who had seen Henry and Knowles together during the evening of the murder. He did not do so.

After lunch, Marsal resumed his cross-examination.

"So, Mr. Knowles, you testify that the sole purpose of the two of you abducting this young man and going to Baldwin County and back to Mobile County was because he was black. Is that what you tell us?"

"Yes, sir."

"That's the sole reason," Marsal demanded.

"That and to show the strength of the Klan."

"To show the strength of the Klan?"

"Yes, sir," Knowles said. "To show that they were still here in Alabama."

Marsal asked about the FBI agents to whom he had confessed.

"And what did they do then?" Marsal asked sarcastically. "They kiss you good night?"

"No, they did not," Knowles said.

WHEN DEES LEFT the courtroom that afternoon, he and Bill Stanton from KlanWatch walked together the few blocks to the Malaga Inn. The old hotel had a quaint courtyard, latticework railings, outdoor stairways and halls. It was Dees's favorite place to stay in the city.

Dees had first come down to Mobile in 1958 when he had taken off a semester before starting law school to work in George Wallace's first unsuccessful race for governor. He had spent a lot of time on the waterfront in dives full of drug dealers, petty crooks, mobsters, prostitutes, longshoremen, and other low-life types looking for trouble. These were dangerous places with a scent of evil to them, and he loved it. And he loved coming back and walking near those streets.

In the lawyer's room at the hotel, Stanton said he had been able to talk to Bennie, Frank Cox, and some of the other Klan members. He hoped he would be able to lead them into implicating themselves in the lynching or saying other things useful in a civil suit, but they weren't going to be pulled into such admissions.

Dees understood the risk Stanton was taking to infiltrate the Klansmen in the courtroom. He knew what happened when you investigated the Klan. Arsonists had tried to destroy the SPLC offices the previous July. If the perpetrators had opened the windows, the whole building likely would have gone down, but starved for oxygen, the fire had burned itself out. The arsonists had focused their efforts on the KlanWatch office full of investigatory files. The fireproof file cabinets that the SPLC had invested in did their job and the crucial research was safe.

Dees's instincts told him that Joe M. Garner, the Snowden, Alabama, volunteer fire chief and a Klansman, was behind the fire. Dees believed the SPLC would have to get the evidence to convict the perpetrators, or it would go down in history as just another unsolved Klan crime. When he got back to Montgomery, he knew he would have to do whatever had to be done so Garner would be brought to trial. It was not, however, until February 1985 that Garner and two of his associates pled guilty to setting the fire and went to prison.

Earlier in 1983 Dees had successfully won a court fight stopping a group of Klansmen and their supporters from harassing and destroying the boats of immigrant Vietnamese fishermen in Galveston Bay. Louis Beam, the Grand Dragon of the Texas Knights of the Ku Klux Klan, was so angry he threatened to kill Dees, and if that didn't work to challenge him to a duel. "Your mother, why I can just see her now," he wrote Dees in 1983, "her heart just bursting with pride as you, for the first time in your life, exhibit the qualities of a man."

Beam told his fellow Klansmen that he had "come under attack by the forces of evil . . . Morris Dees, an anti-Christ Communist Jew." Many people thought the Baptist-raised Dees was Jewish. He was named Morris Seligman Dees Jr., after his father, whose own father named two of his three sons after Jewish businessmen.

Now as he and Stanton discussed the Michael Donald case, Dees said he was convinced that almost everything was going the prosecutor's way. Marsal had attempted to discredit Knowles, but Dees felt that the young killer had walked off the witness stand largely unchallenged. Harrison was prosecuting this case as just another street crime, the sort of matter that came up week after week in the Mobile County Courthouse.

Dees said that if he had been prosecuting this case, he would have treated the murder as a political assassination and an attempt to revive the practice of lynching. He would have talked too about the evil of the Klan and how it had led these two young men to commit this crime. But he also understood Harrison's strategy. The best way to get a conviction was to keep the jury focused on the crime itself, and it was politically astute not to talk of the Klan.

Hours later, Dees and Stanton were still chatting about the case when the telephone rang. It was Danny Welch. They had known each other since Welch was a boy, and he and Dees liked to ride motorcycles together. The former top homicide investigator for the Montgomery police, Welch had left the force to join a private security firm. That's when Dees hired him as a security consultant.

"Morris, I got a call from the FBI," Welch said. "They've got credible evidence that you've been targeted by a white supremacist group, and they might be coming down to kill you."

"Who is it?" Dees asked.

"Confidential source. You know the way it is. But I'm on my way down there, Morris, and I'm bringing a couple of boys with me."

Dees thought he could take care of himself, and he had hired Welch primarily to work out security for the SPLC office. He figured he could outthink and outshoot—he carried a pistol for this very reason—anyone who might try to harm him. He liked to come and go as he pleased. Normally, he would have waved Welch off, but there was an ominous tone in his friend's voice that Dees couldn't ignore.

"Sizzling of the Flesh"

EARLY THE NEXT morning, Dees arrived at the courthouse with Welch and the two other members of his gun-toting security detail. The three men sat in the courtroom and monitored the halls. Dees would never admit he was afraid, but he was glad they were there.

After a short while, Dees stopped thinking about the death threat and turned his full attention to Harrison's questioning of Teddy Kyzar. The Klan had been the best and most exciting thing in Kyzar's life, but the word had gotten out that he had talked to the FBI and he was devastated that he was now considered a traitor. He testified that he had received three death threats, including the first one "from Bennie Hays hisself." Kyzar was so frightened he did not want to tell the court where he lived.

People thought Kyzar was slow, but he had a remarkable memory, and he brought it into the courtroom this day. He recalled Henry and Knowles returning to Henry's apartment about 12:30 P.M., the night of the lynching. "Tiger was the last one to come in the door, and when I looked up, I saw blood all over his shirt," Kyzar said. "I snatched ahold of Tiger and drug him out in the hallway. I said, 'I don't know what y'all been doing. Tiger, you got blood all over your clothes.'

"And he looked down. He had a blue-jean-type shirt that buttoned down the middle, and from the end of the cuffs up both arms, down his chest and his stomach he was drenched in blood, just like if you jumped in a swimming pool with a T-shirt on. He looked down and saw the blood, and he began to snatch the shirt off. He didn't unbutton it. The buttons popped off in the hallway."

DEES KEPT VISUALLY scanning the crowd. He rarely described anyone as evil, but the more he looked at Bennie Hays, the more he thought *evil* was the one and only word that described him. Bennie's right hand cradled his cane. Whenever anyone said something that upset the Klan leader, he tensed up, grasped the cane menacingly, and cursed the witness with his gaze. Dees could not wait to get him into a deposition.

As the trial proceeded, and Dees kept looking at Henry, he was sickened by the thought that he might die in the electric chair. Dees knew that many people would think he was a weak-kneed namby-pamby to be concerned with saving the life of this murderous thug. As the lawyer saw it, the worst was that so many black Alabamans supported the death penalty, even though the electric chair in Alabama seemed to be practically reserved for black men. Dees didn't believe that executing Henry would give the Donald family any sense of closure.

He was so opposed to the death penalty that earlier in the year, he had been in this very courthouse trying, unsuccessfully, to save a serial killer from the death penalty. Now, in the Donald case, Dees didn't believe that Henry should have been charged with capital murder. Dees thought Henry was being railroaded toward the electric chair in what he saw as a "judicial lynching."

In Alabama, it didn't matter how many times a person killed or how vicious or premeditated it was. To be guilty of a capital crime, he must have committed armed robbery in the commission of his crime. If the murderer didn't rob his victim, he could not be electrocuted. As evil as Henry's actions had been, nothing good could come out of killing a man for a crime he did not commit.

As Dees saw it, defending the accused was one of the glories of the law, and he admired the fight Marsal was putting up to save Henry. The Mobile attorney didn't have the pretensions of many big-city lawyers and fought his battles on his own. Dees felt a kinship with Marsal. They were both, in his view, a disappearing breed.

Dees even tried to push his views upon Marsal. During recess, Dees told Marsal how he had recently won a reversal in the Court of Criminal Appeals for Matthew L. Beverly, who had been sentenced to die for a murder involving a robbery.

Beverly had picked up a teenage boy and his girlfriend. One of the three suggested that there would be more room in the car if they placed the couple's backpack in the trunk. Beverly then drove to a secluded spot and shot the young man to death. He drove off with the young woman and later raped her before releasing her on the side of the road. Then the killer drove off with the backpack still in the trunk.

Dees managed to convince the court that Beverly leaving with the backpack was not a conscious robbery, and he could not be given the death sentence. Dees told Marsal that what Henry and Knowles did to their victim was not robbery either, and the indictment was false.

On the first day of the trial, Marsal had spurned Dees's advice that he make all kinds of objections. That's not how he fought a case. His approach was to get up there and tell such a compelling story that when it was over his client was found not guilty and walked out of the courtroom a free man. But the defense attorney was a realist. Marsal knew it wasn't going that well for Henry, and he had to try anything that might work.

"There has been no proof that there was ever intent on the part of any defendant to commit robbery," Marsal told the judge. "There's a complete voidance of any evidence to sustain an attempt to commit robbery."

Marsal went on to talk in detail about Section 13a-5-31a-2 of the Code of Alabama dealing with the definition of capital murder. The argument was hard to follow by anyone but a lawyer, but this was one of the most crucial moments in the entire trial. Henry's life might depend on the outcome.

Marsal asked that Knowles be brought back to testify as to whether he and Henry had robbed Donald. Henry had been driving the car, and if anyone had committed robbery, it was Knowles. In his testimony, Knowles said he'd asked Donald to empty his pockets, but it was clear he had not intended to rob the victim.

"If I had been called back to testify, I would have said 'no, I did not rob Michael Donald,'" says Knowles.

To buttress his request, Marsal brought up the Beverly case. "The supreme court appointed Mr. Dees as the attorney to research and file briefs in that case," said Marsal, nodding toward Dees who sat a few feet in front of him.

Marsal made a compelling presentation, but there was no way to shut local politics out of the courtroom. If Judge Kittrell called for a mistrial based on the state's misguided indictment it would mark the second time the Mobile authorities had botched the case. Black residents had marched through the streets already seeking justice for Michael Donald, and they would likely march again, and it would be a shameful time for the city on the bay.

"Motion denied," Judge Kittrell declared.

OUT IN THE corridor, Bennie told a television reporter that sometimes it was good for a son to sacrifice himself for the sake of other people's happiness. Janet Deem was listening, and she was stunned he would say that about the man she loved. She "took it that he was taking and giving up Henry's freedom for someone else's."

When Henry Hays was sworn in as the final defense witness, his words would likely determine if he would go free, spend the rest of his life in prison, or die in the electric chair. Given that pressure, his account of the day of the murder was a startling performance. He painted an elaborate picture full of exquisitely rendered details.

It all began, he said, that Friday afternoon when Henry was hanging out with his buddy Knowles and his brother-in-law, Cox. "Tiger's car had stalled over on the Interstate there in Theodore, and they needed to get it back over to Grand Bay," Henry said. "Tiger didn't want to leave, you know, the car sitting there on the Interstate, you know, over, you know, overnight." And so after driving to his car "just to make sure they hadn't towed it away or nothing," they headed over to the home of Cox's parents in Theodore.

The three men borrowed a rope from Cox's mother and drove to the stalled car. "Frank got the rope," Henry testified, "and they got out, and they hooked the car up and everything. They tied it on and everything, and we towed it to a service station all the way there in Grand Bay, right there off of Old Highway Ninety."

Henry then drove with his friends to his apartment on Herndon Avenue. Except for going out for forty-five minutes picking up Mountain Dew at the 7-Eleven and playing a little pinball, he said he spent the whole evening having a good time with family and friends, playing spades and Uno. "There was me and Denise as partner, and I think Linda and David was partners," Henry said. "I'm not really for sure, you know exactly. Sometimes I didn't really want to be partners with Denise, you know, I mean that's why, you know, because she gets mad real easy about losing."

On the morning after the lynching, Henry said he got up early and saw police cars arriving and the body hanging from a tree. His immediate thought was how he could be of assistance. "All that day," he testified, "we were trying to help in every way we can, you know, trying to get other people, names, you know, different vehicles, coming and goings of people."

Marsal presented no evidence to document the story, no police account of the car on the side of the highway, no record of service on the vehicle at the gas station, no witnesses who had seen any of this, and no testimony from Cox verifying what his brother-in-law had said.

BUBBA MARSAL HAD been fighting two trials: to have Henry found not guilty, and to save him from the electric chair. As the days went by and the prosecution built its case, Marsal became more concerned with that second trial.

Before the two lawyers made their closing arguments, Marsal asked to speak to the judge outside the presence of the jury. Judge Kittrell had already turned down the defense attorney's attempt to have the indictment for capital murder quashed, and there was almost no way at the end of the trial he was going to change his mind. But Marsal was haunted with the idea that his client might die in the electric chair, and he felt he had to speak out again.

"There was never any intent for larceny of theft," Marsal told the judge. "I submit to the court that there is not a scrap of evidence that would support a verdict of capital murder. None whatsoever."

Judge Kittrell again denied Marsal's motion, but the defense attorney could not let up. "You know how little sleep I have gotten in the past few nights," Marsal continued. "I've tried this case longer with my head on the pillow than I have in the courtroom. And I'm constantly concerned, look what we are faced with. We are faced with a young man that's charged with an offense that can be punished by the electric chair. Death. The pulling of the switch, the sizzling of the flesh."

Then the jury returned, each lawyer made his final arguments, and the judge issued his instructions. Now it was time for the jury to leave the courtroom and begin its deliberations.

The prosecutor had presented a powerful case, and it wasn't just Knowles but also a parade of knowledgeable, compelling witnesses who linked Henry to the murder. With all of that, a guilty verdict should have seemed almost inevitable. But this was Mobile, Alabama, and the crime was the lynching of a black man, and there was no certainty about this verdict.

A Verdict

THOMAS HARRISON WAS utterly exhausted. The weary prosecutor trekked upstairs to his office and tried to read the newspaper.

He believed he had proven the case beyond a reasonable doubt. The jury for the first case he had ever tried had come back with a guilty verdict in just four and a half minutes. He didn't expect it to be like that this time, but he figured it wouldn't take the jury long to decide.

After three hours and forty-two minutes, the jury summoned the bailiff to inform the judge that they had a verdict. They had taken long enough to give Bubba Marsal some hope and yet had come back quickly enough for Harrison to believe that Henry was going down for capital murder. When Henry stood up to hear the verdict being read, he had a distant look in his brown eyes. His look did not change when he heard the jury foreman say that Henry's twelve fellow citizens were convicting him of capital murder.

In Alabama, the jury first decides the guilt and innocence of the accused. If the jurors find the defendant guilty, they return to the jury room to agree upon an appropriate punishment. Now the jury was deciding if they believed Henry should die in the electric chair or spend the rest of his life in prison without the possibility of parole.

For everyone in the courtroom, this was the most unnerving wait of all. Marsal had done his best, but his case had been buried under powerful evidence. The defense attorney was haunted by the vision of the electric chair.

Harrison believed in the death penalty, and he thought this was a crime that deserved the ultimate penalty. Beyond that, he did not want to win in this courtroom and then have a weak sentence that led to rioting in the streets.

This time the jury was gone for only forty minutes before they came back. The jury foreman stood and announced that they had decided that Henry should spend his life in prison. When Mrs. Donald's children and other relatives heard the verdict, they were grievously disappointed that Henry would not suffer what Michael had suffered.

When Henry heard the words that he would live he showed

no sign that he was thankful. The shackled prisoner looked only at Deem as he shuffled out of the courtroom to begin his sentence of life in prison.

The jurors left that day without talking to any reporters, and no one knew why they had decided to spare Henry's life. In fighting what would be the last major defense of his long career, Marsal had somehow convinced these twelve jurors that Henry deserved to live. But Bennie was livid that his son had not walked free and thought Marsal had done a terrible job.

MOST PEOPLE'S REACTIONS outside the courtroom and across the city were relief that after nearly three years justice had been served. But Morris Dees felt that if others involved with the crime were not punished, it was only half justice, which to him meant no justice at all.

As Dees and Stanton drove back to Montgomery at eighty miles per hour, cruising speed for the lawyer, he thought about the potential civil case. He knew that if he went ahead, he would be enhancing his reputation as someone who pushed his way into legal cases and concerns where almost no other white southern lawyer would even think of going.

Harrison had said Michael Donald's murder wasn't a Klan crime, but a crime committed by two Klansmen, and it was unlikely the D.A.'s office would want to indict anyone else. Many in the Mobile establishment believed that only a rabble-rouser would try to link their city even more to the Klan.

Dees didn't care. He vowed to do whatever he could so that Bennie Hays would go to prison as the leader of a murderous conspiracy and the primary instigator of the crime. He believed that Frank Cox also deserved to spend the rest of his life in a cell. The law dictated that if Cox had contributed the rope, knowing it was for a lynching, he was as guilty of murder as if he had pulled its strands tightly around Donald's neck. As for Bennie, Dees was convinced he was the primary instigator of the murder and should be punished as severely as his son. There were other Klavern members who likely should reside in prison as well.

And if true justice was to be won, Dees believed he could not rest there. Robert Shelton's UKA inspired the killers, and Dees would have to find a way to bring down the Klan organization. He was convinced that when Henry and Knowles lynched Donald, they were doing precisely what Shelton would have wanted them to do. But Shelton kept just enough distance from the Klan's violent actions to make sure that he could never be accused of being responsible.

Dees had won many difficult struggles in his career but nothing of the magnitude of what he would be attempting here: to link Shelton and the UKA directly to the murder. He vowed to take on a daunting but possibly historic task: destroying the most powerful and dangerous Klan organization in America, and then having a revival with chapters in more than twenty-five states. To do so, he would have to set a legal precedent that organizations promoting hatred and violence were responsible for the criminal actions of their members. If he did that, he could use the model against other racist organizations, and his lawsuit might prove the beginning of the end of large-scale white supremacist groups.

"Look, Bill, it would be easy to sue the two convicted murderers," Dees said as he talked almost nonstop on the two-hour drive north to the Alabama capital. "Hell, any jackboot lawyer could do that. Henry and Knowles don't have any money anyway, and we're not doing that. What we're going to do is to sue the UKA, bring Shelton into court. And push to get the other conspirators indicted.

"The D.A.'s not going to want to indict anyone else. It's all over. But we're going to find the other conspirators and push the D.A. to do what has to be done. And we're going to bring Robert Shelton to justice. And I'm telling you none of this will be easy."

Dees realized that if he went ahead and tried to destroy the UKA, the death threats against him would probably get worse. From now on, he would have to drive as he did today, periodically checking the rearview mirror.

He kept thinking about how these Klan members had been led to equate the lynching of a black man with justice. No one had done more to create the atmosphere in which such an attitude could prosper than Governor George Wallace and UKA leader Robert Shelton. The Imperial Wizard had been proud that his Klansmen had been Wallace's foot soldiers in the battle to preserve segregation, and the two men had worked in tandem. They had not been present that night when Henry Hays and James Knowles pulled the rope tight around Michael Donald's neck, but their ideas had been there.

As Dees thought on all this, he reflected that at one time he too had been not only a segregationist but also friendly with Wallace and Shelton. And now he was the Klan's biggest enemy. How had he begun as he had and still become the man he was now? It was not an easy question to answer.

PART TWO

A Time of Judgment

"Where in the Hell . . ."

ON MONDAY MORNING, February 6, 1956, the nineteen-year-old Morris Dees hurried across the broad quadrangle at the University of Alabama in Tuscaloosa. As he rushed to his next class, coeds smiled at him. It was better than feeding hogs at dawn, as he had done all through high school, but he had not a moment to enjoy life with the seven thousand undergraduates.

The teenager had arrived the previous fall as a freshman with his pregnant wife, Beverly Crum Dees, beside him. Teen marriages, even with a sixteen-year-old bride, were not unheard-of in Alabama. He was lucky that the university had special married student housing, some of it large enough for students with children.

The previous week Dees's wife had given birth to their son Morris III, nicknamed Scooter. The new father had to get on with life. He was not sure how he was going to do it, but despite having little money he intended to propel himself through college and law school year-round and earn both degrees in a little over four years.

Standing on the steps of the student union, Dees looked down across the grassy expanse ringed by white classical revival buildings where a riot was unfolding. The previous evening when he had gone to the dormitories selling sandwiches, all anybody was talking about was how a black woman named Autherine Lucy was trying to become the first Negro student to study at the University of Alabama. Now hundreds of students and others were screaming and ranting, doing whatever they could to force

Lucy to give up and leave. "Hey, hey, no. Where did Autherine go? Hey, hey, no. Where in the hell did the Nigger go?" was one of the many rallying cries.

As Dees watched, he saw a single black face moving through a gauntlet of white men slinging verbal abuse at her. Anyone would have been scared, but Lucy didn't show it, at least not as far as Dees could detect.

It was nearly two years since the Supreme Court's *Brown v. Board of Education* school desegregation decision, and two months since the Montgomery bus boycott had begun, triggered by Rosa Parks's refusal to give up her seat to a white man. More than one thousand black students had already entered segregated universities across the South. Lucy was the first black person attempting to attend a segregated institution of higher learning who faced premeditated violence.

At the end of her class, Lucy exited the building and walked to a car driven by Sarah Healy, the dean of women. They drove through a jeering mob that smashed eggs on the windshield, and heaved rocks. As Lucy got out and hurried through the narrow gauntlet to her next class, a rock narrowly missed her head, and an egg splattered her dress and stuck in her hair.

After her last class of the day, Lucy sat surrounded by close to two thousand screaming protesters. Three hours later state troopers escorted Lucy out of the building and drove her off campus.

That evening the university board of trustees voted unanimously to "exclude Autherine Lucy until further notice from attending the University of Alabama." When Lucy's attorneys accused the university of conspiring with the mob in failing to protect her, the administration siezed on the "baseless" charge as an excuse to expel her. She could have continued the legal battle, but she had done all that she felt she could do.

Among the protesters that day was Robert Shelton. The young Klansman had found comradeship at Klavern meetings, but there had been nothing like this brotherhood of action: students and Klansmen working together to keep the university white. For Shelton it was an exhilarating, transcendent moment.

The rioters included a number of other young men who would be Shelton's comrades in the long struggle ahead against integration. One of them, Asa Carter, was, like Shelton, a man of intelligence and ambition. Another was Robert Chambliss, whose life had been given purpose when he saw *The Birth of a Nation,* and decided that he wanted to ride through the southern night like the night riders of old.

Chambliss had begun to make his name through his expertise with explosives and his willingness to make bombs. Just the week before there had been two bombings a hundred miles away in Montgomery. The massive explosions targeted the homes of two of the leaders of the bus boycott in the Alabama capital, Reverend Martin Luther King Jr. and E. D. Nixon. Chambliss likely had nothing to do with the bombing, but it was the kind of action that inspired him. The destruction was devastating, and no one was ever arrested for the bombings.

The struggle for civil rights continued in Montgomery, but at the University of Alabama, the segregationist militants had won at least for now, with Lucy forced off campus. Shelton and those like him had a great victory and a model that they would try to replicate in the years ahead.

Shelton had not begun life as an avid white supremacist. His father, Hoyt Shelton, ran a small grocery in Tuscaloosa that served a white-only clientele, and he grew to adulthood having little to do with the town's black residents. In 1952, the twenty-year-old Shelton married nineteen-year-old Betty McDaniels. Betty fancied she had married a man like her father. When they had gone out together, Shelton never said more than a few words. To Betty Shelton that was a sign of manly strength. She adored her father above all men. He was a foundry worker legendary for ramming the biggest pipe, and never slowing down. He never said much and never had to, and that was the man Betty fancied she had married, a bold, protective figure who would watch over her.

Like Wallace before him and Dees afterward, Shelton was studying prelaw at the University of Alabama. The pregnant Betty imagined a bright future with her lawyer-husband going to church each Sunday with their children. After less than a year, however, Shelton dropped out of college. He joined the United States Air Force and soon shipped out to Germany. When he returned, he could have gone back to school on the GI Bill and finished up his law degree. Instead, inexplicably to his wife, he got a job as a manual worker at the B. F. Goodrich Tire Plant in Tuscaloosa.

Shelton had returned from Europe full of implacable anger. He talked to his wife how in Germany he saw black soldiers arm in arm with white fräuleins. To him, that was the American future if the white race did not wise up and defend its heritage. It was understandable why a young man brought up as a segregationist would be upset observing mixed racial dating, but it was not enough to fill him with this inchoate, all-consuming rage. There almost had to have been something else that happened, some trigger that set off this constant anger, but Shelton never talked about whatever it may have been.

The husband who had returned to Betty Shelton frightened her, and she feared what he might do. One day she heard him talking about joining the Klan. Worried that would bring great harm to her and the family, she begged him to back off. But he did not listen, and as her husband became involved in the racist organization, Betty retreated to her family and her faith. She raised their three children and went to church every Sunday, often with her husband. That was all that remained of the dream she once had for her life.

Shelton was violent in his proclamations and in his philosophy, and likely violent in his home life. "Somebody told me, 'Well, why don't you get a divorce?' Mrs. Shelton reflected in 2014. "You didn't get divorced back then. No matter what went on. Women got beat up all the time. Like it was their fault."

When Shelton told his fellow tire workers what was in store for them, he had a receptive audience. The growing affluence of the postwar era had reached down even to them. They had boats that they sailed on the Black Warrior River, modest hunting lodges, indoor plumbing, and new cars bought on monthly payments they could afford, all things that their fathers' generation would not have dreamed possible. Almost everything boded well, but many had begun to worry that it wouldn't last. They had begun to dread that the good times would be wrenched away from them, and they feared anyone who might come to take them away. They looked across town and saw the abysmal circumstance in which most black Alabamans lived. The good times hadn't touched that part of town. That worried them even more.

Shelton said that black men would first take their jobs, and then their wives and daughters in a licentious assault on Christian civilization. Only the brave knights of the Klan could prevent this. With this rhetoric, he signed up many of the tire plant employees. As he went around recruiting new members, it was clear that he had the purpose, vision, and ambition to help lead the growing movement.

Alabama's country club set looked down disdainfully upon the Klan, but the gentry and their ancestors had created a system in which the Klan was the unacknowledged enforcer. "The Klan was just the shock troops, the guerilla warriors for preservation of the order," reflected Birmingham-raised civil rights lawyer Charles Morgan Jr. in Howell Raines's *My Soul Is Rested: The Story of the Civil Rights Movement in the Deep South.* "That allowed for the leading citizens who were segregationists to condemn the acts and the others to perform the natural result of their philosophy."

Sunday School

ON THE SUNDAY after Lucy attempted to enter the university, Dees decided that he would speak to the assembly of married students at the on-campus Calvary Baptist Church about the segregationist demonstrations. Although most of the young marrieds were a good five years older, the minister had appointed him the superintendent of the married couples Sunday school. He opened a big leather-bound black Bible and addressed the married men in blue and black suits and their wives in prim dresses.

"I'd like to read from First John," Dees said looking out on the congregation. "'If a man say, I love God and hateth his brother, he is a liar: for he who loveth not his brother whom he hath seen, how can he love God whom he hath not seen.'"

Dees believed in segregation the same way he believed in gravity. It was part of the natural law. Every white person he knew was pro-segregation, but they had widely varying feelings toward the black race. Some were full of such unbridled hatred that they could not even look at a black man without loathing. Others were convinced that African Americans were naturally inferior and incapable of walking the same pathways as a white person. Still others, like Dees, had known enough black people to realize that they were not treated right or fairly.

Dees believed in segregation as much as ever, but that did not mean that this black woman should have been greeted with hatred. "Autherine Lucy tried to get on this campus," Dees went on. "We might not have been out there joining those opposing her, but I think all of us didn't want her to be there. How can we feel that way and be good Christians?"

A few days later Reverend Williams paid Dees a visit. "We're going to make some changes in the married students Sunday school," he said. "We need someone with a little more experience than you have to plan the programs."

Dees and his wife returned to church the following Sunday. As far as anyone could tell, he had happily accepted Reverend Williams's decision. Although still a teenager, he already understood that politics wasn't just about government. It was about how you dealt with people to get what you wanted, and he had no time or intention to speak out anymore. Not that he had regrets. He had spoken what was in his heart: all people deserved to be treated with decency.

That's how Dees had been brought up in the cotton country outside Montgomery. Though he was white, almost all his friends were black. In the summers he went skinny-dipping with them and stood naked beneath the railroad bridge waving at trains passing by. He picked cotton beside them, and it upset his entrepreneurial spirit that when he went to school in September and looked out the window, his black cohorts were still out there in the fields, making money.

As a boy in the 1940s, Dees liked to go into town. Saturday mornings he would get up in the back of the rusty, bedraggled open-bed truck that took African Americans to Montgomery for a dime a head. Those riding in with him from the village of Mount Meigs right after World War II were mainly farmhands and sharecroppers. They headed for Monroe Street, where white merchants stood outside hawking cheap clothes set out on racks.

They could get a zoot suit with wide padded shoulders tapering down to the narrowest of pegged pants and a couple of dressy shirts on credit for fifty cents a week, and often they left with new clothing. If they did not keep up their payments, the attorneys hit them with lawsuits, and if that did not shake the coins out of their pockets, the sheriff came knocking. Young Dees didn't say anything, but he believed that what the white merchants were doing was wrong, and it troubled him.

Dees's family firmly believed in segregation, and they would not have thought of a black person sitting down with them at the dinner table. But in comparison to most of their neighbors, they were known for treating black people well. His father had black laborers on the land he rented, and when it got so blazingly hot that you could fry an egg on the hood of his pickup, he had them sit down, drink the water that he had brought out to the fields, and wait until it cooled off a little before they went back to work. Dees Sr. had a small cotton gin, and black farmers knew that when you came to Mr. Dees, you received fair weight.

Morris's mother, Annie Ruth Dees, treated black folks decently too. She was the symbol of civility in the Dees family.

Unlike her husband, Annie Ruth had graduated from high school in Montgomery where she grew up. She would have gone on to college if the Great Depression had not taken her family into its grip.

Annie Ruth cooked for the family, clothed and bathed the children, and when it was time to harvest cotton, she was there at the gin, tabulating the totals for the farmers, and in the evenings she was back home working on the books. Things got a little easier in 1947 when the Alabama Power Company finally ran electric lines out to the Dees home, and Morris and his siblings had their first baths in a bathtub.

Young Dees got interested in politics when he met one of his father's friends, Governor James Elisha "Big Jim" Folsom, who served two terms, from 1947 to 1951 and from 1955 to 1959. Dees Sr. may have been a tenant farmer, but he was as concerned with power and politics as his wealthy neighbors in their antebellum mansions. During the governor's first term in office, Folsom often came out to the Dees home. As Folsom sat in the modest living room drinking bourbon, he discussed politics nonstop.

The six-foot-eight-inch, 280-pound Folsom was the most progressive governor in Alabama history. The populist politician talked about how he wanted to tax wealthy Alabamans and corporations at higher rates to improve the schools and pave the country roads. As the governor saw it, the problem was that conservative politicians raised the specter of race to keep the poor white man from focusing on his common interest with the poor black man. One day, Folsom believed, white tenant farmers and garage mechanics would see their kinship with deprived black Alabamans, and together they would change the world.

Folsom condemned his enemies and praised his friends until his words slurred and Morris could hardly understand them. Then Winston Craig, the governor's black chauffeur and valet, gently helped Big Jim get up, put him in the backseat of the black sedan and drove him back to the governor's mansion.

Despite his drinking and the corrupt acts of several of his underlings, Folsom could have been reelected easily, but in those years Alabama governors could not serve two consecutive terms, and he had to wait out four years before he could run again for another term.

Dees was delighted when his father took him to Folsom's second inauguration on a cold January day in 1955. He and his father had great seats to watch the parade. Leading things off was a contingent of motorcycle police, followed by the color guard, and the parade marshals, notably Judge George Wallace from Barbour County in the southeastern region of the state.

Despite the weather, Wallace sat in an open car, relishing his moment passing in front of the 75,000 to 100,000 parade watchers. As he shouted out the names of the people he knew and waved to everyone else, the judge might have been the one being inaugurated.

Young Dees was impressed with Wallace's bravado and was excited to be there among all kinds of Alabamans. Coal miners and steel workers. Manufacturers and clerks. Cotton and peanut farmers. Men in hundred-dollar Hickey Freeman suits and those in overalls. Black Alabamans too, come to celebrate the man they thought was their governor as well as the white man's. Folsom not only pointedly invited Negroes to the inauguration but also for the first time in Alabama history had a special ball just for their race that he attended before the gigantic whites-only ball.

Dees Sr. envisioned his son entering politics one day, and as they tried to keep warm, he told Morris about Wallace and how he had started with nothing and how far he had gotten. Like Folsom, Wallace was an instinctive politician with a visceral disdain for the high-living, richly dressed elites who looked down on poor whites. He also knew how to count, and he saw early on there were more of the poor than there were of the rich. When he was first elected to the state legislature in 1946, the striving young politician seemed to be Governor Folsom's populist heir.

That evening in the inaugural ball at the mammoth Alabama Coliseum, Dees met Wallace for the first time. "This is young Morris, my eldest," Dees Sr. said as the judge gave the young man a fierce handshake.

The scrawny, five-foot-seven-inch Wallace was a man of feisty intensity. He was constantly twitching, chewing on his nickel Tampa Nugget Cigar, spitting on the ground, and running his fingers through greasy hair. He had flown as a flight engineer on bombing raids over Japan during World War II. Wallace had suffered an apparent nervous breakdown that merited a partial disability check from the government each month, and by the way he fussed and fidgeted, it seemed well deserved.

"Bubba, Judge Wallace is going to be governor someday," Dees Sr. said, a thought that did not seem to offend the young politician. Wallace nodded a good-bye and set off, cutting a swath across the coliseum, joshing with the folks, pounding on backs, and shaking every hand he could reach.

Wallace was born in 1919 in a shanty in Clio, Alabama, in a neighborhood with many black residents living in similar conditions. His father, George Wallace Sr., scraped together a living as a farmer. The son of the town doctor, the senior Wallace had only one working lung, a poor heart, a deviated septum, and migraine headaches that lasted for days. He drank heavily. To damper his hangovers, he often went to Jackson's General Store in Clio, where he'd chase down Goody's Headache Powder with a Coke. On top of it, he had a violent temper that led to any number of fistfights. When he died in 1937, he was only forty, but he looked like an old man.

Wallace couldn't stand his mother, who in his mind tried to turn him into a prissy dandy. Mozelle Wallace had been brought up in an orphanage, and in marrying a doctor's son, she thought wrongly she was marrying up. She had studied music for a short time, and when she finished putting meals on the table and cleaning up afterward, she gave music lessons that taught civility as much as anything else. Young George hated squandering his playtime trying to make music. At the annual recital of Mozelle's students at the schoolhouse auditorium, George sat down at the piano, pounded his fists angrily on the keys, and walked off the stage.

For Wallace to embrace culture and self-conscious civility was to embrace his mother. Instead he remained his entire life a proud vulgarian. Another mother would have felt that if she could not have the life she deserved, she would work so her children could have it. But Mozelle was too bitter for that, and as the oldest, George felt the onslaught of her disdain. Mozelle did not tell George she loved him. She rarely held him. She made him feel inadequate. "I think Mozelle had more impact and effect on the psyche of George Wallace than anyone could ever imagine," says his son-in-law, Mark Kennedy.

Turning Back the Tide

A POOR BOY made his way in life sucking up to his betters, at least for a while. Wallace had been loyal to Folsom, but a man took his chances when he got them, and a year after the governor's second inauguration, it was time to move on. The thirty-five-year-old judge saw that in the fight to prevent Lucy from entering the University of Alabama a new resistance was aborning, and the ambitious politician saw that as the vehicle for his advance.

Elected to judicial office in 1952, "the fighting little judge" treated black people with fairness in his courtroom and never expressed negativity toward their race. But nobody understood the fears and aspirations of the working-class white man better than Wallace, and what he feared most of all was the advance of the black man into his world. The politician knew that in the wake of the Supreme Court's historic school decision, segregation would not last much longer, but if he denied what he knew to be the truth, he could likely ride the white man's fears to the governor's mansion.

It was this shrewd, cynical assessment that defined Wallace's political career. He understood what lay ahead infinitely better than Robert Shelton did, who believed segregation could go on forever and intended to devote his life to that fight. The politician also grasped what was going to happen far better than the young Morris Dees, who thought the solution to racial problems was segregation with a bit more dignity.

"I think Wallace knew from an early age that segregation was going to end," says his son-in law, Mark Kennedy.

"I know that my father believed integration was inevitable, and clearly he used that issue to gain political power," says George Wallace Jr.

Wallace's authorized biographer Stephan Lesher agrees and says that from the time he was in college, the aspiring young man understood segregation was doomed.

Nobody in Montgomery or the media was watching this brash young judge with much interest, but Wallace had an exquisite sense of political timing. He saw that the integration attempt at the university had put segregationists on alert, ready and eager to hear the message he had for them.

On the very day that newspapers across the state had front-page stories about Lucy fleeing the Alabama campus, Wallace announced on those same pages that if the FBI showed up in Bullock County seeking to investigate the racial content of grand juries or courts, he would lock them in jail. He said he would do so because "such conduct in my considered opinion is contemptuous."

The Justice Department was not investigating Bullock County and had no intention of sending FBI agents to the county. When FBI director J. Edgar Hoover heard about Wallace's false assertions, he called the young politician a "rat" and said the agency was to have nothing to do with him.

For the first time in his life, Wallace received considerable publicity. The *Montgomery Advertiser* conjectured that if he carried out his threat "the judge might himself be jailed and prosecuted, though this would certainly be tantamount, in these times of reasserted state sovereignty, to his election as governor if not U.S. senator."

A few days after rioters ended the attempt to integrate the University of Alabama, Wallace drove from his home in Clayton seventy-five miles northwest to Montgomery. He was planning to run for governor in 1958, and he had made another crucial decision. He was not about to have Governor Folsom's progressive racial record hanging around his neck.

When Wallace believed he had something urgent to say, he got up so close that the listener could see the spittle in the corner of his lips, and he spoke with such force that the words carried far across the room. That's how he spoke this day, traveling from the Jefferson Davis Hotel where the pols and lobbyists hung out to the corridors of the capitol. He grabbed on to any acquaintance he knew, telling them that Folsom had "gone soft on the nigger question" and was betraying the white race.

A few weeks later, Wallace was invited to a Citizens Council meeting in Clayton. He joined 4,500 of his neighbors at the Clayton football stadium to hear Georgia governor Marvin Griffin praise his "courage in informing the do-gooders and meddlers that he would put the [FBI] scalawags in jail."

Wallace could see what a powerful issue the fight against integration was becoming. If he played it right the segregationists would raise him to their shoulders and might celebrate him as they did no other politician of his generation.

"Who Is Shelton?"

DEES SUPPORTED GEORGE Wallace's run for governor in 1958, but the college student had little time for politics. He was incredibly busy, and only a small part of it was his studies. He and his fellow student and best friend Millard Fuller were involved in several businesses. The fledgling entrepreneurs sent out letters to parents saying that for a mere six dollars, 'Bama Birthday Cake Services would deliver a cake with a personal message on their son's or daughter's birthday. They were soon selling 350 cakes a month, at a three-dollar profit per cake. The two partners then got the rights from the Student Government Association to publish the annual student telephone directory. That project earned them more than twenty thousand dollars.

With their business ventures, Dees and Fuller spent more time with one another than they did with their young wives. "Being around Morris Dees is like being around a whirlwind," recalled Dees's former wife, the late Beverly Betak. "He just doesn't stop. He's just going, going, going and you have to go, go, go. And when he met Millard, it was double, two of them go, go, go. From the day they met, they were never apart. And Millard's wife, Linda, and I were doing whatever they told us to do. It was just type, type, type, both of us."

If the pace of their life was troubling, so too was the difference in their temperaments. Beverly noticed that her husband could not stand to be alone. With Morris, there was always somebody there, always something going on, always some plan being concocted. It didn't help that Beverly's mother had no use for Morris. She thought her son-in-law had stolen her daughter away and robbed Beverly of the carefree joys of youth while turning her into a servant devoted to Morris's ceaseless advancement.

As busy as he was, in the fall of 1957, Dees founded a society at the university for students interested in becoming lawyers. The young man was always thinking ahead, and he decided to invite Judge George Wallace to speak to the organization. Sidling up to the politician afterward, the prelaw student offered his services in the upcoming gubernatorial campaign.

Wallace had a special reason to pay attention. As broke as his father was, Dees Sr. had paid the politician's gubernatorial $500 filing fee. That alone would have made Wallace listen with interest to Dees Sr.'s namesake, but he knew a comer when he saw one, and he named the single-minded young man his statewide student campaign manager.

This was a great opportunity that any of the hotshot campus politicians would have fought to have, and Dees had won it without even running for student office. He was supposed to start law school in the spring of 1958, but he took the semester off to set off on the campaign trail.

Like Wallace, the would-be law student loved to jaw with people, and he could talk to anyone about just about anything. He traveled from town to town, handing out cards and banners and talking to folks about voting for Wallace in the primary that in the overwhelmingly Democratic state was tantamount to election.

While working for Wallace, the twenty-one-year-old Dees also became the de facto campaign manager for MacDonald Gallion, the segregationist candidate for attorney general. His friend and business partner Fuller was Gallion's West Alabama campaign manager. Fuller recalled in his autobiography, *Love in the Mortar Joints,* giving scores of speeches in which he preached segregation, including one "to a huge gathering of robed Klansmen." Dees did not give as many speeches, but he appeared to have the makings of a segregationist politician.

There were more than a dozen candidates in the wide open primary for governor, but the contest came down to thirty-eight-year-old Wallace and thirty-six-year-old Attorney General John Patterson. The campaign was almost as much about Patterson's father as it was the candidate himself. Soon after winning the Democratic nomination for attorney general on a pledge of cleaning up Phenix City in 1954, Albert Patterson was shot dead in the streets of the vice-ridden city. The younger Patterson inherited his father's nomination and, playing the role of a martyr's son, was elected that fall. Four years later he was still playing the part. "I'm running against a man whose father was assassinated," Wallace fumed. "How'm I supposed to follow an act like that?"

As attorney general, Patterson made race his all-consuming issue. He went on to campaign for governor as the uncompromised, uncompromising champion of the white race. When Dees looked back on those days, he liked to think that the Wallace he had worked for had run as "a populist in the Folsom mood" with his racial stance "much closer to that of Big Jim Folsom than Patterson." The truth was that Wallace was every bit as much of a segregationist as Patterson.

Wallace's campaign slogan was "Keep Alabama Southern." Every white man and woman in the state knew what that meant. The *Montgomery Advertiser* headlined: WALLACE VOWS WAR ON MIXING. In a televised speech in Birmingham, the candidate warned U.S. Attorney General Herbert Brownell Jr. that if he sent "the Brownell Brownshirts" south to enforce integration, the federal troops would be greeted by closed schools and endless litigation. Wallace discovered on the campaign trail that the audience tuned out when he talked about building schools and tarring country roads, and only came alive when he talked race.

LIKE WALLACE, ROBERT Shelton understood that race was the preeminent issue of his time. In the two years since being one of those thwarting Autherine Lucy's attempt to integrate the University of Alabama, the twenty-eight-year-old had risen meteorically to become the Grand Dragon of the Alabama Ku Klux Klan, the highest official in the state. Unlike his predecessors, Shelton saw an overtly political role for the Klan in which he one day would sit proudly at the table of power.

The Grand Dragon originally backed Wallace's candidacy, but he changed his mind and started promoting Patterson. Shelton took three weeks off from his job making tires and drove around the state in his 1956 Chevy station wagon festooned with Patterson stickers. His Klansmen were the most important grassroots organization working for Patterson's election. They weren't sitting around the campaign offices or hanging around rallies. "Not only can they nail your signs up all over Alabama in one night," Patterson reflected. "They can also tear 'em down in one night, too."

The Klansmen had an impact far beyond their numbers, and the night before the primary election, Wallace knew it was not going well. Although Patterson did not win outright, he received over 35,000 more votes than Wallace. That was an almost impossible number to make up in the runoff election unless something dramatic happened.

A week later, Wallace changed the tenor of the campaign by charging in a televised interview in Birmingham that "the KKK are supporting my opposition." Three days later, the *Montgomery Advertiser*, Wallace's biggest journalistic backer, set out the particulars in a front-page story. The article included a copy of a letter Patterson had sent on the attorney general's official letterhead seeking the support of the state's prominent white supremacists. Patterson said their "mutual friend, Mr. R. M. (Bob) Shelton," had referred him.

Patterson first said he did not know Shelton. The candidate did his best to disappear from journalistic scrutiny. So did Shelton. When a reporter and photographer from the *Birmingham News* walked into Patterson's Birmingham headquarters the day after Wallace made his accusations, they found the Grand Dragon huddling with Patterson's brother, Maurice. When the Klan leader saw the journalists, he bolted from the room.

"Who is Shelton?" asked Patterson's state campaign manager, Charlie Meriwether. "I don't know him. What does he do?"

Realizing he had his opponent flustered, Wallace implored Patterson to tell the Alabama people "that he would never appoint a Klansman to public office." Pointing his finger, he said, "If Mr. Patterson is elected, there will be a revival of the Klan. My opponent's election would put starch in all those dirty bedsheets." Wallace seemed to be speaking of Shelton's clear objective when the candidate said, "The Klan wants to grow until it makes every office seeker in Alabama doubt that he can be elected without the Klan's seal of approval."

At the same time that Wallace condemned Patterson for his Klan association, he attacked his opponent for not being tough enough fighting for segregation as attorney general. The integration of the Montgomery buses was a settled matter, but not to Wallace. He criticized Patterson for his "lack of diligence" in using his legal authority to fight for continued segregation. And he accused Attorney General Patterson of not only failing to use his office to prevent Lucy from entering the University of Alabama but also for leaving it to protesters to prevent the integration of the state's premier university.

Wallace's assault on Patterson for his Klan support probably only added to those voting for his opponent. In the four years since the Supreme Court decision in *Brown v. Board of Education*, resistance to integration had grown into the overwhelmingly political reality.

In that struggle the Klan was a worthy ally, albeit not necessarily a publicly acknowledged one. Betty Shelton remembers that in those years many prominent Alabamans visited the Shelton house outside Tuscaloosa. For the most part these visitors were not Klan members and wanted no public association with the Klan.

The Klan leader oversaw an empire largely of low-life misfits. Many of them lived on the fringes of society, and some were sociopaths. They were men like those in Hitler's paramilitary units who fought pitched battles in the streets of Munich and Berlin in the 1920s as the führer rose to power. Like these German fascists, they found an identity, excitement, and purpose in the Klan that they found nowhere else. The Klan was the great adventure of their lives.

Patterson defeated Wallace by 65,000 votes, almost twice the margin as in the first go-round. Without the Klan the victory would not have been so resounding, and Patterson conceivably might not even have won.

After Wallace heard most of the results, he waited outside Montgomery's Greystone Hotel in the backseat of a car, smoking a stogie. Discussing the debacle with campaign aide Bill Jones, Wallace could not bring himself to go inside and publically declare himself a loser before whatever diminished, dispirited troops were still there. He wasn't going to speak a loser's words no matter how much Jones argued that he had no choice.

Wallace finally realized that his aide was right. He would have to speak. The defeated candidate opened the back door of the car and stepped down onto the street "Well, boys," he said as he ground out the cigar, "no other son-of-a-bitch will ever out-nigger me again."

The Day of Reckoning

THE LOSS HAD been devastating for George Wallace, and disappointing for Morris Dees, his student campaign manager.

But for Robert Shelton, the youthful Grand Dragon of the Alabama Ku Klux Klan, it was a glorious victory. His Klansmen had worked diligently to elect John Patterson, and the politician would be *their* governor.

Shelton was now an adviser to the Patterson administration, talking with the governor on matters of mutual interest. He was often seen sitting in the governor's outer office waiting to "pop in" or on the floor of the legislature where he had guest privileges.

Patterson rewarded Shelton for his campaign efforts by giving Goodrich the exclusive state contract for tires, worth $1.6 million. That got him promoted off the floor in the Goodrich Tire plant. Now in charge of the state tire account, he had plenty of time to drive around Alabama giving talks and building up the Klan.

Later in his career, Shelton was careful not to promote violence in any of his public statements, but in these years he was far more outspoken. In 1957, an FBI informant heard the Klan leader saying that if Montgomery Negroes continued trying to integrate parks and restaurants, he had more than enough Klansmen to put down Negroes all across Alabama, "much less the bunch in Montgomery who were causing trouble. Now is the time for violence." And in the early years of the Patterson administration, Shelton told the *Mobile Press* that if attempts to integrate Montgomery schools "were carried out, it would bring bloodshed in Alabama." In 1960, after eleven crosses burned across the capital, he led a sixty-eight-car motorcade of robed men to Montgomery where he said that "if need be, citizens should take up baseball bats to prevent schools from being integrated."

Full of vitriol, Shelton spoke of the "Jew-controlled NAACP," the "bayonet rule enforced by Eisenhower's storm troopers," "the Jew-founded propaganda mechanism, known as the Pulitzer Prize," and the "Yankee lynch mob in its campaign to persecute the Klan, the Citizens Council and its members."

Still, for all of Shelton's influence in the new administration, the governor tried to keep their frequent talks secret. When the newspapers learned about the tire contract, they made such a fuss that Patterson canceled it. To exacerbate matters, the Klan leader was fired from his job at Goodrich. Hidden within Shelton's racism was a core of anti-Semitism that grew larger as the years went by. He told his bosses that they were getting rid of him because they were letting a few Negroes and Jews run the company.

The firing was more than just a blow to Shelton's ego. He wasn't yet making enough money from his authorized cut of monthly Klan dues to support his growing family. Finding it necessary to supplement his income, he pumped gas at a filling station on the University of Alabama campus. As he filled tanks he scoped out which of the professors seemed to be liberals and jotted down the names of those in the few racially mixed groups that drove into the station.

Shelton was making plans to be ready when the day of reckoning came, a ritual he continued during his entire career as a Klan leader. "We are keeping a list of people who have violated certain sanctions, such as interracial marriage, and committed other racial crimes; the day will come when they'll be punished," he told author Patsy Sims for her book *The Klan* in 1976.

As Shelton observed the increasingly tense racial situation in the state, the Klan leader anticipated a time when the white man would forcibly drive the black man back into his separate world where he would live forever. For Wallace, however, race was simply a fantastic political issue that he intended to parlay as far as it would go. He spent most of his time making speeches and talking to various supporters, preparing to run for governor again in 1962.

At one time Dees had also thought about running for governor or senator himself one day, but as much as he had enjoyed campaigning for Wallace, he had given up on the idea of entering politics. Making money was more fun. He was convinced that he would be a millionaire by the time he was thirty years old. He had another reason to get hopping to make his fortune. In October 1957, Beverly had given birth to their second son, John.

Once enrolled in law school, Dees worked with Fuller developing various businesses. When they graduated, the two young men owned debt-free apartments that they rented to forty-four students and had, as well, started a nationwide direct-mail business selling fund-raising products in forty states to groups such as the Boy Scouts.

Upon getting their law degrees in 1960, Dees and Fuller set up practice in a three-room suite in Montgomery's new Washington Building. Just down the hall were the new law offices of George Wallace.

AS DEES FOCUSED on getting rich, Shelton faced a serious setback. In early 1960, E. L. Edwards, the Imperial Wizard of the U.S. Klans, accused him of financial improprieties and fired him as head of the Alabama branch. Edwards replaced Shelton with Alvin Horn, a Talladega minister. Horn had previously resigned as Grand Dragon in 1957, after marrying a fifteen-year-old parishioner, and he hardly seemed the choice to move the organization to firmer moral grounds.

Losing his leading post turned out to work in Shelton's favor. Having driven those country roads, talking to one Klavern after another on behalf of the U.S. Klan, paid off. Most of the Alabama membership joined him in a new organization that evolved into the United Klans of America, the largest, most powerful Klan group in the country. There were perhaps fifty thousand Klan members across America with ten times that number of sympathizers.

As head of the UKA, the FBI believed Shelton oversaw about ten thousand members. Only a few hundred of these were willing to involve themselves in the most militant and violent of actions, but that was enough. With the complicity of the police, they could carry out their actions largely with impunity.

As the Imperial Wizard in his own separate national organization, Shelton was the unquestioned leader. His vision was to create a broadly based, quasi-military national organization with discipline as rigorous as that of the United States Marines. For the first time in his Klan life, he received a regular salary and worked out of a UKA office in downtown Tuscaloosa.

An amateur historian, Shelton had bookcases filled with history books in his modest ranch-style brick house on a small lake outside the college town. Many of them were about the Civil War and its aftermath and had been written in the nineteenth century. He felt you had to go back that far to find people daring enough to write what he considered the truth.

Shelton believed "slavery was the greatest thing that ever happened to the Negro people." Until then, for thousands of years, "the Negro was walking on diamonds in Africa and even though they glittered in the sunlight, he didn't realize their value. Even though Africa was surrounded by water, he sailed nowhere beyond his own boundaries. He didn't build himself a house other than wood and mud even though there were stone and lumber."

It was a blessing for these "flesh-eating tribes" to bring them to America and introduce them to civilization, but they were still on the bottom rung of the ladder of civilization. You could not defy nature by trying to raise them to the same level as whites. All you did was pull the white man down to the debased level of the Negro. If that was not terrible enough, the Negroes were taking over and in conspiracy with the "Zionist Jews, the money changers and the financial wizards," who, in connivance with Communists, were their prime supporters. With their help, the Negroes were taking over everything, even "so-called rock and jazz." That was nothing but Negro music: "the rum-tum-tum version of jungle music that brings out sex and drugs in people."

Although Shelton no longer shouted threats of violence publicly, as he had a few years previously, he had become a far more dangerous man, and so were the actions of the UKA militants. In Birmingham his minions got on buses, and when they found black riders sitting too far forward, they picked them up and threw them to the back. They did not care if it was a confused old man or a weary maid coming home after a day working in a white family's house. There were no excuses. And over the years some of the Birmingham Klansmen had bombed and set homes and businesses on fire, not to kill anyone, just to make black Alabamans pay attention and stay in their place.

All these incidents advanced the struggle, but only dramatic actions made the front pages of the newspapers and inspired his Klansmen, and there had been nothing of such magnitude since Shelton and his cohorts had joined with students to prevent Lucy from integrating the University of Alabama in 1956.

As the Imperial Wizard scanned the horizon looking for opportunities to deploy major actions, he feared that the FBI might have infiltrated the organization. His worries about the federal agency were well taken. The FBI had at least thirty informants within the UKA, including a person "employed in a very sensitive position in the national headquarters of the UKA."

Shelton knew that he had to weed out informers. One evening in 1960 he drove over to Birmingham to attend the regular weekly meeting of Eastview Klavern, Palace 13. Afterward most of the members cleared out, leaving a select few Klan officers along with a new recruit, Gary Thomas Rowe Jr.

The rumor was that Rowe had been driving around with state liquor agents. One of the Klansman pulled out a shotgun to confront Rowe, a husky high school dropout, who liked nothing better than a bar brawl. The Imperial Wizard accused the recruit of being an FBI snitch. Rowe insisted on his innocence and checked out on several crucial matters.

Although several other Klan members remained suspicious, Shelton decided that Rowe was not a "cockroach," his term for informers. The Imperial Wizard became Rowe's protector and confidant. "We want you," the Klan leader said, "but we have to be sure about you."

The Imperial Wizard was tired of Klansmen who mouthed the sacred words in the Klavern gatherings but outside the confines of the meetings did little to stand up for the white race. He believed he needed men like Rowe, who would fight the fight that had to be fought, and drive black people into enclaves from which they would rarely venture.

Freedom Rides

ROWE TURNED OUT to be an even better Klansman than Robert Shelton had ever imagined. In mid-April of 1961, Rowe had meetings with two Birmingham police officers, Sergeant Thomas H. Cook and Detective W. W. "Red" Self. The officers told him they had learned from the FBI that an integrated group of CORE (Congress of Racial Equality) "Freedom Riders" would be descending on the city riding interstate buses. Cook's mentor was T. Eugene "Bull" Connor, the Birmingham commissioner of public safety, and it seemed clear that he was the guiding force behind this meeting. Cook told Rowe the Klansmen would have fifteen minutes to do whatever they wanted to the protesters.

The information was passed on to Shelton. He was infuriated that black and white activists intended to confront the South's sacred institutions by riding together from Atlanta to Birmingham and beyond. Rowe set up a secret meeting for Shelton to speak directly with Cook. "You've got time to beat them, kick them, burn them, kill them," Rowe recalled the police sergeant saying. "I don't give a shit. We just don't care. We don't ever want to see another nigger ride on the bus into Birmingham again."

The Imperial Wizard and his minions would be there to meet them and to send them back north. But first he issued a public warning that if these "professional agitators" did not turn back, "he had no choice but to call on the Klansmen all over the state and all other true white people to stop them any way they can."

Three days before the Freedom Riders were scheduled to arrive, Shelton met in Birmingham with other Klan officers. The Imperial Wizard also spoke by telephone to Kenneth Adams, the head of the Klan in nearby Anniston. Adams and his cohorts were delighted to take part in their town.

When the first of the two buses carrying Freedom Riders arrived in Anniston at 3:20 P.M. on Sunday, May 14, 1961, the Klansmen and others descended upon the bus and went to work puncturing the tires, denting the sides of the vehicle, and smashing the windows. An FBI informant said he had seen Shelton driving around the Anniston bus station before the Klan attacked.

The Greyhound bus limped out of Anniston protected by a police escort that dropped off at the town line. A few miles out in the countryside a flat tire forced the bus to stop, and a mob surrounded the vehicle. A young rioter threw a flaming rag into the bus, and when the Freedom Riders fled the vehicle for their lives, they were beaten unmercifully.

When the second bus arrived in Anniston, there was no mob there to greet them, and the Trailways driver continued sixty-five miles west to Birmingham. As the bus reached the outskirts of Birmingham, a television newsman spotted the UKA leader outside the Birmingham Greyhound Station. Shelton drove around the bus depot in his cherished Cadillac, guiding reporters "to places where the action was taking place."

Just after 4:00 P.M., a police contact told Rowe there would be no bus filled with Freedom Riders arriving at the Greyhound

Station, but one was coming to the Trailways Bus Depot, and it was arriving imminently. Rowe shouted out an order to his fellow militants to hurry the three blocks to the other bus station. The Klansmen and their frenzied followers ran through the silent, deserted streets, carrying clubs and chains. Favorite weapons were "head-knockers," hollowed-out baseball bats that had been filled with molten lead and then sealed back up so they looked like normal athletic equipment.

Shelton drove the few blocks to where the action was and parked near the Trailways Station. He stood far enough away to ensure he would not be implicated, but close enough for him to admire the violent assault he had so carefully orchestrated.

The bus arrived in the Trailways Station at 4:15 P.M. Only seven Freedom Riders, four black and three white, got off the bus. The Klansmen not only attacked the Freedom Riders but also beat up a young black man who had come to the station to meet his fiancée, and they bludgeoned a *Birmingham Post-Herald* photographer. After a quarter hour, they received a warning that the police would soon be there. Their work finished, the Klansmen departed to celebrate their victory.

This was not a mindless attack by a mob but a systematic effort to end the threat of integration. As Raymond Arsenault writes in *Freedom Riders*, "With the apparent connivance of law enforcement officials, the organized defenders of white supremacy in Alabama had decided to smash the Freedom Ride with violence, in effect announcing to the world that they had no intention of letting the law, the U.S. Constitution, or anything else interfere with the preservation of racial segregation in their sovereign state."

The Kennedy administration wanted to end the Freedom Rides and hold the Klan back from further violence. Neither side was listening. The activists intended to show that nothing, not even their own deaths, would stop the movement. As for the Klan, they had tasted blood and there was nothing sweeter. And as for Governor Patterson, he was not going to be intimidated into protecting the hated intruders. He said no one could "guarantee the safety of fools."

Three days later, on Wednesday, May 17, 1961, a new group of student Freedom Riders set out from Nashville on their way to Birmingham and Montgomery, and then from the Alabama capital to Mississippi and on to New Orleans. In Birmingham they were rudely pushed out of the Greyhound bus station and led away to a night in jail under "protective custody." The next evening, they were led out of their cells into a limousine and two unmarked police cars that drove them to the Tennessee state line. Their colleagues drove them back to Birmingham in private cars where that Friday they waited in the Greyhound depot for a bus to take them to the Alabama capital.

Outside the bus station stood about a thousand raucous, milling white militants and in the waiting room a number of Klansmen, most notably Shelton, wearing a silk-like black robe emblazoned with an embroidered snake. The Klansmen could not thrash the Freedom Riders with police and reporters present. So they settled on petty harassment, stepping on their feet and pouring drinks on them as the Freedom Riders waited for Greyhound to find a driver willing to take the wheel of a bus headed to Montgomery.

Friday night, exhausted and anxious and with the writing room cleared, the Freedom Riders slept—or tried to—on the wooden benches in the waiting room until Saturday morning when they set out for Montgomery.

As the bus arrived in the Alabama capital, no police protection around the bus terminal awaited them, just an eerily foreboding silence. At least two hundred people, including a number who had been there a week ago in Birmingham, stood a few hundred yards away from the station. Some couples had brought their children. Leading them was thirty-five-year-old Claude Henley, Shelton's liaison aide in Montgomery.

Henley had been a highway patrolman and was friendly with

Drue Lackey, a top Montgomery police officer. As officials had done in Birmingham, Lackey promised Henley that the police would stand back and let the Klansmen beat up the Freedom Riders.

And so they did. Car salesman Henley was dressed in a short-sleeved white shirt and tie, as if he were going to work. He stood at the front of the irate crowd, initiating the proceedings by beating up an NBC cameraman and then James Zwerg, the only white male Freedom Rider. Several men lifted up a battered Zwerg so their wives and other women could claw away at his face with their nails.

A mother held up a young woman Freedom Rider so her son could beat her into submission. Others ran to pound John Lewis, the leader of the activists and later a U.S. congressman, to the ground. William Barbee had not been on the bus. He had arrived earlier to make arrangements for the group, and he too was attacked. Once the rioters knocked Barbee to the ground and held him down, one of them drove a knife-like stanchion of pipe into his ear, and another beat on his head with a base-ball bat, causing injuries from which Barbee never fully recovered. When there was no one left standing and the police finally moved to end the bloody chaos, the rioters slowly drifted away, leaving injured men and women lying in the street.

A Personal Brawl

THE WEEK AFTER the Montgomery riot, Claude Henley came into Morris Dees's office looking for legal representation. The car salesman wore blue-and-red-checked pants, a white shirt, and a tie. Puffing assiduously on a thin cigar, he was wreathed in smoke. Henley said he had been referred by one of the young lawyer's cousins.

Dees had read about the attack on the Freedom Riders in the *Montgomery Advertiser*, but he had not spoken out against the vicious actions. "It would be bad for business if rising young lawyers and businessmen spoke out for social justice and equality," his partner Fuller wrote later. He and Fuller were making a fortune selling everything from tractor seat covers to cookbooks in promotions for groups such as the Future Farmers of America and the Future Homemakers of America clubs. Fighting for civil rights was not on their agenda.

Although he spent most of his time conducting business, Dees still liked to think of himself as a practicing lawyer, even though that part of his professional life wasn't going so well. Fuller considered their early legal practice "little more than ambulance chasing," and there weren't that many ambulances out there.

Henley had been named in a federal civil lawsuit arguing that he had violated the constitutional rights of the Freedom Riders. The other defendants included some of the biggest players in the state, from Shelton to the police chiefs of Birmingham and Montgomery. That was ominous enough, but what frightened Henley most was the possibility that the Feds might also indict him criminally for beating on the newsman. A guilty verdict could result in him serving a long prison term.

Dees was so excited to be sitting with a potentially paying client that he didn't think about what he was doing getting involved with Henley. Dees had been taught in law school that everyone deserves a lawyer. Those may have been noble sentiments, but as the fight against integration revved up, people watched where you stood, and if you stood next to Claude Henley, most observers would figure that you were a supporter of militant, even violent resistance to integration.

Henley said he was not a member of the Klan and just happened to be there that morning. He explained how he had strolled up to the journalist, who used his camera as a weapon, poking it in Henley's face. That's when Henley defended himself. Henley insisted that after that he walked away from the ensuing action.

It was an absurd defense and among other things showed the paucity of Henley's imagination. Dees should have seen as much, but sometimes lawyers want to learn just enough to defend their client effectively but not so much that they have to grapple with the complexities of the truth. If Dees had done an even minimal job of investigating Henley's background, he would have found ample evidence that Henley was a leading member of the UKA. And he could have unearthed numerous stories about Henley's role in the riot. But he rushed to sign Henley as his client without questioning what Henley told him.

As Henley spoke, Dees was already making up his defense in his head. Henley had busted a newsman who had attacked him first. This had nothing to do with the Freedom Riders, and since Henley had violated no federal statute the Feds had no legal right to corral him into the matter. The more he listened the more he thought he could get some real money out of this, and when the time came he was going to tell Henley his fee was $500, and he wasn't going to budge.

Dees was startled when Henley started throwing out figures far beyond the lawyer's dreams. "Why that John Blue Hill," Henley said, mentioning a well-regarded defense attorney. "I went to him first, Morris, and he wanted fifteen thousand. Fifteen thousand. No way can I pay that."

"You know what, Claude," Morris said. "I'll tell you what I'm gonna do. I'll do your case for five thousand."

"You got yourself a deal," Henley said, shaking the hand of his new lawyer.

Dees had never earned so much money as a lawyer. This was the highest-profile case he had ever been involved in, and for the first time in his life, his name made it onto the front page of the *Montgomery Advertiser*.

Attorneys who defended Klansmen were usually members themselves or sympathetic to the Klan. And newspaper subscribers weren't the only ones who had reason to think that Dees was a Klan supporter. For his appearance in the Federal Courthouse, Dees sat next to his client. Alongside them were other defendants, including Robert Shelton.

The Klan leader assumed that Dees was a Klan adherent and made note that Dees was somebody he might find useful one day. For Dees it was an exciting day. For the first time in his life he was arguing a case in a federal courtroom, in front of Judge Frank Johnson, the most controversial jurist in the South, without whose rulings segregation would have continued longer.

When Shelton was called to the witness stand, he tried to invoke the Fifth Amendment, saying that he could not answer any questions from Assistant Attorney General for Civil Rights John Doar because his words might incriminate him. It was a ploy employed by Mafia dons, American Communists, and anyone else who felt that a few wrong words might send them to prison, but Judge Johnson was not going to let anyone easily hide behind the constitutional privilege. In this proceeding, he had already sent one witness to jail for refusing to answer questions, which didn't look good for Shelton, who was trying to be just as nonresponsive.

"I have no records involving any names," Shelton said. "I know nothing of the inner work of local meetings."

"That's not responsive," Judge Johnson said. He called a recess during which he made it clear to the Imperial Wizard that he might soon be bundled off to jail for contempt. When the proceedings resumed, Shelton was a little more forthcoming, but he acted as if he knew next to nothing about the organization he headed.

Later, eighteen-year-old Freedom Rider Patricia Ann Jenkins took the stand. "The riots started when a man in a white shirt, with a cigar in his mouth, attacked a photographer," Jenkins testified. "Others joined in, and the photographer's camera was snatched from him and smashed."

When Dees got up to cross-examine the witness, he tried to suggest that Henley's fight with Zwerg was nothing but a "personal brawl," unrelated to the Freedom Riders. He hoped Judge Johnson would rule that his client's case could be separated from the others. The judge, however, was not buying what Dees was saying. That meant Henley would continue as a defendant in this case.

Dees talked to Doar and said his client would accept an injunction that he would no longer engage in activities such as the attack on the Freedom Riders. Dees could spin anything to his advantage, from tractor seat covers to legal verdicts, and he boasted about what he had accomplished for Henley. In fact, after four days of testimony when Judge Johnson issued his fifteen-page order, he enjoined all of the defendants from ever again interfering with interstate travel. And although he acknowledged that the Freedom Riders might well be within their rights as American citizens, they were causing "an undue burden and restraint on interstate commerce," and he ordered them to stop trying to end segregation by riding on public transportation in Alabama.

When Dees left the federal courtroom on the last day of the trial, a number of Freedom Riders and their supporters milled around the corridor as the lawyer and Henley passed by. "How can you represent people like this?" one of them asked. "Don't you think that black people have rights?"

"Yes, I do," Dees said as Henley listened. "I agree with you a hundred percent."

Dees hated having the Freedom Riders look at him with such disdain, as if he were no better than Henley and the worst of the Klan. He vowed that he would never stand in such a place again, but it was not easy to extricate himself from this world. A week later he stood beside Henley when he was convicted of assault in city court, given thirty days in jail that he never served, and a hundred-dollar fine.

Riding Again

ROBERT SHELTON WORE a splendid silky robe as he entered the first Klonvocation (convention) of the United Klans of America in Indian Springs, Georgia, in July 1961 surrounded by his security guards. The eight men wore new uniforms: white trousers, red ties, and paratrooper boots, their black color set off by white laces. At their left hip, they carried swords hardly bigger than daggers, and on the right side affixed black nightsticks.

Many of the Klansmen in the audience were seeing their ultimate leader for the first time. When the Imperial Wizard addressed the five hundred UKA members from across the South, he was not like some old-time preacher revving up the faithful with gut-wrenching exhortations. He was more subdued and serious, but the words brooked no compromise with the rigid rules of segregation, and he laid out plans to expand the UKA dramatically.

The first Klonvocation occurred two months after the Freedom Riders had showed the kinds of opposition the white supremacist militants would likely face as they continued to defend segregation. It was a propitious time for what would become an annual event. Shelton sought to create a Klan full of power and purpose in which every rule and ritual was followed in minute detail. The great ceremonies, the cross burnings, and the march of hooded Klansmen had to be orchestrated properly to strike awe and wonder in white observers, and fear and trepidation in black Americans and those who walked with them.

In the following months, the Imperial Wizard was on the road, traveling from Klavern to Klavern, talking not only to UKA members but also to politicians and police. Some of the police were Klansmen, and others thought of the UKA as a quasi-militia helpful in defending public safety and order.

As important as his presence was, Shelton realized that he needed other devices to interest people in the UKA if he hoped to expand membership by the tens of thousands. He was printing only a few thousand copies a month of *Fiery Cross*, the Klan publication, at his small press in Tuscaloosa, and he wanted to increase that to run around two million copies.

Shelton knew all about the publishing empire Dees and Fuller were building. Moreover, just a few months earlier, Shelton had seen Dees vigorously defending Klansman Henley in a federal courthouse. He figured that the lawyer-businessman was the obvious person to get the big job. He set up a meeting with Dees and his partner, Fuller, and drove to Montgomery.

In most respects Shelton lived modestly, but he drove a new Cadillac with a big police radio antenna, a kind of car rarely seen on the rural roads of Alabama. When he arrived at Dees and Fuller's office, he suggested they drive around Montgomery. As the three men cruised around town, the ambitious Klan leader talked about the large printing job.

Dees had not risen so quickly in business by making unnecessary enemies. He was friendly to any and all, reaching out to almost everyone with backslapping geniality. Dees knew Shelton was not someone he wanted to offend, so he was unfailingly warm to the Imperial Wizard. But still he wanted no part of the *Fiery Cross*, even if he stood to make a profit from it. He politely but firmly declined, saying that his company did not print newspapers.

Shelton took the rejection well enough. He went so far as to ask the two lawyers to lunch. He did not appear to realize that Dees chose a table far in the corner of the restaurant where he hoped people would not notice that he and his partner were dining with the Imperial Wizard. As disappointed as Shelton was by the turndown, he still considered Dees a friend of the Klan. Preoccupied with all his businesses, Dees gave no more thought to the Klan and whether there might be unforeseen consequences in being considered a friend of America's leading Klansman.

Dees had other personal matters to face. On a Saturday evening in October 1961, his fifty-two-year-old father died in an automobile accident. Dees Sr. had been out visiting his buddies. After a night of drinking, he drove his Mercury into a tree.

George Wallace showed up for the funeral and was solemn and deferential, respecting the occasion. At one point, while Dees and his mother sat in the car, just before they were to get out at Greenwood Cemetery to bury Dees Sr., Wallace joined them and told Mrs. Dees how much he admired her late husband.

But the likely gubernatorial candidate was always politicking, and there was no better place to meet and greet than a funeral. Dees watched Wallace as he shook endless hands, his face locked in solemnity. The jockeying, however, failed to impress Dees. The candidate's former student campaign manager didn't like what he was hearing from Wallace. The politician had grown strident in his defense of segregation, and Dees was not just uncomfortable campaigning for him, he didn't think he could vote for him. He feared that if elected, Wallace would force a confrontation with the federal government that he could not possibly win. That would do great harm to Alabama and the South.

These were strange times, and Dees was in a strange place. He had represented Henley at a time when it mattered profoundly where you stood. He didn't want to stand there any longer. He didn't know quite yet where he belonged, but it was not among the strident segregationists like Wallace trying to hold back tomorrow.

Dees was also bothered by the way Wallace treated women. He had heard the stories about Wallace wanting a different woman at every campaign stop, and volunteers were ready. Dees knew about the politician's conduct personally. A secretary had told Dees she was having an affair with Wallace. The secretary said the first time Wallace came to her apartment, he pulled his pants down without so much as a hello and asked her to perform oral sex on him.

Wallace had an astute sense of those willing to help him and those repelled by his rhetoric. So he picked up on Dees's feelings and didn't even bother discussing the forthcoming gubernatorial campaign with him. Wallace had other far more important people to bring into the campaign.

Well before the start of the race, Wallace sent an aide to Shelton to see if the Klan leader would consider supporting him. The candidate had condemned John Patterson for taking Klan support in his successful 1958 gubernatorial campaign, but he had seen what the Klan could do, and he wanted the Klan riding with him. Shelton understood full well what was at stake.

"I went to him and asked him if he wanted our support," Shelton told Wayne Greenhaw for his book *Watch Out for George Wallace*. "I didn't want to play any behind-the-scenes games." The Imperial Wizard figured it would just be a matter of time before the UKA would be no more controversial to whites than were the Masons or the Rotary Club.

Shelton and his Klansmen worked wholeheartedly for candidate Wallace. As they had in the Patterson campaign, the UKA members performed with devotion beyond other volunteers. They were willing, indeed, delighted, to do things of questionable legality to elect their candidate.

Shelton set out the main themes of the campaign with boldness beyond even that of the candidate. Standing tall in his satin gown, Shelton condemned the "nigger-loving, Jew embracing Kennedys" and praised Wallace by saying that as governor, he would "stand in the schoolhouse door and keep our children from becoming mongrelized by the degenerate races."

In a confidential 1964 memo, the FBI noted a whole range

of UKA activities in support of Wallace: "The UKA worked for his nomination; helped finance his campaign; were seen at his campaign headquarters and instructed UKA members to support him. UKA leaders believed Wallace was a friend of the UKA financially and otherwise. Wallace spoke at a meeting of the Imperial Board of the UKA."

Beyond promises Wallace may have made to the UKA leader, Shelton had another reason to support him. One of the candidate's closest advisers was speechwriter Asa Carter, who was one of Shelton's old friends. In 1956, the two had stood shoulder to shoulder preventing Autherine Lucy from entering the University of Alabama.

Since those days Carter's Klavern had attacked popular crooner Nat King Cole onstage as the singer performed in Birmingham. They had beaten up civil rights leader Reverend Fred Shuttlesworth and then stabbed his wife. They had castrated J. Edward Aaron, a mentally challenged black handyman, and dumped his nearly dead body on the highway outside the city to send a message to black "trouble-makers."

Carter was such a controversial figure that during the campaign Wallace relegated him to giving talks to Klan groups. The Klan members were so important to Wallace's campaign that this was not a trivial assignment.

"As far as I can remember, [Wallace] never did speak at one of our rallies, but Asa Carter came to them and spoke for Wallace," Shelton told Greenlaw. "He'd get the crowds all churned up. Asa spoke to 'em and told 'em George Wallace was the white savior and that he was against no-good Communists on the Supreme Court and no-good scalawags on the local federal benches. It was like a camp meeting down home."

Wallace squandered a few minutes in his campaign speeches on the old populist issues of class and economics, but most of the time he talked about race. The louder the audiences screamed their approval and the louder they shouted out his name, the bolder he made his rhetoric and the more extravagant his pledges.

The candidate promised Alabamans that he would stand so tall, so bold that the hated Feds would turn tail and head back north. He told his audiences the cowardly intruders always backed down. But if these "scallawagging, carpetbagging liars" tried to integrate Alabama schools, Wallace pledged, "I shall refuse to abide by any such illegal federal court order even to the point of standing at the schoolhouse door."

Wallace's wife, Lurleen, had had enough of a husband who was rarely home. While he was off romping on the campaign trail, she was left in a tiny apartment taking care of their three children. She knew her husband was out listening to every would-be voter, but George had no time to listen to her. Lurleen packed up the kids and went to her parents' home in Green County and filed for divorce. That got her husband's attention.

Wallace was planning to campaign as a loving family man and father. A divorced candidate would not be elected governor. Wallace turned his formidable political skills on his most important constituent. He told his wife that the difficult days were almost over. When he was elected, the family would move into the governor's mansion and everything would be better for his wife and their family. Lurleen agreed to stay with her husband.

Big Jim Folsom was running in the primary, seeking his third, nonconsecutive term. Wallace had pillaged Folsom's populist rhetoric, leaving the former governor sounding tired, redundant, and desperate. A few days before the primary, Folsom shouted out that the Klan was "in the Wallace camp." That accusation was true, but it was not an effective way of winning votes in Alabama in those days, and Folsom came in third. Wallace won in the runoff primary by a heady 340,000 votes and became the Democratic nominee. The party was so dominant then that this was tantamount to winning the election.

On election night Shelton and other Klansmen waited in Wallace campaign headquarters, and the successful candidate came to thank them. Shelton's association with Wallace made him an increasingly powerful figure. "Alabama is the only state in which the Klans can claim a political role," wrote the *New York Times* in September 1962 in an article titled KU KLUX KLAN IS RIDING AGAIN. "This is the result of the work of Robert M. Shelton, a former rubber plant worker from Tuscaloosa and the most important Klan leader in the South."

ON THE FRIGID inaugural morning in January 1963, Wallace stood with a silk top hat in his hand as he proudly watched 15,000 Alabamans marching up Dexter Avenue. Not a single black person paraded past him. Nor was a single black person pictured in the 296-page official inaugural program. The tens of thousands of men and women who braved the twenty-five-degree weather to hear the inaugural address were also exclusively white.

The most famous passage in the thirty-six-minute speech become almost as much an anthem of resistance as the song "Dixie."

"I draw the line in the dust," Wallace said, "and toss the gauntlet before the feet of tyranny . . . and I say . . . segregation now . . . segregation tomorrow . . . and segregation forever."

As Wallace's aide Seymore Trammell listened, he thought, "Adolf Hitler must have been weak by comparison." Much of the speech the governor gave that day could have been spoken word for word at a Klan rally.

Shelton believed that Alabama had a white man's governor who would resist the federal onslaught with the last breath of his political life. He was sure that when that great moment of confrontation came, as everyone knew it would come, Wallace would stand up as he said he would, and the Imperial Wizard would be there with the Klan.

Dees had very different feelings. He was appalled at the campaign's rhetoric. It exposed an Alabama he didn't want to believe existed. He wasn't going to speak out, but he was upset. On election day, he and Fuller went out duck hunting on the Tallapoosa River. As they paddled along, it was so unbearably cold that Dees couldn't think about anything else but the weather.

Eternal Vigilance

ROBERT SHELTON STOOD on a flatbed truck in his purple gown between two enormous burning crosses. Bodyguards and other top officials in their Klan garb surrounded him. Even before the Imperial Wizard began to speak, the regalia and ritual should have been enough to charge the 2,500 attendees at this Klan rally in Bessemer on May 11, 1963, with all the energy and enthusiasm of a University of Alabama football game. But the crowd in the working-class iron community outside Birmingham was dispirited this evening.

The event was supposed to have been a demonstration in support of the fight for segregation in Birmingham, but it had ended up coinciding with what Shelton considered the city's capitulation to the integration demands of Martin Luther King Jr. and the activists of the Southern Christian Leadership Conference. The SCLC team had arrived in the city in April to lead mass nonviolent demonstrations against segregation. After faltering during the initial weeks, the campaign finally caught fire in early May when hundreds of black children were recruited, one child only six years old. Commissioner of Public Safety Eugene "Bull" Connor met them with dogs and water hoses.

The city's business leaders realized the bad publicity was costing them money, and they decided to settle. Birmingham businessman Sydney Smyer figured it was "a dollar-and-cents thing." And so the business leadership negotiated with a committee of black leaders to desegregate the fitting rooms and the department store lunch counters, to remove the hated COLORED signs from drinking fountains and restrooms and to hire one black "sales person or cashier." The precise timetable was kept secret, for as Reverend King told his followers, "The Klan, they still live somewhere."

That evening in Bessemer, the working-class steel community outside Birmingham, Shelton tried to reenergize the discouraged legions of Klansmen and their supporters spread out before him. "Good evening, ladies and gentlemen, and fellow Klans people," Shelton said. "Now just let me remind you of this, and regardless of what the news media says, regardless of what television or Martin Luther King or the businesspeople say, Martin Luther King has not gained one thing in Birmingham because the white people are not going to tolerate the meddlesome, conniving, manipulating moves of these professional businessmen."

Likely at Shelton's direction, his subordinates were about to carry out an action to reassert the segregationist imperative in the most violent way. His minions bombed the suite at the Gaston Motel where Reverend King was staying as well as the home of King's younger brother, Alfred Daniel King. But somehow the bombers didn't know that Reverend King had flown to Atlanta earlier that day, and no one was in the room when the bomb exploded. As for A. D. King, he was in bed when the bomb went off, and he was not hurt either.

The men who placed the bombs were never found, but the FBI had evidence suggesting that the bombing was a UKA effort, planned at the highest level, and that meant Shelton. Diane McWhorter in *Carry Me Home,* her definitive account of the Birmingham civil rights movement, writes that an FBI informant said that UKA Klansman Chambliss threatened that if any of his colleagues talked about his likely bomb maker's role in the Gaston Motel bombing, he would rat out Shelton, who had supervised the operation, and name those who had taken part, including the Imperial Wizard's subordinate, Gary Thomas Rowe.

In the aftermath of the night of bombings, young black people took to the streets to riot and throw rocks. Shelton and his Klansmen hoped their action would create such turmoil that integration could not proceed. It seemed clear. All it took to change history was a few bold men and a few well-placed bombs.

The Schoolhouse Door

ON A SATURDAY afternoon in June 1963, state police stopped and arrested a carful of Klansmen at a roadblock outside Tuscaloosa. They were driving to a Klan rally south of the college town protesting the attempt to integrate the University of Alabama. The militants carried an arsenal that included loaded pistols, shotguns, a machine gun, hand grenades, dynamite sticks, a bazooka, swords, and bayonets. It was enough to start a small war. "Jesus Christ!" exclaimed one of the troopers. "We sure hate to bust you when you came down here to help us keep the goddamn niggers away from the school!"

A few hours later, Robert Shelton stood before three thousand people assembled in a field outside Tuscaloosa as a sixty-by-forty-foot cross burned in the nighttime sky. The Imperial Wizard's hometown had been the scene of the Klan's great triumph in 1956 when it helped to prevent what would have been the first black student from entering the school. In three days two black students, Vivian Malone and James Hood, were scheduled to register for classes at the University of Alabama. Shelton was convinced this time the result would be the same, but it would come quicker with the full authority of the state slamming the door in their faces.

Back when Autherine Lucy knocked on the university door, then Governor Folsom had shied away from playing any role and had instead flown down to Florida for a weekend of fishing. This time Shelton's friend and hero George Wallace had said in campaign speeches that if he had to, he would stand in the schoolhouse door and personally bar any black students from entering. Wallace had been in office only half a year, and he vowed he was not backing down. "They will have to arrest me before they integrate the University of Alabama," the governor told columnist Drew Pearson. Shelton planned to be right there beside Wallace, along with his Klan brethren.

Shelton owed Wallace big-time. The governor had set Shelton up on the payroll of Dixie Engineering, a company that did a lot of business with the state. Five hundred dollars a month was big money to the Klan leader, and the governor put Shelton's father on the payroll as well. Wallace was keeping his promise to the Klan in other ways. The only Alabama Klan members to spend significant time in prison were the Birmingham Klavern members who castrated J. Edward Aaron. The governor's appointee to the parole board saw to it that they got out on early parole.

Shelton knew his constituency as well as Wallace did his. In his speech, he attacked the Jews and the northern radicals who, he said, had taken over the *Crimson White*, the Alabama student newspaper, and were writing mealymouthed editorials advocating integration. Despite what Shelton said, many of the reporters and editors were Alabama born and bred, including several attending the event to write about it in the student paper.

The audience expected Shelton to ask them to come when the two black students arrived at the university and do whatever must be done so they would not spend one full day on the campus. But he surprised them by saying they must stay away and let the governor do what he must do to prevent integration.

The Imperial Wizard was giving up his own right to lead his troops into confrontation, and he was proud, even flattered, to be so intimately a part of the governor's game plan. He had faith that Wallace could do things that even his Klansmen could not do.

"I see in Wallace the ability to rewrite history in Tuscaloosa in the next three or four days," Shelton told the assembled that evening. But the governor needed space to achieve their common goals. "I have talked to Brother George, and Brother George has asked me to tell you-all that he's going to stand up for you-all, and you can mess everything up that he's worked for if there's any violence at all."

This was Shelton's hometown, and he wasn't going away. His fellow Klansmen drove through the streets of the city in cars with KKK written on the side and waved Confederate flags out the windows. Every time one of these vehicles drove near campus tensions ratcheted up. That wouldn't do, and Alabama state detective Ben Allen met with the Klan leader downtown at the Bell Café and asked him and his people to stay away.

Shackled to the rhetoric he had spoken during the campaign and at his inauguration, Wallace could hardly budge from his unyielding position. But with Shelton keeping his people at a distance, the governor could appear to be the defiant, unrelenting segregationist champion without the likelihood of violence.

Wallace had to figure how to exit from this self-made crisis with his segregationist honor and his polls intact. So far everything had gone brilliantly. He had flown up to New York to appear on the NBC Sunday-morning news program *Meet the Press*. The reporters asked questions as if they thought the man was a know-nothing redneck. He replied with acumen, wit, and originality and left the North with new admirers. They would be watching Tuscaloosa, and so would millions of others.

Reporters arrived in the college town from across America and the world. That was all part of the governor's scheme, but one misstep and his aspirations could be burned to ashes, the debacle chronicled by scores of scribes and cameras.

Things became even more complicated for Wallace when

Seybourn Harris Lynne, a judge on the United States District Court for the Northern District of Alabama, issued an injunction saying that while the governor could show up on campus, he could neither try to prevent the two students from registering nor could he block the door. Lynne was a federal judge, but he was equally a citizen of Alabama, and in taking the stance he did, he risked being ostracized and worse.

"I love the people of Alabama," Judge Lynne wrote. "I know that many of both races are troubled and like Jonah of old, are 'angry even unto death' as the result of distortions of affairs within this state, practiced in the name of sensationalism."

The Alabama judge was planning another contingency that would have made him so hated by Wallace stalwarts that his name would have been anathema for years. The state constitution said that when a governor stayed out of Alabama for more than twenty days, he was removed as governor. If Wallace violated the injunction, Lynne intended to spirit him out of state and keep him in a federal facility for twenty-one days. After that he could go free. The one duty left to him in Montgomery would have been to vacate the governor's mansion.

What Judge Lynne did not understand nor did most of the journalists assembled in Tuscaloosa was that the governor was fighting this war with blank cartridges that made lots of noise but caused no damage. It was all a game, a mockery.

Wallace did not intend to go to jail even for a night. He was planning to do in Tuscaloosa what he always did: push things as far as they could go and then back away. The scheme was workable largely because Shelton's Klansmen were not there to riot if the two students were admitted.

Wallace saw it as a gigantic game, a daring provocation. Shelton, however, believed the governor and thought his political hero knew best and through the sheer force of unyielding will would force the black students to leave campus for good. It was not a game to the U.S. Army either, which had been training in the countryside outside Tuscaloosa on just how they would arrest Wallace. They would grab him from behind and shuttle him into a car before he hardly knew what they were doing.

On the night before the confrontation, Wallace stayed in a Tuscaloosa hotel. The next morning he dressed in a gray suit and mismatched brown and blue tie and got in his chauffeured old Ford to be driven over to Foster Auditorium where 125 state police, revenue and game agents, 150 journalists, and a national television audience waited for a moment that many believed would end up in the governor's arrest and possibly a full-scale riot. The furnace-like Alabama summer had arrived early this year, and everyone sweltered in the hundred-degree heat.

As Wallace waited inside for Hood and Malone and their Justice Department representatives to arrive, he was visibly edgy. He was not good in situations like this. He feared that this time he had gone too far, and he would face a terrible humiliation. "Ben, do you think they'll actually arrest me?" he asked state police officer Ben Allen, who had no idea how to respond.

When the cars carrying the Washington officials and the students arrived, Wallace stepped out in front of the massive door and stood behind a lectern wearing a microphone that would amplify his words to everyone present. The Justice Department did not indulge Wallace's gaudy theatrics by asking Malone and Hood to walk up the steps to confront the governor by their very presence. Instead, only Deputy Attorney General Nicolas Katzenbach met the governor.

Katzenbach started reading a proclamation signed by President Kennedy calling for Wallace to end his defiance. "We don't need your speech," interrupted Wallace who gave his own speech in words crafted by Asa Carter.

"Governor, I am not interested in a show," Katzenbach said, though that's precisely what it was. "I don't know what the purpose of this show is . . . I ask you once again to responsibly step aside."

Wallace stood in petulant silence, his lips tightly pursed. Katzenbach turned, walked down the steps, and got into the car where Malone and Hood sat waiting. The two students were driven to college dorms, Malone had lunch in the cafeteria where she was warmly welcomed by any number of students.

After listening to the morning charade with mounting anger, Attorney General Robert Kennedy decided to nationalize the Alabama National Guard and send them on campus to see if that would end Wallace's posturing. In the afternoon, the governor stepped outside again in front of the cameras. National Guard General Henry V. Graham told him it was his "sad duty" to use the Guard to force the governor to back off.

That set Wallace off on a minitirade about "military dictatorship" in the United States. "We shall now return to Montgomery," he said in his exit line, "to continue this constitutional fight."

When the governor got back to Montgomery, he did not have to wait for the fan mail to come pouring in from all across America to realize that he could spin this as a great victory. He had stood up in the schoolhouse door and in doing so had become the face of resistance to what he considered federal tyranny.

Wallace felt himself wildly popular among white Alabamans, and it wasn't only southerners who admired him. He was a hero to millions of Americans all across the country who before this day had not even known his name. It didn't seem to matter that a few minutes after Wallace left campus, Malone and Hood walked over to Foster Auditorium to register as students. The little judge had stood up for the white race.

Wallace's daughter, Peggy Wallace Kennedy, says, "My father did wrong standing in the schoolhouse door. But by the end of the day, he was a household word in every household in the United States. He took advantage of the moment. That's what he was, an opportunist."

Wallace backed down physically at Tuscaloosa, but he did not tone down his rhetoric, and that was what people believed. The governor took exquisite pleasure in the emotions his words instilled. Most students treated Hood and Malone well, but some did not, and that hostile attitude had been nurtured in part by Wallace's intemperate language.

It was difficult for the two students always being on view and not knowing how the next white person would treat them. That fall Hood had a nervous breakdown and dropped out. A few days later a bomb went off in front of Malone's dormitory and a caller left a message that if she did not leave the next bomb would target her dorm room.

University of Alabama's vice president Jeff Bennett drove to Montgomery to try to get Wallace to do what he could to prevent a tragedy. The governor listened but Bennett said the governor was more concerned with what measures they could take "to get that nigger bitch out of the dormitory."

Wallace did not talk to his wife or children about what he was doing or what he believed. "My father was so consumed, so preoccupied, that to some extent, he was gone even when he was with us," reflected George Wallace Jr. years later.

After the confrontation at the University of Alabama, the life Lurleen and the children hoped they might have was gone forever. On three different nights in April bullets had been fired into the mansion. The assailants were never found, but Wallace's list of potential enemies was endless. From then on, the children were warned not to stand by the windows. And when they went to school, they had police protection. "His ambition and the bargain he had made were bringing home consequences he never imagined," said Wallace Jr.

To ensure victory, Shelton would have had his Klansmen fight to prevent the two black students from entering the university, and he could have considered the result little better than Wallace's capitulation. Shelton was an astute politician in his own right and he made his peace with the unsatisfactory results. He knew Wallace was planning to take his campaign nationally, and Shelton hoped to go with him, elevating the Klan to an unprecedented place in American life.

Dees watched all of this with growing distress, but he was also consumed with the meteoric rise of his business career. He believed that what Wallace was doing was wrong, but it was not a good idea for a prominent young businessman to get involved in such controversial matters. Two years out of law school, Dees and Fuller were earning more than $500,000 a year profit from their cookbooks. They were building their operation up so quickly that they would soon claim they were the largest publishers of cookbooks in the nation. It was heady stuff for the son of a tenant farmer whose home mortgage on the day he died was the same as on the day he purchased it.

Good Working People

SHELTON WAS CONVINCED that the upcoming March on Washington scheduled for August 28, 1963, was a manifestation of the Communist conspiracy. He wanted to be there so he could film the leaders and their duped followers, documenting the interracial gathering.

To witness the largest civil rights demonstration in American history, Shelton flew up in a rented Cessna 182 Skylane and brought thousands of KKK pamphlets with him. Three-hundred-and-fifty-pound Alvin D. Sisk, the Imperial Kligrapp, or secretary, of the UKA, flew the rented plane. There was one other passenger, Frederick G. Smith, who like the other two men was from Tuscaloosa. As they flew north through heavy fog, the plane crashed on Medlin Mountain near Walhalla, South Carolina. Smith had minor injuries. Shelton survived with a broken right arm, but Sisk died in Oconee Memorial Hospital. The

On March 20, 1981, the body of Michael Donald was found
hanging from a tree in Mobile, Alabama. It was the first lynching
in a quarter century. (MOBILE POLICE DEPARTMENT)

On the morning of the lynching, Klansmen Bennie Hays, Henry Hays, and James Knowles watched from across the street.
(MOBILE POLICE DEPARTMENT)

Above left: James "Tiger" Knowles in May 1983.
(MOBILE POLICE DEPARTMENT)

Above right: Teddy Kyzar, a member of UKA Klavern 900 in Theodore, Alabama, lit a Klan cross the night of the lynching of Michael Donald. (COURTESY SOUTHERN POVERTY LAW CENTER)

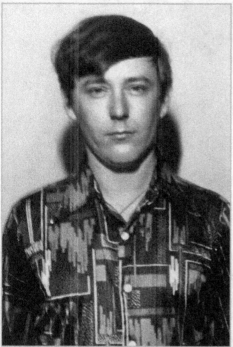

Henry Hays in May 1983.
(MOBILE POLICE DEPARTMENT)

Henry Hays, arrested for the
murder of Michael Donald on
June 16, 1983.
(MOBILE PRESS-REGISTER)

ABOVE: Upon the death of her son, Beulah Mae Donald aged overnight. (GILLES PERESS-MAGNUM)

LEFT: Nineteen-year-old Michael Donald. (COURTESY OF THE DONALD FAMILY)

The young Morris Dees in a cotton field. (MORRIS DEES)

Morris Dees with Governor George Wallace and his daughter Janie Lee in 1972, at George McGovern headquarters where Dees was finance director. (MORRIS DEES)

Imperial Wizard Robert Shelton (second from left) at a United Klans of America rally on April 23, 1965.
(COURTESY OF THE W.S. HOOLE SPECIAL COLLECTIONS LIBRARY, THE UNIVERSITY OF ALABAMA)

The United Klans of America 1977 march in downtown Mobile.
(*MOBILE PRESS-REGISTER*)

In 1980, two of the Klansmen who firebombed the SPLC offices,
Joe Garner (1) and Tommy Downs (2) marched in a Klan parade in
Birmingham. (GARY NUNGESTER)

A Klan cross burning.
(MICHAEL MCVAY/CORBIS)

Morris Dees was the Klan's most hated opponent.
(COURTESY SPLC)

From left, SPLC cofounder
Morris Dees, chief
investigator Joe Roy,
lawyer Richard Cohen,
and Klanwatch director Bill
Stanton preparing for the
Michael Donald civil trial.
(PAUL ROBERTSON)

In July 1983, Klansmen firebombed the Southern Poverty Law
Center's office in Montgomery, Alabama. (PAUL ROBERTSON)

United Klans of America Grand Titan Bennie Jack Hays and Opal Hays in February 1984. (*MOBILE PRESS-REGISTER*)

A cartoon in the Fiery Cross, the UKA newspaper that was a crucial exhibit in the 1987 civil suit against the UKA. (SPLC)

Mrs. Beulah Donald and Morris Dees outside her new house bought with the proceeds of the civil suit against the UKA.

(JOANN CHANCELLOR)

Rosa Parks, whose action set off the 1955–56 Montgomery bus
boycott, with Morris Dees in 1995.

(ALABAMA TOURISM DEPARTMENT)

Michael Donald's older brother, Stanley, unveils a street sign for Michael Donald Avenue in 2006. (LYLE RATLIFF)

The Southern Poverty Law Center's fourtieth anniversary in 2011. From left: cofounder Morris Dees; Civil Rights Memorial Center director Lecia Brooks; President Richard Cohen; SPLCL's first president, Julian Bond; and co-founder Joe Levin. (DAVID BUNDY)

Morris Dees at the Civil Rights Memorial. (VALERIE DOWNES)

TO KILL A
Mockingbird

To Morris Dees:

Because you spoke when good
men were silent and acted
when good men did nothing,
You changed our lives.

With all good wishes,
Harper Lee

Harper Lee wrote this dedication in Morris Dees's copy of
To Kill a Mockingbird. (MORRIS DEES)

Klan leader believed someone had tampered with the altimeter, but the accident report said otherwise.

Shelton could not make it to the March on Washington, but his Klan colleague Ralph P. Roton filmed the event. The tenth-grade dropout had been working as the Imperial Wizard's investigator when George Wallace recommended that he be hired as an undercover operative for the state's new Peace Commission. The agency was charged to investigate anyone who posed threats to the "southern way of life." This was an all-encompassing term that included anyone favoring integration, including activists, teachers, ministers, and reporters. Roton made copies of many of the dossiers the new agency collected and passed them on to Shelton.

Wallace viewed the gigantic civil rights event as an opportunity to mock the 200,000 Americans who had come to hear Martin Luther King Jr. give his "I Have a Dream" speech from the steps of the Lincoln Memorial. The governor said it was being led by "Communists and sex perverts." He had no grasp that something enormous was happening at the March on Washington. A small mark of it was that hundreds of black Alabama farmers left the state for the first time in their lives to ride fifteen hours in stiflingly hot buses to the nation's capital. There was a great awakening, and whether or not the governor acknowledged that fact, he would one day have to deal with its power and resolve.

Dees wasn't close to the Montgomery progressives who had flown up to attend the march. Beyond that, he simply wasn't a demonstrator, and he had not gone to Washington. But he was moved by Reverend King's speech, and Dees felt his lethargic unconcern for the events happening all around him increasingly untenable.

Soon after the plane crash, Shelton headed to Birmingham. The federal courts had directed a number of Alabama cities and towns to integrate their schools when they opened in September 1963. Local officials reluctantly conceded that their only rational choice was to go ahead with integration, albeit in a limited way. Only five black children were scheduled to enter two Birmingham high schools and one elementary school.

Two days before the scheduled integration, Wallace addressed ten thousand supporters in Birmingham's Ensley Park, a forlorn facility in the scruffy working-class white neighborhood. He condemned the March on Washington as "planned and led by Communists and atheists," including "sex offender" Bayard Rustin, a prominent civil rights activist who in 1953 had been arrested for having sex with two other men in a car in Pasadena, California.

The governor employed the same ploy he used in Tuscaloosa earlier in the year, saying he had "other secrets for Birmingham," undisclosed means that only he would use to end this attempt at integrating the schools in Alabama's largest city.

It was not what the governor said that evening that made the event unique, but that he had Edward Fields, the national information director of the National States' Rights Party (NSRP), sitting on the speaker's stand behind him. After four NSRP members were charged but not convicted of dynamiting Atlanta's largest synagogue in 1958, the neo-Nazi organization had moved down to a working-class neighborhood in Birmingham, where the white supremacists had more of a welcome.

The cover of the NSRP monthly publication, *Thunderbolt*, had a symbol taken directly from Hitler's SS guards. Fields laced the pages with illustrations taken from prewar Nazi publications. In Birmingham, the NSRP passed out Nazi propaganda that probably had not been seen in such profusion in America since the Amerikadeutscher Bund in the 1930s.

Fields was not merely copying Hitler. He had his own ideas: Supreme Court justices should be executed, Jews shipped to Madagascar, and black people to Africa. Only then would America be right again.

A few days earlier, Fields had led a convoy of seventy-five Confederate-flag waving cars to Montgomery to deliver a petition with thirty thousand names on it calling for Wallace to shut down public schools instead of integrating them. This was the kind of effort that Shelton once would have led. It suggested that the Imperial Wizard risked being replaced in Wallace's heart and mind by a pro-Nazi militant. To maintain what he considered his rightful place next to the governor, Shelton needed to assert the supremacy of the UKA in their Alabama world.

ON SEPTEMBER 4, 1963, protesters tried to prevent five black children from registering in Birmingham's all-white schools. These demonstrators were not the parents of white schoolchildren: they were nearly all NSRP partisans. They ripped out the police lines, threw rocks at the school, and kicked and beat a motorcycle officer. Out in front stood four NSRP security guards dressed like Nazi storm troopers with thunderbolt arm belts. As they rushed forward, police arrested them and bloodied one with a billy club.

This was the first time a white supremacist group attacked Alabama police, whom until then they had always considered their supporters. Whatever doubts Shelton had about the NSRP, he condemned the "police brutality."

That evening, for the second time in two weeks, a bomb went off at the home of Arthur Shores, a prominent black activist lawyer involved in school integration. That set off protests that the police dealt with by openly firing at the demonstrators, killing one man, John Coley.

Wallace, who had provoked the violence, then came rushing in to save the situation, like an arsonist putting out the fire he has set. The events in Birmingham were Wallace's perfect scenario—creating such turmoil and uncertainty that he could then come to the rescue.

The next morning after the death in Birmingham, the governor decided it was time to call in a few reporters. He enjoyed putting on northern journalists, spitting tobacco juice into a wastebasket not six inches from their shoes. He was as good at hitting the target as Bob Cousy was at making layups, but the hacks sat there, not daring to pull their feet away but worrying that they might leave the interview with an unwanted gubernatorial souvenir on their Gucci loafers.

As Wallace kept spitting away, he often threw at them such wild rhetoric that they almost broke their pencils getting it all down. When they asked what they considered thoughtful questions, he rolled over their queries as if such pretentious philosophizing was beneath him. These meetings with often-hostile reporters were a seductive pleasure the governor almost always performed before an approving audience of two or three of his crony aides.

For this meeting, Wallace arrived in his office wearing dark glasses. He said he was wearing the glasses because he had been up all night in discussions that ended with the Birmingham School Board doing what the governor insisted they do: end the violence by shutting down the schools instead of going ahead with planned integration.

It all sounded perfectly rational, but before the reporters had time to explore that, Wallace was lecturing them that those who stood up forcefully against integration "are not thugs; they are good working people who get mad when they see something like this happen. . . . It takes courage to stand up to teargas and bayonets."

Wallace had a way of rolling over reporters with such unseemly haste that at the end of their interviews they looked down at their scribbled notes and could hardly understand what had happened. The governor wanted the journalists to think that the fight against school integration in Birmingham was the spontaneous uprising of a beleaguered people. He didn't give the scribes time to note that these "good working people" were neo-Nazi members of the NSRP out in the streets doing what in effect was his dirty work.

The governor was soon boring into the reporters with his familiar routine that outsiders were causing the troubles and if these troublemakers would just go away, everything would be okay. Many of those NSRP demonstrators were themselves outsiders. And as much as the governor rebuked the federal intrusion, he was himself stepping on the rights and decisions of the local leadership.

What Wallace did not say was that closing the Birmingham schools was a temporary expedient, and the issue of integration still loomed large over the city and the South. He believed that what was happening across the United States was untenable, and in that there could be little disagreement. "What this country needs is a few first-class funerals," Wallace said, "and some political funerals, too."

Wallace enjoyed provoking his enemies, spewing rhetoric rarely heard in public life. In the end, he always backed off, but in toying with words, he toyed with human lives. Words were actions, and when he provoked people to do their fearful deeds, he was as much morally responsible as if he had struck the blow, planted the bomb, or shot the bullet.

On Saturday evening, September 7, 1963, Wallace gave the keynote address at a Klan fund-raising dinner in Birmingham for a group called United Americans for Conservative Government. Shelton was present, as was the neo-Nazi Edward Fields, who sat at a privileged table right in front of the dais at the Redmont Hotel's Emerald Room.

Wallace told the gathering there had been forty-seven bombings in Birmingham since 1947, and no one had been hurt. There was only one possible reason. The "nigras" were dynamiting themselves, and they were doing it to raise at least a million dollars. As he spoke, the governor looked out on a room where almost unquestionably sat Klansmen who had participated in these bombings.

Black homes had been bombed in Birmingham with seeming impunity since the 1940s. The establishment acquiesced and in some cases celebrated these bombings as Birmingham's racial greeting card, an efficient device to keep black residents in their place.

Nobody had ever gone to jail in the bombings. Unchallenged by the police and tacitly accepted by the power brokers who ruled the city, the bombings were the preferred way that the Klan sent messages to black civil rights lawyers to back off or chastised black families who had moved into white neighborhoods.

The bombs were effective tools, but nobody considered that they were playing with dynamite.

"Seeds of Hate"

THE MOST IMPRESSIVE black-owned building in Birmingham was not a bank, a store, or a private residence but the 16th Street Baptist Church. It was from the altar of this imposing brick church that Martin Luther King Jr. had exhorted the multitudes to continue their struggle. It was from here the black children of Birmingham had marched into the downtown streets to be confronted by Bull Connor's dogs. And it was to this church that the black elite of the city came each Sunday.

To destroy this building would be a great victory for the Klan and the resistance. With this one action, Shelton could prove himself the true man of initiative and action, not Edward Fields, the leader of the NSRP. And Shelton knew just who could build the bomb that would do the job. He had known Robert Chambliss for almost a decade. Just a couple of months earlier, the Imperial Wizard had spent the evening with Chambliss. They had disrupted a meeting that sought to advance the peaceful integration of the Birmingham schools.

The FBI reported "various informants advised that Shelton allegedly ordered the bombing and that he allegedly attempted to place the blame on other individuals." All kinds of shadowy, often secondhand information linked Shelton to the bombing. A witness said that Chambliss's niece or nephew had told her that she or he had overheard Shelton talking to Chambliss about the bombing. McWhorter writes that James Hancock, a state investigator "would insist to investigators that a wiretapped conversation among several Klan units revealed that Shelton had said the bomb had to go off at midnight."

Chambliss had built many bombs before, but at the church the detonator apparently misfired, and the bomb did not go off in the middle of the night when no one was in the building. Instead, at 10:22 A.M. on Sunday, September 15, 1963, the large bomb destroyed a corner of the church, killing four girls: fourteen-year-old Addie Mae Collins, Carole Robertson, and Cynthia Wesley, and eleven-year-old Denise McNair; twenty-two others were injured.

The explosion sent a wave of flames streaking above the church, filling the building with smoke and debris. Out on the street, it blew a driver out of his car. It was the worst single act of violence in the history of the modern civil rights movement.

Although they did not dare to express this openly at the time, some members of the business establishment blamed Wallace, who had orchestrated the crisis that allowed these deaths to happen. "There wouldn't have been any trouble if Wallace had stayed out," reflected businessman Syd Smyer after the bombing. "Why did he do it? Why didn't he let us alone?"

If anything, the murders spurred on the Klansmen and their followers. An antiintegration rally that had been planned for later that Sunday at the Dixie Speedway outside the city went ahead. Shelton was among those present. So were two of the men thought to have had primary responsibility for the bombing, Troy Ingram and Thomas Edwin Blanton Jr. They had left a horrendous mess from which the Imperial Wizard now had to extricate himself.

After the Dixie Speedway rally, a large motorcade was supposed to proceed into the city, but the police convinced the organizers to cancel it. Two white teenagers, one of them an Eagle Scout, had been looking forward to being part of the motorcade. Upset at the cancellation, they drove into black neighborhoods on a motorcycle carrying a Confederate flag. When they came upon two black boys on bicycles, one of the white youths fired his pistol at thirteen-year-old Virgil Ware and killed him.

Later that day, a group of white teenagers drove into a black neighborhood near the 16th Street Baptist Church, honking their horns, waving Confederate flags, and taunting people on the street. When the black residents started throwing rocks in return, police opened fire, killing a sixteen-year-old black youth fleeing the scene, Johnny Robinson Jr. That night fires burned in several streets, gunfire sounded, and it appeared that the bombing might set off a racial war.

The next day at noon, at the weekly Monday luncheon of the Young Men's Business Club, Charles Morgan Jr. got up to speak. The Birmingham lawyer said that he was tired of all the apologists who said the bombing was an isolated incident committed by a few sick persons. He believed that the entire community was culpable from "every little individual who talks about the 'niggers' and spreads the seeds of hate" to "all the Christians and all their ministers who spoke too late in anguished cries against violence." When Morgan began his speech, he was a likely candidate for governor one day. When he finished and his talk became international news, he was ostracized and ended up leaving Birmingham for good.

Morgan received around thirty letters from other southern lawyers condemning him, and only a few letters in support. One of those was from Morris Dees. He wrote to Morgan: "You are indeed a great man. We all need your courage. Your remarks are a faint glow on the horizon of a brush fire we must start."

Wallace said that he agreed with the assessment of many white Alabamans; black activists had probably destroyed the church and killed the girls themselves. Dan T. Carter writes in *The Politics of Rage*, his powerful Wallace biography, "A substantial minority—probably a majority—believed the bombing to have been a tragic miscalculation by civil rights 'fanatics' who had set the device to go off earlier (or later) when the church was empty in order to drum up support for a faltering campaign."

Wallace was intending to run for president in 1964. He needed to spin this bombing business as best he could, and get out of it before it could ravage his plans. If the investigation led to Shelton or anywhere near him, it would likely expose the governor's relationship with the Klan leader. And it might well unmask how Wallace had orchestrated the demonstrations and the turmoil, all to allow himself to play the hero.

Wallace directed the Alabama public safety director, Al Lingo, to move quickly to arrest someone for the crime. One of Lingo's associates in this was none other than Shelton. FBI agents were stunned to see the Imperial Wizard riding around with state investigators. An FBI source said that she had seen him "at the Alabama Highway Patrol Office interviewing individuals they were bringing in." Lingo met with Shelton and several other Klansmen on the evening less than two weeks after the bombing, when Chambliss was arrested along with his Klan associate, Charles Cagle.

Wallace went on television to brag that his police investigators had solved the crime. But these hasty indictments forestalled an FBI investigation that would have moved in directions that would have been troubling for Wallace and his ambitions. The FBI agents were bewildered by the arrests. They knew that there was not enough evidence. It was all too soon.

The two UKA Klansmen were charged with possession of dynamite. They pled guilty to the misdemeanor and were sentenced to six months in jail and a hundred-dollar fine. The judge, however, made sure they didn't spend a day behind bars. That was the end of it as far as Wallace was concerned.

FBI agents interviewed Shelton, who blamed the bombing on activists in the NSRP, his greatest competitor. The FBI had sources saying the Imperial Wizard was behind the bombing. But two and a half years later, the agency removed him from its lists of suspects, saying, "It was established he was not near the scene of such bombings." No one alleged that Shelton had personally planted any bombs, and it appeared that J. Edgar Hoover had no more interest in establishing Shelton's connection to the bombers than did Wallace.

IN MONTGOMERY, WHEN Dees read about the death of the four girls, he felt that he was a stranger to what truly mattered. The Sunday after the bombing, Dees and his wife, Beverly, drove over to attend services at the all-white Pike Road Baptist Church not far from his childhood home. He liked to worship in this country church that his father had helped to build, among people with whom he'd grown up. Most of them had known Morris since he was a child. They knew him as a man who could speak the word of God with the best of them.

This was a church where anyone who felt the calling could get up and speak, and Morris felt the calling. The congregation sat waiting to see what biblical lesson he would have for them this morning.

"Brothers and sisters," he began. "There's another Baptist church that needs our help."

"Tell us, Bubba," someone said.

"You've heard of it," Dees said. "It's the Sixteenth Street Church in Birmingham where those four little girls were killed last Sunday and the church was destroyed."

Silence and anger filled the pews.

"This ain't none of our business, Morris Jr.," said an elderly woman who had been a missionary in Africa. Several parishioners nodded their heads in agreement. "This ain't nothin' we want to get involved in."

Dees looked out across the pews and saw not a single face looking up at him with encouragement.

"Won't you join me in a prayer?" he asked. "We all have children. No matter how you feel . . ." His words dribbled into nothing.

Dees bowed his head and tried to pray, but rustling sounds and footfalls bothered him. He kept his eyes shut for the longest time, and when he opened them, his wife had gotten up and stood beside her husband. Everyone else had exited the church.

A Race Thing

WHEN WALLACE SET off for the north in early 1964 to run for president, he discovered millions of people across America who believed the way the white people of Alabama believed. He toned down his racial rhetoric and spent much of his time attacking the pending civil rights bill that outlawed discrimination based on race, color, religion, sex, or national origin as "a federal power grab." The crowds applauded his statesmanlike utterances, but many of them believed he was really talking about race and stopping the advance of black people.

Unlike other presidential candidates, Wallace didn't have a team of aides churning out speeches and position papers. He had only a few speeches that he gave over and over again, tweaking the particulars depending on where he was. To his audiences, Wallace seemed refreshingly raw and authentic.

Most of those who came to his speeches roared their appreciation when he pointed out what he considered the overwhelming hypocrisy of so many northern politicians and professors. He strutted across the stage wiggling his fingers as he mocked lefties in Berkeley calling him a racist when that town had just voted down a fair-housing bill. And he derided the two-faced Washington politicians who sent their kids to private all-white schools, yet forced integration of the capital's public schools, which ended up 90 percent black.

Wallace had hooked into anger among working-class and lower-middle-class whites who thought the American Dream was no longer within reach. They felt that government was wired against them. They did not want to be forced to send their children to public schools with black students or live next to blacks, especially while well-off Americans lived in suburbs where there were almost no black residents.

But Wallace also had protesters come to his events and hold up signs and placards and boo and scream. He loved to taunt them and to hurl invective at them. His rallies always had an undertone of potential violence. He loved that and needed it. This was all a marvelous game to him, as long as it did not go too far. He did not want to be smashed on the shoals of blood and violence, and as always he knew just where to stop, holding his people back from beating up the protesters, who included reformist students, progressive union members, and liberal activists.

"There are more good people like you in this country today than there are those little pinkos running around outside," Wallace told an audience in Cincinnati. "When you and I start marching and demonstrating and carrying signs, we will close every highway in this country."

The candidate was speaking directly to those who thought themselves disenfranchised. Even in liberal Wisconsin, Wallace won a third of the Democratic vote in the presidential primary against President Lyndon Johnson. Then Wallace moved on to Indiana. During the 1920s more than 30 percent of adult white male citizens in Indiana belonged to the KKK, and a Klan member, Edward Jackson, had been governor. Wallace had every reason to think he could resurrect these dormant beliefs across Indiana.

To advance his campaign in the Hoosier state, Wallace brought in Shelton as well as speechwriter and former Klansman Asa Carter. The two men did not go to the Rotary Clubs and Kiwanis to make their Wallace pitch, but out among the Klansmen and their kind. For Shelton, these days in Indiana were deliverance. The previous year, Wallace had embraced Edward Fields and the neo-Nazi NSRP and left him standing in front of the stage looking upward.

Shelton had played a crucial role ending the fallout from the Birmingham church bombing, allowing Wallace to focus on the presidential campaign. And now the Klan leader was acting as a real political player, up front and in public, proudly advancing the Klan and its causes. "We found our people throughout the state," Shelton said. "They're good people, tired of being shoved around, wanting something different, and seeing what they needed in George Wallace."

Against President Johnson, Wallace won nearly 30 percent in Indiana and 43 percent in the Maryland presidential primary. But, not surprisingly, Johnson was the party's nominee and went on to defeat Republican Barry Goldwater in a landslide victory in the general election. Wallace had no impact on the general election except for Goldwater appropriating part of his rhetoric, but the governor returned home to Alabama a victor in the eyes of the white population.

MILLARD FULLER AND Morris Dees hosted a fancy Christmas party for their staff in December 1964 at the ballroom of the Jefferson Davis Hotel, one of the ritziest places in the city. Despite the signing of the Civil Rights Act on July 2, 1964, the hotel was still segregated, as was everyplace else in Montgomery. Nonetheless, Dees and Fuller invited *all* their employees.

The two young businessmen thought it was the right thing to do, but that it was no big deal, a private matter at a private party. They had no awareness that they were crossing a bridge that would collapse once they reached the other side. In these tense, unsettled times, everyone was watching everyone else, and there was no going back.

Dees felt that some of the white employees were unhappy about the integrated event. One of them, Alice Ortega, headed the proofreading department, overseeing a group of about a dozen employees of both races. Ortega checked off on the invitation that she and her husband did not plan to attend. A few days before the party, Dees took Ortega into his office.

"Why aren't you coming, Alice?" Dees asked.

"Morris, I'm a southern girl raised in the southern manner," Ortega said. "It's all right to work together, and even to play together as children, but as adults, you just don't mix. You don't party together."

"You're married to a man from Latin America," Dees said. "Have you ever gotten any flack about that?"

"Well, yeah. In Texas there were places we couldn't go, hotels where we couldn't go. My husband's from Guatemala. But as far as they were concerned, he was Mexican."

"And what about you, Alice?" Dees asked, knowing that Ortega had childhood polio.

"Because my one leg is shorter than the other, and I walk with a limp?"

"Yeah."

"Sure, when I was growing up, kids made fun of me, and I had all kinds of problems."

"Well, how do you think blacks feel?" Dees asked. When Ortega started to cry, he gave her his handkerchief.

Ortega and her husband ended up going to the party, and so did almost everyone else at the company. The staff at the hotel was queasy, the black waiters stunned. For the most part everything went well, though there was palpable nervousness when Dees and Fuller danced with a number of the black women.

"It was delightful, great fun," remembers Ortega. "And now, a couple of my best friends are black. And I have a mixed granddaughter. So it was Morris who really helped me grow up."

But Dees was still far away from the person he wanted to be. He could not go around talking much about his strange discontent or he would seem self-indulgent, petty, and unappreciative of his good fortune. Fuller was even more dissatisfied, moaning about the burdens of money.

The partners were running what most people would have considered an honorable business, but Fuller felt otherwise about the company and his life. "Under a thin veneer of honesty, respectability, and Christian character lay a pile of rottenness," he wrote in his autobiography.

Both men were energized and excited by the civil rights movement. To the deeply religious Fuller, it was a spiritual crusade led by men of God and full of those willing to accept martyrdom for their cause. Dees saw it differently. He had this profound, yet dormant, sense of justice. He had come to believe that segregation was morally and constitutionally wrong. He was no protester, no placard-carrying activist, and he was fitfully, painfully figuring just how he could play a role in helping to change the South.

Dees watched as George Wallace remained unyielding on racial issues. The governor's presidential run had given him a newly exalted status. He planned to run again in 1968. He might have thought on racial matters it wise to back off a little, or at least to make sure not to get caught in another situation like the Birmingham church bombing. But the governor had become so obsessed with black people that he could not pull back.

When Wallace was a judge, he had glommed onto segregation as the most viable political issue on the southern horizon. That calculated stance had become a profound belief in black subservience. He had grown up having no special hostility against black people. But he had one now.

The governor sprinkled the *n* word throughout his conversations. "It was race—race, race, race—and every time that I was closeted alone with him, that's all that we talked about," said Tony Heffernan, who in the 1960s was a UPI reporter assigned to Montgomery. "Didn't talk about women. We didn't talk about Alabama football. Somehow no matter what you were talking about, the race thing got into the conversation, and he was off and running with it."

Wallace did not grasp that racial attitudes were changing even within his own home. His daughter Peggy was precocious and held her own firm convictions. One of them was that segregation should end. But her father never once asked her what she thought.

The children were growing up in the governor's mansion attended by black convicts with long sentences who because of good conduct were allowed out of prison to serve the governor's family. These trustees were not career criminals but for the most part were men who long ago had committed crimes of passion that they were unlikely to commit again. "They were our family," says Peggy Wallace Kennedy. "We saw them more than we saw Mom and Daddy. We loved them very, very much, very much."

Wallace's son George Jr. learned to play guitar from Robert Woods, a trustee who had murdered his wife. He was a brilliant blues musician, and his training gave George Jr. the beginnings of his career as a country music singer.

But no matter how much the governor's namesake learned or his other children adored their keepers, Wallace did not change his belief in the natural inferiority of an entire race.

AS PROUD AS Robert Shelton was to be associated with presidential contender Wallace, all kinds of strange things had begun to happen to him. The Imperial Wizard received an unsigned letter saying that one of his subordinates was secretly after his job. A letter accused one of the Klansman of once having been friends with Fidel Castro. That was enough to get the entire Florida Klavern thrown out of the UKA. Some of the members opened their mailboxes to find postcards containing the words "Trying to Hide." Anonymous phone calls made all kinds of troubling accusations.

Shelton rightfully suspected that the FBI was behind these actions. In August 1964, the FBI had authorized what it called a "new counterintelligence effort [that] will take advantage of our experience with a variety of sophisticated techniques successfully applied against the Communist Party, USA, and related organizations since 1956."

The program, known as COINTELPRO, involved agitprop of the sort used against Nazi Germany and the Soviet Union. The FBI initiatives "to expose, disrupt and otherwise neutralize the activities of the various Klan and hate organizations, their leadership and adherents" often violated the civil liberties of Klansmen accused of no crimes, and were sometimes against the law.

In this regard, Shelton and Martin Luther King had one thing in common: they were both targets of undercover FBI campaigns. Hoover considered King a dangerous Communist dupe. An FBI monograph "Communism and the Negro Movement" stated, "as the Communist party goes, so goes Martin Luther King, and so also goes the Negro movement in the United States." King had associated with several activists who were alleged Communists, but the Christian leader was far from a fellow traveler.

Thanks to the FBI director's paranoia about Communist infiltration, the agency had stood back, doing little when the Klan and its kin attacked the civil rights activists. The violence had startled not only America but also most of the world, and with a liberal Democratic president in the White House,

Hoover had little choice but to take some sort of action against the Klan.

FBI agents conducted a self-styled "smear campaign" against Shelton, whom they called "probably the most well-known Klansman in America." They forged Shelton's name, placed false articles in newspapers, invented fake organizations, and conducted any number of bizarre initiatives, including having an undercover source propose to Klan members that they "wear female attire for the purpose of luring Negroes into a trap." Beyond that, Klan attorney Matthew Hobson Murphy told Shelton the FBI had a special program called "Operation Nancy" involving Alabama prostitutes recruited to pass on whatever they learned from their Klan clients.

To combat the FBI efforts, Shelton paid $1,000 per month for a special phone that made it hard to tap his conversations. Despite the work of dozens of FBI agents, the bureau could not find substantive compromising information on the Klan leader. Not only did he not drink, but he also disliked anybody who did. They learned that, rare for a southerner, he did not like grits, but that wasn't enough to destroy the man.

J. Edgar Hoover became personally involved. The FBI director proposed publishing an attack on the Imperial Wizard that supposedly would appear to be written by George Lincoln Rockwell, leader of the American Nazi Party.

Hoover wrote the Birmingham special agent in charge: "For example, if Rockwell printed a report that Shelton has some Negro ancestors, it would be necessary for us to know the names of certain ancestors who could, perhaps, have been an illegitimate child related to Shelton. As another example, if we were to show that Shelton had some abnormal sexual tendencies, it would be necessary to give specific information as to whether he was associated with any persons who would have those tendencies."

The FBI decided "to secure information that Shelton could be stealing money for the UKA and misappropriating it." Shelton lived a modest lifestyle, and they came up with nothing substantial. But no matter how thin their results, the FBI continued to throw massive resources into their quest to find something to bring him down.

Scrawny Pine

ON THE EVENING of February 18, 1965, about five hundred black protesters got together in a church in the little town of Marion, sixty-two miles northeast of Montgomery. They were seeking the right to vote and to eat in restaurants where their white neighbors ate. At the end of their meeting, they decided to march to the county courthouse to protest the arrest of one of their leaders, Southern Christian Leadership Conference (SCLC) field secretary James Orange.

Waiting for them in the darkness were troopers in twenty-one state police squad cars led by Alabama director of public safety Al Lingo; county deputy sheriffs; Marion police and civilians armed with clubs and ax handles. The police rushed forward, batons flailing, beating to the ground every one of the protesters they encountered. State Trooper James Bonard Fowler shot and killed civil rights marcher Jimmie Lee Jackson, claiming he had assaulted the officer. (It was not until 2010 that seventy-seven-year-old Fowler pled guilty to a charge of manslaughter and was sentenced to six months in prison.)

George Wallace had authorized his troopers to be there, and he was not going to criticize them for beating a few black heads and shooting one of them. The governor repeated his familiar refrain: "career and professional agitators with pro-Communist affiliations" had orchestrated the riot.

Reverend King preached at the funeral and fervently agreed with those who had been beaten and others in the movement that there should be a march from the nearby town of Selma to Montgomery. They would carry Jimmie Lee Jackson's body to the capital and leave it on the steps of the capitol. In the end, they decided to march—and to leave a petition with the governor—but not to carry the body.

ON SUNDAY, MARCH 7, 1965, about six hundred marchers set out for Montgomery. Many of them arrived after church, still wearing their Sunday clothes. Contrary to Wallace's repeated assertion that black protesters were puppets in the hands of outside agitators, the event was largely planned and peopled by Selma locals.

As they walked in two double lines toward the Edmund Pettus Bridge leading out of town, Reverend King was not among them. He said he had to preach at his church in Atlanta, but his aides may have convinced him that he would have faced serious death threats if he participated. And so it was left to another SCLC leader, Hosea Williams, to stand at the head of the march along with John Lewis, chairman of Student Nonviolent Coordinating Committee (SNCC).

As the overwhelmingly black marchers looked across the Edmund Pettus Bridge, they saw a long line of state police donning gas masks that would not only protect them from the ravages of the noxious C-4 tear gas, but also hide their features like Klan night riders. Lingo was there under Wallace's orders to direct the sixty-five state troopers. Sheriff Clark waited with at least ten of his deputies, several of whom were Klansmen. Behind the Alabama officers stood a line of fifteen men mounted on horseback.

The officers came forward through clouds of tear gas with their clubs and truncheons ready. They drove the marchers off the bridge, and a mile up the road, many of them fled into Selma's First Baptist Church. The police went into the church and beat them there too. And when the officers were spent, they left the marchers where they fell, bleeding, wounded, crying, rubbing their eyes and vomiting from the tear gas. And some were left with the marks of horse hooves embedded on their legs and shoulders.

That evening ABC broke into its Sunday-night movie, *Judgment at Nuremberg,* for a fifteen-minute bulletin showing footage from the Selma march. If viewers listened closely, they could hear Sheriff Clark saying, "Get those goddamned niggers! And get those goddamned *white* niggers!" Millions watched that evening, including President Lyndon Johnson.

Three days after the march, three local white men clubbed to death James J. Reeb, a white Boston Unitarian minister, in the Selma streets. The murder of Reverend Reeb—a crime for which the men were later found not guilty—only exacerbated the anger over all that had occurred. To protest the killings, a thousand multirace demonstrators protested in Montgomery, an unheard-of scene in the Alabama capital. And downtown in the federal courthouse, Judge Johnson heard petitioners asking for the right to march from Selma to Montgomery.

Wallace decided to fly to Washington to meet with President Johnson to tell his story. The president would not accept the governor's contention that he did not have the power to register black voters.

"George, don't bullshit me," Johnson said. "Who runs Alabama? Don't shit me about your persuasive powers. I had on the TV this morning, and I saw you and you were talking and you was attacking me, George."

"Not you, Mr. President," Wallace replied. "I was speaking against federal intervention."

"You was attacking me, George. George, you and I should not be thinking about [election year] 1968. We should be thinking about 1988. We'll both be dead and gone then. What do you want left behind? You want a great, big marble monument that says 'George Wallace: He Built.' Or do you want a little piece of scrawny pine laying there that says, 'George Wallace: He Hated.'"

. . .

MORRIS DEES WAS appalled by the Selma violence, but when Judge Johnson authorized the Selma-to-Montgomery march to go ahead, he never considered joining the marchers. Hundreds of people—everyone from celebrities to schoolteachers—were flying in from all across America, but Dees still didn't feel he was part of this movement.

Despite feeling so disconnected, on Sunday, March 21, 1965, Dees drove out to Selma with Fuller, who was ferrying several northern Church of Christ ministers to take part in the march. Before a joint session of the Alabama legislature, Wallace called the demonstrators "mobs, employing the street-warfare tactics of the Communists" and said he wasn't about to protect them. That's why Johnson ended up federalizing the Alabama National Guard.

With all these outsiders and the full range of journalists protected by guardsmen and the U.S. Army, it seemed unlikely there would be a repeat of the violence that had occurred just two weeks before. But there was just no telling. As they drove toward Selma, state troopers stood on the sides of the roads taking down the license plate numbers of all the vehicles that passed by.

Dees and Fuller led the ministers up to the start of the march. The 3,200 marchers stood in a column that stretched along the main street of Selma for about a mile. The celebrities, national politicians, and outsiders threatened to overwhelm the marchers from Selma. But they all seemed to meld together as they stood waiting for Reverend and Mrs. King to lead the way.

Before the marchers took their first steps across the Edmund Pettus Bridge, they knelt in unity for a silent prayer. Fuller had turned to God, and he was ever ready to pray. Dees had left the Pike Road Baptist Church of his childhood and had started attending services at Montgomery's tiny Unitarian Church. It was more like a discussion group than a church service, and he did not feel that rich old Baptist faith any longer. Dees was reluctant to kneel. But he was not going to stand there by himself, and so he got down on his knees and pretended to pray.

Dees and Fuller drove back to Montgomery together. Soon after Dees got back to town, his mother called him. A deputy sheriff had come to the house to tell her, "Morris is going to lose his reputation fooling around with niggers and Communists."

Dees hadn't thought he was part of the civil rights movement, but as far as many of the white people of Alabama were concerned, he had already made his choice. When it came to race, move one step beyond the narrow parameters of acceptable behavior, and everything you did was duly noted.

Sitting in Montgomery, Dees followed the progress of the four-day march through the Alabama countryside. The lawyer feared the protesters would meet with violence as they moved through "bloody Lowndes," a county notoriously hostile to African Americans. But with the 2,000 U.S. Army soldiers and 1,900 members of the federalized Alabama National Guard, the activists walked an average of ten miles a day along the old Jefferson Davis Highway within a cocoon of safety.

A FEW DAYS before the second march, Shelton had attended the weekly meeting of Eastview 13, the most violent Klavern in America and one of the Imperial Wizard's favorite places. After the formal meeting, Shelton got together with a few UKA members to discuss future strategy. He held court in a stage area separate from the meeting room. The next most important person at the meeting was Robert Creel, who was both the Exalted Cyclops of the Bessemer Klavern and the Grand Dragon, the top UKA officer in the state. Also present was Gary Rowe, who Shelton treated as his assistant in many serious matters.

Shelton was itching to attack the activists. Earlier in the year, the FBI reported that he had "requested that a severe beating be administrated to two racial agitators in Birmingham." The marchers in Selma deserved more of the same.

"Damn it, we have to go down there [to Selma] and get that shit taken care of," Shelton said, not specifying the actions he was proposing. "It's getting out of hand down there. If necessary, you know just what you have got to do. There will never be another time in the country that we will be so pressed as the whites is right now."

Two days before the march, Shelton met with Wallace and Alabama public safety director Lingo. The Imperial Wizard generally did whatever the governor wanted him to do. He agreed to keep his Klansmen away from Selma, so the marchers could cross the Edmund Pettus Bridge into the countryside without challenge.

Given how important Shelton considered his relationship with Wallace, it is unlikely that Shelton would have ordered any further Klan actions without the governor's approval or acquiescence. On the first day of the march, Shelton drove to Montgomery for a rally. He had the 250 or so present form a motorcade to harass the marchers on the highway. They had not reckoned, however, on the strong presence of the National Guard and federal authorities. A white minister in one of the advance cars was beaten when he got out of his car on the roadside, but other than that, no one could get close enough to threaten the marchers.

On their way home, one car of Klansmen stopped in Selma to leave some crates containing land mines and hand grenades with a local Klan militant. A number of them returned in the next two days to figure out just where the marchers would be sleeping out at night and how they could use those mines and grenades to best advantage, but the marchers were well protected, and it was just too dangerous to try to attack them.

When the marchers arrived in Montgomery after four days on the road, around twenty thousand supporters joined them the next morning in the parade to the capitol. Wallace had warned Montgomery citizens to stay away. The governor gave female state employees the day off because of what he called "danger."

He thought of taking down the Confederate and Alabama flags over the capitol, and replacing them with a black flag of mourning. But he ultimately decided not to do that.

Troopers holding rifles lined the roofs of the office buildings, and the sky was full of helicopters and spotting planes. Behind the podium stood a hundred blue-helmeted troopers to protect the capitol from defilement. To further that effort, the United Daughters of the Confederacy had covered over the bronze star marking the spot where Jefferson Davis was sworn in as president of the Confederacy.

Dees and Fuller stood on Dexter Avenue just beyond Reverend King's old church as the marchers moved up the wide boulevard to the capitol. The two friends were there as King walked past. Then Dees saw a one-legged black man limping along on a crude wooden crutch. Attached to the crutch was an American flag that fluttered in the wind.

"Tears of patriotic pride filled my eyes," Dees says. "I cannot say at that moment I made any major commitment to justice, a path I was already treading, but I felt this flag bearer was a symbol of all that our democracy represented for the oppressed and the powerless."

Wallace could not see the marchers from his office windows because they had plates on them to protect him from assassins. And so, as this multiracial stream walked up Dexter Avenue, the governor walked into the office of his executive secretary, Cecil Jackson, opened the venetian blinds, and looked out.

"That's quite a crowd," Wallace said

"In a few years, that may be the way the inauguration crowd looks," an aide said.

"Don't say that," Wallace said.

Wallace had been told that the marchers had behaved in such a perverse, wanton manner that it marked the beginning of serial miscegenation in the southern heartland. These black radicals had bonked white women in the muddy woods, leaving their condoms and other filth behind. It didn't matter that the story was not true, for it was true to his fears.

Dees and Fuller were among the few local whites who showed up that day. Dees had a way of getting wherever he wanted to go, and he and Fuller worked their way toward the front of the crowd.

Standing there, Dees noticed his uncle, James Dees, about a dozen feet away standing under a tree. To his uncle and others in his family, Dees was as much a participant as if he were up on that podium speaking this afternoon.

James Dees walked over to Dees and Fuller. "I know all about you," he said angrily. "You're nothing but a bunch of nigger lovers." Then he pulled open his coat to display a .38 stuck into his belt. "I oughta take this gun and kill you both here on the spot."

"Millard, get away from him," Dees said urgently, trying to pull his friend away. Fuller stood his ground, and Dees walked off and stood fifty yards away, waiting for his business partner to join him.

Dees had known Uncle James all his life. He considered him something of a coward. He felt his uncle had probably come here to try to provoke some of the marchers. Indeed the men around Reverend King feared men like James Dees and what they might do. Several death threats had been made that day, and half a dozen black ministers had dressed in the same kind of blue suit that Reverend King wore. They thought that a would-be assassin might mistake them for their intended victim and shoot the wrong target.

WHEN REVEREND KING got up to speak late that Thursday afternoon, he looked down past the great crowd and saw the Dexter Avenue Baptist Church where he had preached in the mid-1950s and where this movement had begun during the bus boycott.

By that time, Wallace had gone back to his office to watch the speech broadcast live on television. Wallace was always interested in what people were saying about him, and Reverend King did not mention him even once, as if he and his agenda were of no account. But when the minister talked about the populism of old, he was in some measure evoking the young Wallace, who was gone forever.

"Toward the end of the Reconstruction era, something very significant happened," Reverend King said. "That is what was known as the Populist Movement. The leaders of this movement began awakening the poor white masses and the former Negro slaves to the fact that they were being fleeced by the emerging Bourbon interests. Through their control of mass media, they [the white elite] revised the doctrine of white supremacy. That crippled and eventually destroyed the Populist Movement of the nineteenth century."

That had happened again in mid-twentieth-century America when Wallace took Big Jim Folsom's all-embracing populism and transformed it into racist pseudopopulism. Despite Wallace's claim that he was the people's governor, the Alabama he governed was becoming one of the most regressive states in the union. The big mules from which Wallace had refused to take money in his first campaign dominated the state, and as long as the governor played his race card bold and true, most poor white Alabamans seemed not to care.

A Follower of Christ

EVERY TOWN IN Alabama had at least one bar where the Klan hung out. In Selma, it was the Silver Moon Café. That's where, on the evening of the vast assembly in Montgomery, four members of the UKA Bessemer Klavern—Gene Thomas, E. O. Eaton, Gary Rowe, and Collie Leroy Wilkins—sat having dinner. After eating, they set out in their car to the black part of Selma.

In setting out to make an example of a black person, they thought they were doing what Robert Shelton wanted them to do. When they reached the A.M.E. church, where some out-of-town entertainers were putting on a show, they saw a black man holding hands with two young white women. The four Klansmen had blackjacks, a small, easily concealed weapon that can deliver devastating blows, and leaded baseball bats. Just as they were about to show the trio a measure of Klan justice, they saw some army trucks and decided they better scram.

The Klansmen drove back into town and were waiting for the light to change at the Edmund Pettus Bridge when they saw in the next lane a car driven by a blond white woman. Sitting next to her was a young black man. They set out after them. The faster they sped up, the faster the woman drove, but finally they managed to pull up beside the car and pointed their guns out the lowered windows. The woman turned for an instant and looked at the Klansmen. They fired their guns, and as she slumped over the wheel, the vehicle drove on for at least two hundred yards before plowing into some bushes by the side of the road and coming to a stop.

Viola Gregg Liuzzo, the woman who was murdered that evening, was a thirty-nine-year-old community activist from Detroit who was married to a Teamster business agent and had five children from two of her three marriages. When she heard Reverend King's appeal for people from all across America to come to Selma for the march, she had driven down from Michigan in her 1963 Oldsmobile. She walked the long march to Montgomery in her bare feet. And when the police pulled her body from her car, she was still in bare feet.

Liuzzo's passenger was nineteen-year-old Leroy Moton, an SCLC activist from Selma. After King's speech, they had been ferrying people to the airport and to various towns. After taking several marchers to Selma, they were heading back to Montgomery when Liuzzo was killed.

Klan crimes were rarely punished. It usually took months even to indict a suspect. But the very next day FBI agents arrested the four Klansmen. That happened because Rowe was an FBI informant. He claimed that he had not fired his weapon at Liuzzo. In return for his testimony and cooperation, he was not indicted for the crime and was instead hidden away in the Federal Witness Protection Program.

Rowe had been on the FBI payroll since 1960. For half a decade, the informant had been out in front on the UKA's most violent activities. All those years he had been alerting the FBI to Klan actions, yet the federal agency had done nothing to stop them. Many people had been hurt, and Liuzzo had been killed on a country road.

FBI director J. Edgar Hoover decided that the best way to divert criticism of his agency was to attack the victim. So the agency leaked an internal memo stating that Liuzzo "had puncture marks in her arms indicating recent use of a hypodermic needle." Hoover met with President Johnson and told him that Liuzzo's husband had "a shady background" and that the woman was sitting so "very close to the Negro" that it had "all the appearances of a necking party."

To Wallace, Liuzzo symbolized all of the busybodies who had come down to Alabama to try to change white folks' ways. The state officials gave their investigative files to Shelton, and he went to work.

The Imperial Wizard called a press conference in Birmingham where he claimed that the killings were part of a "trumped-up Communist plot to destroy the right wing in America." He alleged that Liuzzo was being investigated as a possible Communist and from what he had heard "hasn't been home most of the last several months, but has been around the country on these demonstrations." As for the murdered Reverend Reeb, he "had been dying of cancer before he ever came to Alabama."

On other occasions, Shelton said Liuzzo had a "liberated relationship" with her husband. Wallace's people spread the story that Liuzzo had driven down to Alabama to have sex with black men, and that young Moton had shagged her good.

Moton was an introverted young man. He was adamant that nothing like that had taken place with this overweight mother twice his age. It was irrelevant to the murder whether they had sex or not, but many white Alabamans were convinced that the couple had lusted after one another, and to them that justified what had happened to Liuzzo. They believed that if a white woman was having sex with a black man and she was shot to death, that was pretty much what she deserved—and this story might well stop others from violating the moral standards of the South.

Major W. R. Jones, the head of the Alabama Department of Public Safety's antisubversive unit, which investigated civil rights activists and anyone favoring integration, became involved in the inquiry into the murder. Like Shelton, Wallace, and so many other segregationists, Jones was obsessed with black sexuality. They believed that black males were instinctually predatory and ready to pounce on the purest of southern maidens.

That fear had its beginnings during the long slavery era when a growing mixed-blood population resulted from slave masters' relations with the women that they owned. In the post–Civil War era, a myth emerged that black men were to blame for the mixed population—they were raping white women. What the segregationists feared beyond all else was the notion of white women willingly desiring and sleeping with black men.

That almost hysterical fear of black sexuality had a long history. In 1892, in Tennessee, eight black men were lynched within a short period, five of them because they were accused of raping white women.

At the time, an anonymous editorial in a black newspaper, the *Memphis Free Speech*, said: "Nobody in this section of the country believes the old threadbare lie that Negro men rape white women. If southern white men are not careful, they will overreach themselves, and a conclusion will be reached which will be very damaging to the moral reputation of their women."

Most had assumed that the writer of the editorial was a black man who had the audacity to suggest that white women might want to sleep with black men. A white paper, the *Memphis Evening Scimitar,* editorialized that if the Negroes did not take care of the writer, "it will be the duty of those whom he has attacked to tie the wretch to a stake, brand him in the forehead with a hot iron, and perform upon him a surgical operation with a pair of tailor's shears."

When it was learned that a black woman, Ida B. Wells, who became one of the most celebrated and bravest journalists of her time, had written the offensive editorial, castration was no longer an option. "Whore" was one of the kinder names that Wells's critics had for her. A mob burned down the offices of the *Memphis Free Speech*, and Wells left Memphis for good.

Wells continued to speak out in the most daring and provocative ways. She told audiences how despite all the laws and immense social pressure, white southern men had "so bleached the Afro-Americans that a race of mulattos, quadroons, and octoroons had grown up." This provided white racists with more reason to lynch black men who were alleged to have gone with white women—or even looked at them.

This fear of black male sexuality stood at the center of Shelton's belief system. In 1965 he told the readers in his *Playboy* interview that wherever the civil rights movement was strong in the North, black men came out to rape white women. "Why else do you see so many attacks being made in New York and Chicago, where the nigra thinks he is strong with the civil rights movement?" Shelton asked. "Why do we see all of these assaults and rapes being committed against white women?"

W. R. JONES, the head of the Alabama Department of Public Safety's antisubversive unit, ordered Dr. Paul E. Shoffeitt, the toxicologist and assistant director of the Alabama Department of Toxicology and Criminal Investigation, to perform an autopsy of Viola Liuzzo. Although the victim had been shot in the head, the autopsy included an examination of Liuzzo's vagina. After probing the most private parts of the victim's body, Shoffeitt took a vaginal smear.

The results showed that Liuzzo had not had sexual intercourse in the hours before her murder. The state chose not to release the information to the press, allowing the scandalous whispering to continue. They did leak it to Shelton and others that Liuzzo was not wearing panties, and that information was broadcast across the state and beyond.

IN MAY 1965, two months after the murder of Viola Liuzzo, the first of the defendants, twenty-one-year-old Collie Leroy Wilkins, went on trial for the murder of Liuzzo before an all-white jury in Lowndes County, one of the most racially reactionary counties in the state. Shelton had helped to raise $200,000 to defend the three Klansmen accused of the killing, and was in the Lowndes County Courthouse for the trial.

Shelton brought in the UKA lawyer, Matthew Hobson Murphy, to defend Wilkins. The 235-pound, fifty-one-year-old attorney had two fingers missing on his right hand. In his summation to the jury, Murphy focused not on defending his client, but on attacking Liuzzo, her driving companion Moton, and the civil rights movement.

"You remember what that nigger Moton said on the stand," Murphy said. "You notice his eyes? Oh, I did. Eyes dilated. You see them? You see them staring? Pupils dilated. You see him talking under the hypnotic spell of narcotics? You know that [Liuzzo] was in the car with three black niggers? One white woman and three black niggers. Black nigger Communists who want to take us over.

"I am proud to be white, and I stand here as a white man,

and I say we are never going to mongrelize the race with nigger blood, and the Martin Luther Kings, the white niggers, the Jews, the Zionists who run that bunch of niggers, the white people are not going to run before them. I urge you as patriotic Americans not to find this young man guilty."

The jury quickly decided to take first-degree murder off the table. They ended up deadlocked voting ten to two to convict Wilkins of manslaughter, a crime that carried a ten-year sentence. Wilkins was tried again and found not guilty. His alleged coconspirators got off scot-free as well.

As in the deaths of the four black girls in Birmingham, Wallace had a moral complicity in the murder of Viola Liuzzo. It is unlikely he directed Shelton to have someone killed in Selma, yet his uncompromising rhetoric created the climate and his political ambition the situation that allowed the murder to take place. The governor likely knew of Shelton's plans to take Klan action during the march and, at minimum, had not opposed them.

After leaving the White House, President Johnson said: "I don't believe you would have had any Wilkinses, Thomases, or Eatons [the murderers of Viola Liuzzo] if you didn't have leadership that gave them that idea that they could do what they did with immunity."

Shelton may not have specifically ordered his Klansmen to kill someone, but he had told them to go to Selma and take strong action. Gary Rowe said that on the day of the murders, Shelton's own deputy had ordered them to deal with the marchers. Shelton had prodded them to do what they had done, and he knew they had murdered Liuzzo.

That December after the murder, Shelton flew up to Boston, where he gave a lengthy interview to WNAC radio. The Imperial Wizard wanted the northern audience to know that he and his fellow Klansmen were nothing like the image some people had of them. They did not wear hoods or masks. They were not violent. They were god-fearing, Communist-hating American patriots.

"Our polar star is Christ," Shelton said. "The Lord Jesus told his followers, 'Suffer little children to come unto me,' and on the occasion of the Last Supper, he added His commandment to the Commandments saying, 'This is my Commandment, that ye Love one another, as I have loved you.'

"I am a follower of Christ. The structure of the United Klans of America is patterned very much after the structure built by Christ to carry His message to the world. The Son of God had twelve disciples. The UKA has twelve imperial officers."

A Pain in the Stomach

MORRIS DEES FELT that he and Millard Fuller had not done much to advance the cause of civil rights. Yet in holding an integrated Christmas party and driving a group of ministers to the Selma march, they had done enough to be considered traitors and enemies. The rumor in town was that at night they secretly printed Communist propaganda for Martin Luther King Jr. Many people believed the story, but the two partners were far too busy publishing popular cookbooks to print missives for the SCLC or any other activist organization.

Unlike his more congenial partner, Dees had an in-your-face belligerence toward anyone he considered an enemy. After his confrontation with his uncle James at Reverend King's speech, Dees challenged him to a shootout at Barney Pinkston's Store in the countryside. Almost anyone else would have dismissed the idea of two grown men taking out their pistols and shooting at each other until one of them lay bleeding in the gravel. But Dees's wife, Beverly, knew her husband was perfectly capable of carrying through on his pledge. So she called Fuller and got him to get his partner to back down.

One evening in 1965, Dees got a call informing him that there was a cross burning in front of his company offices. He knew that meant the Klan, and he and Fuller hurried to get there in time to see the flames. They stood wondering what they had done to merit this. As they were contemplating what to do, Beverly Dees arrived home to find someone running through the house. They never figured out who it was, but the events together made Beverly nervous.

For all the difficulties Beverly was going through, she saw that Morris was having tough days too, and it wasn't the time to bring her problems to her husband. For a decade, he had been closer to Fuller than to anyone else, spending hours with him each day. But Fuller had gone through a profound religious conversion and decided to spend his life devoted to Christ by doing good works. Later that year, Fuller sold his partner his half of the business and gave up most of the money to charity.

Dees had never had such a close friend in his life. And now Fuller was condemning himself and his former partner for the way they had lived and made their money. Without Fuller, Dees continued to build his empire, but he was going through a transformation. Even as he made even more money, he began to feel that making money wasn't enough. He felt increasingly compelled to help those he considered exploited.

As Dees saw it, local merchants were taking advantage of black customers from the countryside, just as they had when he was a boy in the 1940s. Only now it wasn't clothes the customers wanted but television sets so they could watch *Bonanza* and *The Ed Sullivan Show* from their living rooms. The storekeepers set them up on credit with interest rates that guaranteed they would likely never be able to pay off their debts. Their lives were just like those of sharecroppers in the old days. No matter how much cotton they picked, they always ended up at the end of the year owing the man money.

Dees thought the interest rates and other charges disgraceful, especially because well-regarded Montgomery businessmen imposed them. He began to take on many cases in which he charged that these businesses were setting unfair and usurious interest rates. He did this for free, and he generally won, but it upset the business community that a man who was supposedly one of them was sticking his nose in places where it might get bitten off.

Dees didn't like these businessmen with their highfalutin ways, fancying themselves better than most of the people who came into their stores, bought their merchandise, and made them well-off. Dees had a poor boy's disdain for people of privilege. Out in the countryside, as a youth he had driven past the antebellum mansions of the wealthy old families, but he had never been invited inside to sup on linen tablecloths and fine china.

When he entered Lanier High School in Montgomery, the students from upscale Cloverdale, in their starched khaki pants, burnished penny loafers, and country club ways, thought it was *their* school. They could not stand hayseed farm boys like Morris in their jeans and white T-shirts. When one rich Cloverdale youth made a crack about Morris's girlfriend, their battle in the parking lot was so one-sided that Dees's opponent spent a week recovering in the hospital.

In September 1954, when Dees was a senior in high school, he met Beverly Crum, a statuesque tenth grader with a quietly beguiling manner, and gave her his black and pink business card: MORRIS DEES DATING SERVICE: MY BEST ADVERTISEMENT IS A SATISFIED CUSTOMER. Beverly had never seen anybody so brash, and she threw the card right back in his smart-alecky face.

Beverly had already heard all about Morris from her girlfriends. They had warned her to stay away from the senior. He was just overwhelming, and she was not the only girl who had been given his business card. He had dated Governor Folsom's daughter, Rachel, and one of Beverly's classmates, Cornelia Ellis, who years later would become George Wallace's second wife.

Dees irritated some people by his mere presence, or more accurately his lack of presence. He hardly ever seemed to be in class. He had a photographic memory, and he never appeared to do any studying, although he received pretty much straight A's. When he wasn't off as a page in the legislature, he often finagled excuses to be away doing something else. He showed up at school dances driving the odorous truck that he used to haul garbage.

When Dees was old enough to get a horse, he rode it to the juke joint down by the river. He was the one white boy watching the dancers shimmying in moves he never knew existed to music he had never heard before. In high school, he danced the moves he learned at the juke joint—and he was condemned for doing so. In a few years everyone in America would be dancing like that, but not in white Montgomery, and not in the fall of 1954.

Dees was the king of persistence, and he and Beverly eventually began dating. Early the following year Beverly told Dees that her father, a United States Air Force colonel stationed at the Air War College in Montgomery, was being transferred to Germany, and she would be leaving. That's when eighteen-year-old Morris asked sixteen-year-old Beverly to marry him, and she said yes. Without telling anyone, they drove to Meridian, Mississippi, where they married in a Baptist church and spent the night in the best hotel in town.

By the mid-1960s, Dees was no longer known by the local gentry as the son of a tenant farmer, but he still had that visceral disdain for Montgomery's elite, these proud, haughty men and women who benefited for generations from the servitude and virtual peonage of black people and had little understanding why they lived lives of privilege. That reality was a pain in his stomach, and no matter how much money he made, how big a success he became, that pain stayed there. When he fought some of the great civil rights legal battles of his time, he seemed to be fighting over political principles, but it was also a personal battle

against those who once thought they were better than Morris
Seligman Dees Jr.

A Political Prisoner

AS ROBERT SHELTON sat at the witness table at the House Un-
American Activities Committee (HUAC) hearings in October
1965, he looked not so much thin as emaciated, an impression
emphasized by his lean, diminutive wife at his side. He had been
a big fan of HUAC, and he found it hard to believe that he was
sitting there.

He had enthusiastically supported HUAC in the 1950s when
the congressmen attacked Communists and those accused of
being close to them in belief, seeing to it that they were sent
to prison or headed off into exile when they refused to testify.
In the process, many thought that the committee had trampled
upon citizens' civil rights, but Shelton believed HUAC was full
of bold patriots protecting American liberties.

Shelton was therefore startled to learn that the congressional
committee had decided to investigate the Klan. But he should
not have been surprised because after the death of Viola Liuzzo,
President Johnson had called the Klan "a society of hooded bigots," and asked for congressional investigations into the organization, warning Klan members to leave "before it is too late."

When first approached by HUAC investigators, Shelton told
them he would bring down committee chairman Edwin E. Wil-
lis in the next congressional election in Louisiana. He threatened
to take the robe that Supreme Court Justice Hugo Black had
worn as an Alabama Klan member in the 1920s and present it

personally to the Smithsonian Institution. What's more, Shelton said, he would not take the Fifth Amendment like the commies and their defenders were forever doing.

As Shelton prepared to testify, George Wallace had reasons to be worried. He was planning to run for president again in 1968, and his relationship with the Klan leader could prove deeply troubling. People outside the South may have thought of the Klan as low-life kooks running around in sheets, but the governor knew Shelton's UKA was a crucial arm of his movement and a fearless enforcer of segregation. If Shelton ever truly began to talk, spinning tales about what Wallace told him before the tragic bombing of the 16th Street Baptist Church or the start of the Selma march, Wallace's future as a national political figure might be fatally compromised.

It was an immense relief to all kinds of people that at the last moment, with a lawyer at his side, Shelton decided he would assert his constitutional rights and not say anything. In his afternoon session before HUAC, Shelton invoked the Fifth Amendment more than a hundred times.

Wallace had another reason to feel relieved. The committee had an unprecedented opportunity to educate the American public about the true role of the Klan in American life. They could have questioned Shelton in detail about the violence the UKA provoked. The Imperial Wizard was an important political figure in the South, and they could have asked about his friendships with Governor Wallace, former governor John Patterson, other elected officials across the region and the role the UKA played in their elections. The Klan leader probably would have invoked the Fifth Amendment, but the questions would have been answers themselves.

HUAC did none of this. Instead, the questions focused on the Imperial Wizard's personal finances, trying to expose him and his colleagues "as small-time con men." The FBI had already attempted the same thing and came up with nothing substantive, yet the committee portrayed Shelton as an embezzler of UKA monies. The accusations were so petty that when the Intelligence Division of the IRS investigated him, the agent recommended that the case be closed due to "a lack of criminal prosecution potential."

The southern Democratic politicians who dominated Congress were not about to create problems for a Democratic governor wildly popular throughout the South. Wallace would be running for president again, probably in 1968, and no one wanted a prominent place on his enemies list.

"We were out to destroy the Klan, not to investigate southern politicians," said HUAC investigator Philip R. Manuel years later, defending what he calls the committee's "exemplary work."

After the hearings, Shelton was convicted of contempt of Congress for having refused to give the committee the UKA membership list and financial records. Just as the American Civil Liberties Union (ACLU) had fought for the legal rights of left-wingers convicted for not talking before the committee, the ACLU came forward to defend the Klan leader, saying the conviction was "a patent violation of the First Amendment right of free speech and association." Despite the ACLU's defense, the court sentenced him to a year in prison.

As Shelton appealed the verdict, he worked as determinedly as ever to advance the UKA. With the Birmingham bombings, the murders in Selma, the constant negative publicity about the South, and the overwhelming fatigue associated with the struggle against integration, many people wanted to move on. But those who believed in a pure white world were more fervent than ever, and the UKA's revenues increased dramatically. In 1966 the Klan organization received $75,168.12 in gross revenues, more than twenty times what the UKA had taken in four years previously.

There were many other hard-core segregationists in power across the South who still considered Shelton a valuable ally. In November 1966, two FBI informants said that Shelton "had been a guest of Democrat Senator [James O.] Eastland at the Senator's [Mississippi] farm. . . . Eastland had given him some very useful ideas in connections with the operation of the Klan organization." The FBI learned that in August 1968 Shelton met with Alabama senatorial candidate James Allen. The segregationist Democrat won the November election with Klan support. "In return for Shelton's efforts, Allen, if elected, was to employ the Grand Dragon of the UKA in Alabama," the FBI reported.

Despite such meetings, the Klan leader and the UKA had become outcasts to those in the southern political establishment who were making their reluctant accommodation with some measure of integration. That meant that joining the Klan signaled even more of a commitment. Yet among those who felt politically disenfranchised and threatened by integration, the UKA still recruited a remarkable number of new members. At a rally outside Durham, North Carolina, in October 1966, Shelton initiated 644 new members into the UKA, including about 200 women.

Shelton was out there greeting and inspiring his legions, traveling by his own estimate 120,000 miles by automobile on Klan business during 1966 alone. And everywhere he went he talked about his friend Governor George Wallace.

Never

TO RUN FOR president in 1968, Wallace believed he needed the perks of office and all the power and resources that came with the governorship. But Alabama's constitution gave its governors only one four-year term before having to retire for at least a term. So Wallace tried to push through a constitutional amendment that would allow a governor to serve more than one consecutive term. In some ways the proposal made sense, but some in the legislature saw in Wallace the makings of an American Caesar, a power-hungry leader who would do anything to stay in office.

In the end, a few crucial legislators voted against the amendment, destroying their careers in the process. That would have ended the matter for most politicians. All it meant to George Wallace was that he would have to get someone else to run in 1966 who would let him be the *real* governor.

Wallace figured he could not trust even his most loyal supporters in the legislature or even his own younger brother, Jack. The one person he could allow to hold the office was his wife, Lurleen, who had only a high school education and no interest in politics.

In 1961, when Wallace was planning to run for governor, Lurleen had been diagnosed with cancer. Her physician told her husband of the diagnosis but not his patient. George withheld almost everything from his wife, including the fundamental facts of her health. So four years later when Lurleen's doctor told her she had uterine cancer, she did not realize it was a recurrence. She had a hysterectomy that sought to remove all the malignancy, but Lurleen was in a weakened, vulnerable state. She was, however, a self-effacing, self-sacrificing woman who lived for her children and her husband. If George wanted her to run, she would run.

Given his wife's condition, Wallace might have sought another paper candidate, but he was perfectly willing to risk his wife's health and perhaps her life so that he might have control over the governorship for another four years.

The campaign was a down-home coronation in which Alabamans hardly pretended that Lurleen was the actual candidate. It was a gigantic public conspiracy in which the voters willfully and happily abrogated the laws of their state so that they believed Wallace could serve a second consecutive term. On the bunted platforms, the supposed candidate said her few scripted words before George came roaring out to take over for the evening. Often at the various venues, Shelton and his Klansmen handed out the *Fiery Cross* and NEVER buttons.

Lurleen did her part valiantly, but it rankled her that wherever they spoke in public, George's young mistress, a state employee, sat in the front seats smiling up at her husband. "If she's there tonight," she finally told one of his aides, "I'm walking off the stage. You understand me. I'm walking off the stage." From then on the woman no longer attended campaign events.

Lurleen won the election in a landslide, and after her inauguration Wallace and his aides stage-managed most of what his wife did. He had people telling him what Lurleen was doing. One state trooper refused to report on her activities. So the former governor had Director of Public Safety Lingo remove the trooper from the detail and put another officer in his place.

This trooper was the only person Lurleen felt she truly could trust, and now he was gone. Then she thought of Morris Dees. She had known him for years, and she figured maybe he could help her situation.

"Morris, they're just controlling me," Lurleen told Dees in a telephone conversation. "I've got a right to have the people around me that I want. I need this trooper. I trust him. And they got rid of him, just like that, said it was none of my business. And I'm the governor. Right?"

"That's right, Lurleen," Dees said. "They got no right to do that, I'm telling you."

"Well, what can I do?" the governor asked.

"Don't do nothing. Just give me some time."

It took only a couple of calls threatening a lawsuit and publicity for Wallace's people to back off, and the governor to have the trooper back at her side.

. . .

ALMOST EVERY SUNDAY Dees attended Montgomery's tiny
Unitarian fellowship. He was instrumental in getting the services moved from a hotel room to a rented auditorium at the
downtown YMCA. Many Y members came to the segregated
institution to work out on Sunday mornings. When they asked
what black families were doing there, they were told it was for
the Unitarian Church, and when they asked who was responsible, they were told it was Morris Dees.

Bill Chandler, the Y director, called Dees into his office and
told him, "Morris, we're Christians at the Y, and you Unitarians
aren't Christians and you're gonna have to leave."

"Well, Bill, you're a good Christian," Dees said. "But you
know last time I looked the chairman of the Y was Jewish and
lots of members are Jewish and a bunch of our church members
are Jewish too. What are you going to do with them?"

"Well, you're building your own church," the Y director
said, "and you can stay until your building is finished."

That summer of 1966, Fuller & Dees held a company picnic
at the YMCA camp on Lake Jordan outside the city. Dees had
gone there as a boy for summer camp. He had marvelous memories of that long-ago time. There was a large recreation building,
a mess hall, a gym, and cabins scattered throughout the woods.
Since his childhood days, many summer homes had been built
on the lake, and the seasonal people often passed by the Y dock
and swimming area in their motorboats.

It was a hot day, and Fuller & Dees employees of both races
went into the water. The Y had black employees back in the
kitchen, and there was no objection to the occasional black guest
up front, but not swimming in the water.

The staff could hardly order the black swimmers out of
the water, creating a controversy that Dees would probably
exploit. So the camp manager hurriedly hand-lettered a large
sign saying PRIVATE PARTY and nailed it on a post on the dock
to be read by those passing by in their boats. Afterward, the

Y official told Dees that he and his employees would not be welcome back.

Dees may have been one of the most successful men in Montgomery, but his actions at the Y camp were just another reason why the country club set turned their backs on him. As far as they were concerned, no matter how high he rose, how much money he made, he would always be the son of a tenant farmer, who was now a cantankerous troublemaker unworthy of joining their clubs or sitting at their tables.

Censored

IN AUGUST 1966 Dees arrived at his office to discover that someone had flooded the computer room and slashed four-foot high *KKK* letters into the Sheetrock wall. The office computers sat on raised blocks, saving the company from total disaster.

As Dees stood surveying the damage, he thought immediately of Shelton. The lawyer-businessman was convinced that if the Imperial Wizard had not personally ordered his Klansmen to go in there and trash the office, he knew who did, and it surely was members of the UKA. He had brushed off the occasional hate letter and other indications that he had a network of enemies out there. But this provocation was too much, and he felt personally violated. He was not about to leave it to the police, who might send over an officer who was a Klansman or at least a Klan sympathizer.

It had been five years since Dees had defended Claude Henley in his attack on the Freedom Riders in Montgomery. Since then, Dees had learned that the car salesman was not only a

UKA member, but also Shelton's closest associate in Montgomery. That led Dees to call Henley and ask him to visit him.

As Henley walked into the large office and saw his former lawyer standing with an intimidating look on his face, Henley knew he had not been invited here because Dees wanted to discuss buying a car. When the lawyer-businessman explained what had happened to his company, Henley said he knew nothing about it or who had done it.

"Dial Bobby's number," Dees said abruptly and put the call on a speakerphone. Then he reached behind the curtain, pulled out his Browning semiautomatic shotgun, and pointed it at Henley's forehead.

"Tell Bobby what I'm doing," Dees said.

Henley's teeth were chattering so much that his omnipresent cigar almost fell out of his mouth.

"He's pointing a shotgun at me," Henley said.

Dees racked a shell into the chamber. The clanging sound was so loud and distinctive that Shelton surely realized what Dees was doing.

"Now *tell him* what I'm doing,"

"He put a shell in," Henley said, finding it hard to speak.

"Bobby, I'm going to blow this son-of-a-bitch's head right off of his goddamned neck. You don't fuck with me now."

"Claude, see if you can find out about this," Shelton said. "And you tell 'em leave Morris alone. Just leave the man alone."

DEES DECIDED THE best way to end the rumors that Fuller & Dees was printing flyers for Martin Luther King Jr. and carrying on all kinds of secret, evil enterprises was to invite people to come and visit. That October Dees held a three-hour Sunday-afternoon open house celebrating his company's enlarged facilities. The fifteen-page supplement in the *Montgomery Advertiser-Journal* promised "free cookbooks and refreshments" at the home of "the largest book publishing business in the South."

Even before the event began, a line of cars formed a mile-long snake on Atlanta Highway waiting to get into the parking lot.

The supplement contained pictures of the well-dressed white employees, the men generally in suits and ties, the woman in heels and dresses. Only on the last page were there three pictures of black employees. They wore work clothes as they labored over the letter folder and printing presses. It was enough to please any Alabama segregationist, the white employees in their proper place, the black employees in theirs.

"We had done enough to antagonize the community, and I didn't want any bad happenings during that day," said George Seitz, then the president of Fuller & Dees. "The truth was we had blacks holding positions that they had never held in Montgomery."

DEES HAD LEARNED how little it took to offend the Montgomery establishment, and he had reached the point where he didn't give a damn what they thought. He forged ahead seemingly oblivious of those who mocked and condemned him.

Most anyone else would have thought twice about linking up with the American Civil Liberties Union (ACLU), viewed by many southerners as legal busybodies swarming south to inflict themselves on matters that should have been left alone. Dees not only joined the Montgomery chapter, but also became its president.

In August 1967, with the backing of the ACLU, Dees filed his first civil rights lawsuit. The case involved the First Amendment rights of Gary C. Dickey, an Alabama college student. Dickey had served in the navy in Vietnam. He had returned wanting to become a journalist. The veteran went to Troy State, a state school that did not have a journalism department. To learn about reporting, he worked for the *Tropolitan*, the school newspaper. In his sophomore year, he was the news editor deputized to write an editorial each week.

Dickey soon had an unpleasant introduction to Troy State president Ralph Adams, one of George Wallace's college friends.

Adams had chosen a path to power that Dees could have chosen, staying close to Wallace until it brought high position. In Adams's case, he worked for the governor until Wallace rewarded his old friend by naming him Troy State president and giving him the money to turn the teachers' college into a university. Adams had no credentials to be a university president except for the only one that mattered: he was close to the governor.

Adams considered it his supreme duty to defend Wallace and the traditions of the Old South. When the college president learned that the student government association had negotiated to bring in a popular rhythm-and-blues group, the Platters, Adams said that no black group was performing at the segregated college. That led Dickey to write an editorial criticizing the decision, which was his first personal acquaintance with Adams's rule that the *Tropolitan* could publish nothing critical of the college or of Governor Wallace, or anything else unseemly or controversial.

At the same time as Dickey wrote his editorial, down the road at the University of Alabama, student journalists published an editorial calling for racial equality. Governor Wallace and a number of state legislators were so piqued that they called for the resignation of President Frank Rose.

Dickey wrote an editorial supportive of the University of Alabama president headlined A LAMENT FOR DR. ROSE. Adams told the student journalist to his face that the editorial could not be published. Dickey ran the headline and beneath it the word *CENSORED* above empty white columns. Adams ordered the papers removed from the stands and vowed that he would shut down the student paper for good.

While Adams fumed, the *Montgomery Advertiser* published a facsimile of the *Tropolitan* page on its front page, and next to it the full editorial. That coverage turned the incident into a major story.

Adams refused to allow Dickey to study at the school the following quarter. That's when Dees filed a lawsuit against the university. Dees won in a judgment written by U.S. District Judge Frank

Johnson that allowed Dickey back into college. It was an important victory for civil liberty, but for many people in Alabama it was their first introduction to Morris Dees. As they saw it, this belligerent busybody had come elbowing his way into an area where he didn't belong. Dees would be a name to remember.

Beverly watched her husband's behavior with a growing sense of disquiet, and it wasn't just about her husband's civil rights activities. She wasn't a complainer, but she was the one who worried when her husband went roaring off on his BMW motorcycle a hundred miles an hour down country roads. He wasn't happy unless he was going so fast that one misstep would send him riding shotgun in heaven. And that wasn't enough. On weekends he was off on the rodeo circuit jumping off his prized horse trying to rope calves. He was never good enough to be an all-around rodeo champion, but he loved playing cowboy, and for Beverly, this was yet another worry.

Her husband was shunned by some of the most socially prominent people in Montgomery, and at times was in physical danger, but Beverly felt she suffered far more than Morris did. She would get telephone calls threatening her and the children, and when she changed the number, it was only a matter of days before the anonymous callers figured out the new number and were back pestering her. She was often alone with the children, wondering how far these people might go.

Then there was their son Scooter, who was ostracized by some of his classmates at the Pike Road School outside Montgomery. Beverly was the one—not Morris—who had to explain to the boy why he wasn't invited to birthday parties along with the rest of his classmates, and when his birthday rolled around, why so few kids showed up at the house for his party.

BACK WHEN LURLEEN had come close to divorcing Wallace, he lured her back by promising that once he was elected, everything would be different. They would live in the glorious governor's mansion. They would have servants to take care of them. And he wouldn't be traveling much anymore but would be pretty much of a homebody. Lurleen already had the mansion and servants, but the rest of it was not true. And now as cancer attacked her and she deteriorated to the point that she could hardly fulfill even minimal duties as governor, it was the moment for George to become the kind of husband he had never been.

Wallace tried in his way, but by this time he was running for president again, and he kept darting back and forth across the country. Each time he returned, he reported to his wife how great the crowds had been, how enthusiastic the greetings.

By mid-April 1968, Lurleen was down to less than eighty pounds. If ever there was a time for Wallace to be there for her, it was then, but he instead headed out for yet another round of campaign speeches, saying his wife "has won the fight." Wallace returned in time to hold Lurleen's hand at her bedside when she died on May 7, 1968, at the age of forty-one.

Wallace had no time to wear a mourner's black beyond the funeral. He had a race to run as a third-party candidate in the 1968 general election opposing Republican Richard Nixon and Democratic vice president Hubert Humphrey. He hoped to gather just enough votes so that neither the Republican nor Democratic candidate would win the majority of the electoral college votes. That way Wallace could then play the kingmaker. In return for Wallace's votes, the winning candidate would end what the governor considered a second Reconstruction.

As Wallace headed out again on the campaign trail, he was not going to have Robert Shelton with him as he had in Indiana in 1964. The Imperial Wizard represented potential danger. Wallace pushed Shelton away as if he had never even known him.

Shelton's career was defined by his friendship and commitment to Wallace. Only the Imperial Wizard knew what the governor had said to him, and to what extent the governor had called for actions that ended in death and bloodshed. But Wallace danced away unscathed, severing his contact with the man who had been so crucial in his rise.

In June 1968, Shelton paid twenty-five dollars to attend a fund-raising dinner for Wallace in Eutaw, an hour outside Birmingham. Afterward, the Imperial Wizard stood in line like everyone else to shake the governor's hand. When he got up to the front, scuffling and shouting broke out as soon as he grasped Wallace's hand. ABC had been filming the event, and Wallace's aides ripped the camera from the cameraman and destroyed the film.

Within a two-month period in the spring of 1968, both Martin Luther King Jr. and Bobby Kennedy were assassinated. If anything, this caused Wallace to rev up his rhetoric even higher. His supporters and detractors confronted one another, throwing chairs and fists. Wallace was pelted with everything from tomatoes, fireworks rockets, Tootsie Rolls, and even a sandal.

In that traumatic year, Wallace's message was heard with greater resonance than it had four years before, but in the last few weeks before the November election, millions of voters turned and walked away from him. In the end, Nixon won the election, with Wallace carrying five states in the Deep South and 13.5 percent of the vote. In a moment of optimism, his campaign rented Montgomery's Municipal Auditorium for an election night celebration. It was as empty, however, as the hotel ballroom had been in 1958 when Wallace lost his first race for governor.

Lowering the Boom

IN FEBRUARY 1969, after the lengthy legal appeals process ran out, Robert Shelton entered the Federal Minimum Security Correctional Center at Texarkana, Texas, for refusing to give HUAC subpoenaed Klan records. The Imperial Wizard was segregated from black prisoners, some of whom might have killed him and been celebrated for doing so.

After serving nine months of his one-year sentence, Shelton was released in November 1969. He told reporters that day, "We are chained to the infested black carcass that's dragging us down to the low morals and disruption that's in this nation today."

"No individual has a basic knowledge of what takes place behind the walls of a prison," Shelton told a radio reporter after his release. "I gained knowledge of what happens in a fully integrated government community. The Negro militants run the prisons just like they rule it on the outside. The Black Panthers and those groups have their meetings weekly, but white groups would be thrown in the hole if they wanted a meeting. I would have to say I'm not the same person I was before prison. I have a little bitterness."

The UKA had lost many of its estimated 14,000 members during the time he was incarcerated, and Shelton set out immediately on a lengthy speaking tour to remedy that loss. His time in prison made him a hero to his fellow Klansmen and sympathizers, and the audiences listened to him with an elevated respect.

He told audiences his familiar tale that the black man had taken over the white man's job, and now he was moving into his bedroom to take over his wife and daughters. And wherever the schools were integrated, and black and white students sat together in the same classrooms, the black teenagers were raping the white girls. This was part of a grand and evil plan devised by the Jews and "the anti-Christ conspiracy." He had decided, he said, not to talk so much about "niggers" any longer but to emphasize the evil of Black Power and the Jews who "were taking all the gold and silver out of the United States."

Shelton believed that 90 percent of American Jews were Communists, and that they "held all the key positions in government." They had taken a docile, easily led black population and manipulated them to revolt against their natural lot in life. Even white children were not safe from their wicked impact. He told a rally, "Textbooks are controlled by Zionist anti-Christians who use them to brainwash schoolchildren." The Imperial Wizard intended to focus the Klan on ending the malevolent Jewish power grab in America and the "Jewish conspiracy to take over the world."

The UKA was full of know-nothing, low-life types who cared little about the philosophy that Shelton espoused. He didn't like spending much time with them, for they compromised his vision. Now that he had no more contact with Wallace, he needed new excitements, new possibilities for action, and sophisticated new contacts. In 1972 an informant told the FBI that Shelton had met with Dr. Sallah El Dareer, an Arab-American leader in Birmingham, who wanted Shelton to help establish a camp to train anti-Israel insurgents. El Dareer told the informant "due to a lack of funds and his inability to satisfy the KKK's material demands, he had not been able to start the training camp."

Another informant told the FBI that Shelton confided to an associate that he planned to turn the UKA into an "out-in-the-open paramilitary organization and would, if necessary, be patterned after the German Gestapo." He met with a group of Arab-American activists and told them that American Jews needed to have "fear put in them by the killing of a few Jewish leaders." The Klan leader agreed to show an anti-Israel film at a Klan meeting and "distribute any available Arab literature."

The Muslim leaders asked Shelton if he would fly to an undisclosed location in the Middle East to meet George Habash, the leader of the Popular Front for the Liberation of Palestine. The left-wing organization had been involved in plane hijackings and political assassinations. Shelton said he was willing to make the trip as long as his flight was prepaid. Two months later, the Klan leader told an informant that an Arab embassy was arranging the trip, but there is no evidence that he ever flew to the Middle East.

In the years after he left prison, Shelton sometimes seemed to be daring the U.S. government to come after him. In early 1971, "a highly placed Klan informant" said that the Imperial Wizard claimed to be writing a book that would cause the government to "lower the boom on us." He would charge that "Hoover is a 'queer' and his homosexual partner is Billy Rose." Hoover received a memo on the supposed project. The FBI director knew the late Rose, a celebrated showman and nightclub owner. There had long been rumors about Hoover's sexuality, and it was wildly provocative to make such an accusation. Nothing ever came of the scandalous endeavor, and given the FBI director's sensitivities on the subject, that was just as well for the Klan leader's future.

Since leaving prison, Shelton had become an even more powerful speaker. Although Wallace would no longer have anything to do with him, Shelton poked his finger in the air and walked across the stage like Wallace and spoke much of the same rhetoric. And like the governor, Shelton wasn't just staying in Alabama. He told his tale from New Orleans to Arkansas, and Michigan to Pennsylvania, and wherever he went, the audiences applauded. Even the *New York Times* wrote in 1970 that the Imperial Wizard "had taken on considerable polish since his pre-prison days" and that he looked "almost handsome."

Private Matters

IN FEBRUARY 1968, a snowstorm forced Dees to spend the night in Cincinnati's airport. Having nothing else to do, he bought a paperback copy of Clarence Darrow's *The Story of My Life* in the gift shop, sat down in a hard plastic seat, and began reading the life of one of America's most famous and controversial lawyers.

Darrow wrote that as a young lawyer hanging out his shingle, "not only could I put myself in the other person's place, but I could not avoid doing so. My sympathies always went out to the weak, the suffering, and the poor. Realizing their sorrows, I tried to relieve them in order that I might be relieved."

As far as Dees was concerned, that was precisely right. It hurt to see suffering. It hurt to see injustice. It hurt to see evil triumph. And when it didn't hurt, you were dead inside. He remembered back when he was sixteen years old, and his father told him that one of the field hands, Clarence Williams, had been charged with drunk driving and resisting arrest. He knew Williams as a serious sober family man, who until Dees's father had paid off his charges had been a virtual indentured servant on a nearby plantation unable even to leave the property without the owner's permission. He was a good worker, and the charges sounded false. Dees walked over to the shack where Williams lived with his wife and nine children and asked him what happened.

"Bubba, you know my car ain't nothin' but a piece of car, and I was driving along there, and this tire rod came loose, and the car ran off and hit that concrete median up there on the road and it knocked me dizzy, and the state trooper came along, and he pulled me out, and he said, 'Nigger, what you doing drunk?' And I said, 'Boss, I ain't drunk.' And I got out and staggered 'round, and next thing I know that state trooper shoved me in the back of the car and hit me upside my head with a blackjack and took me on up to jail in Tuskegee."

Dees had never heard such a preposterous story. "Shoot, Clarence, we can beat that," he said. "You c'mon with me."

The two men got in Dees's truck and drove to Shorter, where Justice of the Peace Metcalf Letcher held court in his country store as he sold Wonder Bread and Nehi orange soda. Entering the cluttered facility, Williams took off his hat and shuffled forward, his head deferentially down. Dees told Williams's side of the story in what he thought was exemplary fashion. Then the state trooper told what "really" had happened, and the judge hit this field hand who earned four dollars a day with a $150 fine.

Young Dees thought the courts were the place one went to seek justice, and he was stunned by what had gone on. "Well, if you don't like it, why don't you go to law school," his father had told him. All these years later, Dees remembered what his father had said and why he had wanted to go to law school in the first place.

While Dees was growing up, he had seen that black lives didn't matter, and until they did, there could be no true justice. He remembered as a boy the horrifying sight of a dead black man with stab wounds in his chest being lifted onto a hearse outside the Mount Meigs grocery store. The man had gotten in a knife fight with another field hand who had already been hauled off to jail. As the hearse drove away Gus Dozier, a wealthy landowner, called the sheriff from the store phone. "God damn it, bring my nigger back," Dozier said. "It was self-defense. I need him on my tractor tomorrow." That evening the deputy delivered the man back to the plantation, and that was the end of that.

As Dees read Darrow's harrowing tales of injustice, he interspersed them with his own memories of how he had seen black people treated. He read how Darrow had been a corporate lawyer before he left to defend workers and the poor, the very people he had once fought against. As the sun rose on a frigid Cincinnati, Dees decided that he could do what Darrow had done.

Dees lived a life that was a manic pursuit of work and play. And whatever was going on, no matter how complicated and convoluted, there was always room for something new, to escalate matters to a new place, to press ever upward his sense of energized excitement.

And always there were women. Dees was not a dozen roses and a pound of chocolates kind of guy, but he attracted all kinds of admirers, both within the company and outside. Fuller & Dees was filled with attractive women, none more than the raven-haired Maureene Bass. Maureene had won many beauty contests before becoming an airline stewardess. She had a husband and two young children, her diversions limited largely to the Montgomery Little Theatre Group where she served on the board with Morris. Maureene went to work for his company and achieved a position of considerable responsibility.

Maureene and Morris flew together to St. Thomas for a cookbook editorial meeting with Poppy Cannon, the *Ladies' Home Journal*'s food editor, who was on the Caribbean island recuperating from an operation. On the plane, Dees reached out to hold Maureene's hand. A few days later at the jewelry store H. Stern, Maureene helped Morris pick out a ring that she assumed was a gift for Beverly, his wife. When they got out of the store, Dees proposed.

As soon as the couple got back to Montgomery, Maureene excitedly told her closest friend, Eleanor Davis, what had happened.

"He asked me to marry him," Maureene said proudly.

"What did you say?" Davis asked.

"I said yes."

"But you're married, and so is Morris."

That was a minor impediment that was soon overcome.

Though she loved him and thought she always would, Beverly was glad that her marriage to Dees was over, and after the divorce, she wished the newlyweds well. When her ex-husband had the time and intention, he could be the most charming man in the universe. But when he came charging into the house, there was often no room for her.

"There's nothing you can do about it except decide you're going to hang on or not," Dees's former wife says. "And I decided not. And it wasn't just that. It's just I was tired of being threatened by what we thought was the Klan. I was tired of the boys being threatened and they had to be guarded, you know."

Their two sons ended up staying with Morris and living in

the countryside they loved. Without any legal wrangling, Dees took care of Beverly, among other things providing her the money she used to buy a home in Louisville, Kentucky, and a summer cottage in Maine. In 1970, Maureene gave birth to Ellie Dees, her and Dees's first and only child together. He had a tender closeness to his daughter.

Dees decided to bring his boys up so they did not come whining to their father when they had troubles. When a group of boys beat up Scooter behind the school gym at the Montgomery Academy, yelling "Take that for your nigger-loving family" as they busted him yet again in the gut, he did not even tell his dad.

In July 1969, Dees and his bride were off in England when someone burned a cross near the mailbox. The boys started hearing what they thought were gunshots and became even more frightened. Afterward, the youths discovered the remains of firecrackers out by the road.

Dees had plenty of warnings that his civil rights lawsuits threatened not only him and his business, but also his new wife and enlarged family of five children. His friends warned Dees to back off from these controversial lawsuits. He had done enough. It was time to grow up and focus on his new responsibilities and to pay full attention to his enlarged family and new wife. But he considered civil rights lawsuits the most dangerous, exciting of challenges. He became even more provocative in filing them.

Earlier that year, students at Auburn University invited Yale University chaplin William Sloane Coffin to speak on campus. Reverend Coffin was an outspoken anti–Vietnam War leader who had been federally indicted for promoting draft resistance. Colleges and universities across America still had great control over whoever appeared on campus, and the administration canceled the event. In doing so, they invoked one of George Wallace's favorite excuses: if they went ahead there might be a riot and even death.

There was overwhelming support across the state for the decision to prevent this cleric from targeting the youth of the region. Anyone who took on the students' case risked being vilified from Birmingham to Mobile. Dees rushed in to defend the students' freedom, and so attained a whole new level of notoriety in the state.

Dees won his case when federal judge Frank Johnson once again made an unpopular ruling, and Reverend Coffin spoke to a polite audience without incident. Troopers in riot gear waited behind a nearby National Guard armory but were never called out.

After Reverend Coffin spoke, there were no state troopers near the Fuller & Dees offices when cars carrying Klansmen drove into the parking lot and sat there. Dees carried a Beretta and walked boldly out of the office each evening. His bravado may have been in part a way to deal with fears so deep and profound that he wanted them never to surface.

Later that year, Dees sold his company to the Times Mirror Publishing Company for $6 million, more than twice what he thought it was actually worth. In 1969, this was a fabulous fortune. The boy who had hitched a ride to the capital in the back of an old truck for a dime was now a thirty-two-year-old man who could walk along Decatur Avenue as one of the wealthiest men in Montgomery.

Maureene had a burgeoning sense of entitlement with the new wealth. She felt they were rich and should live appropriately. She drove a Rolls-Royce, which was as rare in the streets of Montgomery as a rickshaw. Dees could not bear to ride in the ultra-luxury car and drove a pickup instead.

THE MONTGOMERY COMMUNITY might have forgiven Dees's multiple sins, but he took an action that made him an outcast in his hometown for decades. Other than the Montgomery Country Club, the YMCA was the most important white private institution in the city. To most members, the Y was their country club.

In the late 1950s the city had closed down its twenty parks with their swimming pools, tennis courts, and grass enclaves rather than face integration. To meet the vastly increased need, the Y ran a large capital expansion campaign chaired by the mayor.

The organization built five new buildings across the city, including a modest facility in the black part of Montgomery. The most impressive building of all was the new downtown headquarters. It was here at the Central branch that businesspeople and local luminaries came to swim and exercise.

Life could have gone on like this indefinitely if Dees had not filed a lawsuit to integrate the Y. He made enemies of thousands of white Montgomery residents who thought they had every right to choose with whom they wanted to swim and play in *their* private club. That Dees was one of them and not a carpetbagging northern liberal made it even worse.

Dees's action upset even the capital's small liberal community. They had been waging their battles when Dees was either out of the fray or on the other side. It irritated them that he refused to understand that he lived in a community where it was crazy to upset unnecessarily some of the most powerful people in town.

As he took on these lawsuits, he realized that segregation and racism were more deeply embedded and pernicious than even he had ever imagined. "I think it's only a slight exaggeration to say that in 1969, the message delivered by many of the white men who wore suits and ties in Montgomery, wasn't that different from the message from those who wore robes and hoods," wrote Dees in his autobiography, *A Lawyer's Journey*. "It's just that it was delivered differently."

While doing discovery research for the YMCA case, Dees came across a 1958 document dealing with the "City Recreation-YMCA Coordinating Committee." As the city shut down its public pools and parks, it made an agreement with the Y that allowed it to expand dramatically and provide segregated pools and facilities. The city practically gave away the Perry Street Recreation Park to the Y for $18,000. The agreement stipulated that within three years the Y had to spend at least $100,000 building new facilities for "athletic, health, recreational and religious" purposes on the property or the city could buy the park back at the selling price. It was here the YMCA built its new Central branch.

Because the Y was a private institution, it could legally keep pools and sports facilities segregated. A few years later when the mayor chaired a meeting of the committee that dealt with the agreement, he said they should "not include the Negro staff members or board members." The mayor clearly did not want anyone outside the inner circle to know why the city's black children had almost nowhere to swim in the torrid summer months.

Among the elite in Montgomery, the worst crime was to be embarrassed or shamed. And Morris Dees was exposing what they considered the private matters of private people. There were attempts to investigate the lawyer and find something that would force him to back off. But they failed. In the end, federal judge Frank Johnson opened every aspect of the Y to black members.

No one looked at the ruling with more embarrassment than Dees's relatives. As far as they were concerned, he had brought nothing but shame to a once honored name. A family delegation that included his father's brothers Lucien, James, and Arthur, along with his aunt's husband, Hoyt Shepherd, came to see him. They signaled the importance of their mission by wearing suits and ties. The men told him they were tired of hearing about him and his "nigger-loving ways." Shepherd was an unmitigated racist who loved to say the *n* word, letting it roll languorously off his tongue.

The men believed Dees had disgraced the family name and

betrayed his own father. The four relatives told Morris that if he was not going to change his ways, then he should change his name so they could once again carry it with pride.

"If your father were alive today, he would take you to the woodshed and beat your ass," Shepherd said.

Nothing his relatives said diminished Dees's belief that his father would have been proud of him. But when his family left that day, he felt a terrible sense of isolation. The Dees were a close clan, and he was now an outsider even to his own family.

A few months later, Dees's uncle Hoyt called him. "I got a case about them niggers that you ain't gonna take, Morris," Shepherd said, taunting his nephew. Dees asked him to bring over the potential plaintiff, a white man named Wilbur Berry, who arrived wearing work-stained overalls and a greasy Caterpillar cap covering his baldpate.

Berry said he had been the foreman of the school bus mechanics in overwhelmingly black Tuskegee. In the wake of the Voting Rights Act, the newly elected all-black school board ruled that the town employees must send their children to Tuskegee's public schools. As much as Berry needed the $510 a month job, he couldn't see sending his children to all-black schools, and when he refused, he was fired.

For a man staking out a claim as a civil rights lawyer in Alabama, this was hardly the kind of suit that would advance Dees's reputation. But he felt this was unjust, and he took the case.

During a break in the Montgomery proceedings in the United States District Court, one of the Tuskegee board members, Connie Harper, came up to Dees. The lawyer had stood with her and her people on other issues, and he knew and respected the woman. "Connie, I am for you and for all the good reasons you and your people have the rights you do today," Dees told her. "But what you are doing to my client is exactly what the whites did to you over the years." He didn't think she understood what he was saying and she was clearly distressed when the court ruled that Berry's constitutional rights to freedom of speech and association had been violated, and the bus mechanic got his job back.

Fighting the Fight

WITH THE DEATH of Martin Luther King Jr. in 1968, the generally acknowledged era of the civil rights movement drew to a close, and the civil rights battles moved in some measure from the streets to the courthouse. Dees saw that there were few lawyers in the South, black or white, who were prepared to fight those fights. In 1971, Dees and another Montgomery attorney, Joe Levin Jr., founded the Southern Poverty Law Center (SPLC).

In his prototypical fashion, Dees didn't run around asking the NAACP or the ACLU to anoint him in his battle, but just set off blithely on his own. Nor did he ask the liberal muckety-mucks in the city's tiny beleaguered liberal community for their approval. The one measure he took to garner immediate credibility was to bring in civil rights icon Julian Bond as the SPLC's first president. Although Bond was not involved in the day-to-day operations, northern donors saw Bond's name prominently on the fund-raising letters, and that gave the SPLC instant credibility. Dees named himself the chief trial lawyer, the only title at the SPLC he ever held.

Dees was not using his own wealth to fund the center and was relying on fund-raising. The man who had marketed everything from birthday cakes, tractor cushions, holiday wreaths, and cookbooks was astutely aware of how to motivate Americans to buy a wide range of products. He now set out to promote the SPLC in what was by any measure the greatest selling job he would ever do. The letters were raw, desperate in their urgency, screaming for help out of the heart of darkness.

Dees's first mass mailing asked for help in fighting a legal battle for a black man charged with killing a white woman. He had an almost mystical certainty that people would respond to his letter. A few days later, Levin drove downtown to the law firm's post office box and brought back a stack of replies. Here were checks for five dollars, ten dollars, or even twenty-five dollars from people all over the nation, many of them with notes saying how much it meant to be part of such a worthy cause.

Few people in America were as good as Dees at making money through the mails. That's why he was brought in to handle direct mail for Senator George McGovern of South Dakota in his 1972 presidential run. The Democratic nominee raised more than $24 million largely due to Dees's efforts. It was the first time a presidential campaign had been financed primarily by legions of small donors, and it became one of the greatest fund-raising successes in American political history. All he asked in return from the McGovern Campaign was a copy of the list of about 600,000 names. To a fledgling liberal organization, the list was beyond priceless.

Dees cared about the SPLC the way he never cared about tractor cushions or cookbooks, and he wrote fund-raising letters that were sent out by the hundreds of thousands. If he was a direct-marketing folk poet in his writings, he carefully tracked the results of each letter. As he did so, he developed themes that he sent out in one mass mailing after another, touting the SPLC's fierce, beleaguered struggle against evil.

Northern liberals loved the idea that they were receiving mail from the heart of the monster. The least they could do was to send their checks, and about 200,000 of those on the McGovern list ended up doing so.

Some in the South were offended by the letters, thinking they pandered to the prejudices many northerners had about the region. Dees had no qualms about the way he raised money, and he would not listen.

The lawsuits and other legal actions initiated by the SPLC exposed a persistent pattern of segregation and wholesale discrimination. One lawsuit forced the town of Selma to give black neighborhoods the paved roads that only white neighborhoods had. Another lawsuit stopped the city of Montgomery from allowing segregated private schools to use public facilities to provide sports and recreation for their students. A legal action forced the state of Alabama to hire black state troopers. Another lawsuit ended the practice of white funeral homes refusing to provide their services to black people. Thanks to another action, a federal judge declared Alabama prisons so foul that they were "wholly unfit for human habitation."

Many in Alabama were furious at these legal challenges from what they considered northern liberal lawyers camped out in Montgomery. But year after year and case after case, the SPLC lawyers were helping to change the way people in Alabama and across the South lived and worked.

If Dees had headquartered the SPLC in Atlanta or Washington and had come down to the Alabama capital on working visits, his organization might have been barely tolerated. But to many in Montgomery, it was an incitement to plant the civil rights law firm in the Alabama capital just down the street from the house where President Jefferson Davis had lived when Montgomery had been the capital of the Confederacy. Davis's pew was reverently preserved at St. John's Episcopalian Church, and it was a city of proud old customs and unchanging beliefs.

Dees kept the SPLC in Montgomery not to provoke his enemies, but because he loved living in the Alabama countryside. He was as much a proud southerner as any of his enemies, and there was no way he was going to move away.

Dees was not afraid to have the SPLC take cases that most

civil rights law firms would have shunned. In the mid-1970s, the firm funded a lawsuit against Alabama State University in Montgomery, arguing that in the wake of desegregation, the overwhelmingly black school was discriminating against white faculty and staff in hiring and promotions. The plaintiff lawyers maintained that given a choice between a superior white candidate and a mediocre black one, the administration inevitably chose the African American, believing that racial solidarity and advancement were more important than the quality of education the black students received.

The ASU lawyers argued that the university was doing what white schools were doing, and they had some devastating figures with which to buttress their arguments. The University of Alabama, for instance, in 1977 had one black employee among the 144 staff members and 20 black teachers among the 788 faculty members.

The defendant's argument did not go over well with federal judge Frank Johnson. In his judicial math, two injustices did not add up to justice. In finding for the plaintiffs, Johnson took special offense at Dr. Levi Watkins, the pretentious, overweening ASU president, who denied that he had anything to do with the decisions.

Judge Johnson would have none of that. "Dr. Watkins runs ASU like an administrative tyrant," the federal judge wrote in his 1978 opinion in *Craig v. Alabama State University*. "He utilizes his powers over the employment process to maintain a nearly dictatorial grip over the internal life of the university."

Dees had a penchant for controversy, and this time he had managed to offend some of Montgomery's most important black leaders. Even if privately they might admit that Dr. Watkins was a pompous martinet, the university president was one of *theirs*, and what he was doing at ASU was no different from what white people had systematically done to African Americans for generations. They couldn't understand why Dees was squandering time and resources on such a petty matter when black Alabamans still faced discrimination and injustice.

A Wannabe

MANY WHITE ALABAMANS had made their peace with integration and a new kind of South, but George Wallace was not one of them. In 1970 he had won election as governor for a second time applying an overtly racist strategy an aide described privately as "promise them the moon and holler nigger." His administration was rife with corruption, including a series of organized kickbacks that for the most part benefited the Big Mules, the wealthy Alabamans who once had been his declared enemies.

As Wallace campaigned for the Democratic presidential nomination for a third time in 1972, he continued to deny that he was a racist. The governor blamed the press that "got folks believing now that I'm against certain people just because of who they happen to be." Out on the campaign trail, he was on his best behavior, but sometimes things would just creep out, as when he referred to United States senator Edward W. Brooke (R-Mass.) as a "nigger."

Everywhere Wallace traveled across America, he spoke to enthusiastic audiences. In a mocking voice streaked with irony, he told his audiences how the other Democrats in the race were stealing his ideas on everything from opposition to school busing to dramatic all-round tax cuts and knocking the chronic cheats off of welfare rolls. As far as the governor was concerned, the biggest thief of all was President Richard Nixon, whose "silent majority" of hardworking taxpayers were people Wallace considered *his* constituency. Wallace still invoked these ideas louder than any of his opponents, and he won the Florida Democratic primary decisively.

After days on the campaign trail, Wallace was exhausted, his voice half gone on May 15, 1972, the day before the Maryland primary. All he needed was a crowd to energize him, and he had one in a strip mall in Laurel, a town halfway between Baltimore and Washington. He gave the same stump speech here that he gave everywhere, and his themes resonated powerfully with his audience.

No matter how tired he was, Wallace always plunged into the crowds. Despite the wishes of the Secret Service, he was going to grasp every hand he possibly could. The governor was about finished when he heard a voice from the crowd, "Hey, George, let me shake hands with you." As Wallace turned, the twenty-one-year old Arthur Bremer raised his .38 caliber pistol and fired four bullets into Wallace, one of which lodged next to his spine.

The fifty-two-year-old Wallace was left paralyzed by a wannabe who said later that he sought fame by killing a politician. The day after the assassination attempt, Wallace won both the Maryland and Michigan primaries, but the candidate was in a hospital bed and unable to control his bodily functions. (McGovern would win the nomination and be defeated in the general election by Nixon, running for a second term.)

Wallace's recuperation was as much psychological as physical. His aides figured he would be okay when the governor's sense of humor returned.

"Well, I guess I'm gonna die," Wallace told his aide Elvin Stanton just before he was released from Holy Cross Hospital in Silver Spring, Maryland.

"No, Governor, you're going to be fine," Stanton said. "Why do you think you're going to die?"

"Well, these people come in here, and they tell me 'Governor, you're looking great.' I visited a lot of people in the hospital, and those that are just about to die, that's what I would tell them."

Wallace left the hospital in a wheelchair. He would never walk again, and he suffered from debilitating pain. Another man would have retreated into private life, but he had no private life to enter. His second marriage, to sexy, ambitious Cornelia Snively, had not gone well and after seven years would end in an acrimonious divorce. He had never paid much attention to his children, and he had no interest in grandchildren. His true family was his cronies and old friends who traveled with him wherever he went. And so he was left with the only life that mattered to him, the public life he had lived since he was a young man.

Despite his paralysis, Wallace still wanted to run again for president. He had seen the phenomenal job Dees had done raising money for McGovern. Despite Wallace's battles with the civil rights lawyer, his brother Gerald contacted Dees and offered him $1 million to raise money for the governor's 1976 presidential run. No one would even have to know that he was writing the letters.

Dees knew he could have done well for Wallace, but it was a job he could never accept. In saying no, he was unfailingly polite, just as he'd been when turning down Shelton's offer to print the Klan newspaper. The lawyer even suggested that the governor go to Richard Viguerie, a right-wing direct mail expert. And Wallace did just that.

Although he would have preferred to back a more liberal Democrat, Dees signed on as Jimmy Carter's national finance director. Carter's centrist politics caught hold, and he was the southern politician that campaign year who seemed the voice of change and promise. Wallace tried to rev up the rhetoric that had always brought his audiences to their feet. Now talking from his wheelchair, the passages sounded muted, and people at times applauded as much out of pity as passion.

"We had plenty of money to run in '76, but Governor Wallace was having bouts of infection and hospitalization and it was hopeless," says his close aide Elvin Stanton. "We had all kind of problems with his wheelchair, and the media focus was on a crippled man, not on what he stood for."

Wallace lost primary after primary to Carter, even in states that the governor had long since thought of as his. Carter campaign aide Hamilton Jordan called Dees and asked if he thought Wallace would accept a phone call from Carter to discuss endorsing his candidacy. Dees helped to arrange the call, and after a congenial discussion, Wallace agreed to drop out of the race and endorse his opponent. It was enough to put Carter largely over the top, a crucial step to his becoming the thirty-ninth president of the United States.

After the election, Wallace's campaign manager called Dees and said they had been left with large debts. He wondered if the lawyer would be willing to write a letter to the 200,000-person mailing list. Dees said that many of these contributors probably weren't happy that their hero had endorsed a candidate they despised, and he did not know how generous they would be. He suggested a test sample of 10,000 names.

The Wallace people did not listen. They wrote their own letter, and did an expensive mass mailing to all 200,000 names. The money that came back was not even enough to pay for the postage, and it was clear the quadrennial quest for the presidency of "the most influential loser" in twentieth-century American politics was over.

LIKE WALLACE, SHELTON spent a good deal of time looking back at what could have been. As the UKA had tried to fulfill Wallace's mandate to prevent integration, they had participated in Alabama's worst racial violence in the modern era. But the Imperial Wizard still believed that if the Klan had prompted more blood and brutality, the black man would never have dared to stand up to the white man.

"It's unfortunate, really, that there wasn't more violence than what it was," Shelton told journalist Patsy Sims in 1976. "I feel like had there been enough violence, it would have stopped all of this, and we wouldn't be in the position we're in today."

Shelton was still a strong man filled with ambition and purpose. He continued to travel the country gathering supporters and planning for a revitalized Klan. In 1981, in the midst of this, UKA members strangled nineteen-year-old Michael Donald and left his body strapped to a tree on Herndon Avenue in downtown Mobile.

PART THREE

Roll Call of Justice

"Novel, but Unlikely"

IN DECEMBER 1983, when Morris Dees returned to Montgomery after attending the murder trial of Henry Hays for the lynching of nineteen-year-old Michael Donald in Mobile, he called the SPLC lawyers into his office to discuss the case. It was a lean team of only five attorneys, and four of them were available to attend the meeting.

There were few places in America where an idealistic law school graduate could have more freedom and resources to wage the fight for social reform than at the SPLC, and the cofounder of the civil rights law firm had his pick of some of the finest, most passionate young attorneys in America.

The SPLC lawyers listened intently as Dees laid out his theory. He argued that the United Klans of America had a mock military structure, and Robert Shelton, the Klan leader, and his subordinates directed the Klansmen to work as their agents, carrying out all kinds of vicious activities that had led to the death of Michael Donald. Dees was convinced that the UKA could be sued directly for its role in the murder.

As Dees sketched the potential case in broad strokes, the lawyers rustled uneasily. Dees was unlike anyone these lawyers had ever known, and that was one reason for the growing tension on the staff. The then forty-six-year-old attorney lacked the gravitas that a man of his stature naturally assumed. Their professors at Harvard or Stanford dressed casually sometimes, but Dees came roaring in on his motorcycle or driving his pickup truck in the morning wearing jeans and a T-shirt. He went zooming off in the evenings at times to go off to a honky-tonk with some of his low-living buddies.

Dees did not have the top-drawer academic legal education of the young lawyers in the room who were silently drawing upon all kinds of legal precedents and history that could be used to try such a case.

"Novel, but unlikely," said John Carroll, who went on to become a U.S. magistrate judge and dean of Birmingham's Cumberland Law School.

"Can't be done," proclaimed Stephen J. Ellmann, who later became a professor at New York Law School. Ellmann lectured Dees on why his idea was impossible. "You'll never clear the legal hurdles so that a jury can consider the Klan's liability," Ellmann said. "Corporations are not usually liable for the criminal acts of agents. You'd have to prove it was the UKA's official policy, or at least a practice encouraged or condoned by high officials, to commit criminal acts to carry out UKA goals."

Ellmann was right. If Dees couldn't tie in Shelton and his lieutenants to specific acts of violence orchestrated by the UKA, the judge would likely throw out the case.

Dees felt confident because he had successfully tried out his legal theory back when he was presidential candidate George McGovern's finance director. In June 1972, James McCord, security director of the Committee to Re-Elect the President (CREEP), and four accomplices, broke into the Democratic National Committee offices at the Watergate. As soon as he heard about the break-in, he called McGovern's campaign manager, Gary Hart, and convinced him the Democrats should take legal action. Dees filed the suit only three days after the break-in, and long before most people had any idea of the significance of the thwarted robbery.

The suit was against not just the five burglars, but also equally Nixon's reelection organization for sending them. Dees listed one of the causes of action as Title 42 USC 1985, an anti-

Klan statute dealing with "conspiracy to interfere with civil rights," the same law that he hoped to use against the UKA. The CREEP suit settled for $850,000 after Nixon resigned from office.

While admiring Dees's many legal accomplishments, the young SPLC lawyers did not like the way he was pushing them in new directions. In the twelve years of its existence, the SPLC had evolved into a progressive public interest law firm dealing with a wide range of important social issues. These included voting rights, death penalty cases, and occupational health and safety.

There was serious work to be done, and these lawyers wanted to do it, but they feared that Dees's pursuit of the Klan in the Donald case would set them off on a futile quest. These attorneys were for the most part northerners. As far as Dees was concerned, they had little sense of how racism in the South had festered and been nurtured and how it must die.

Several of these lawyers had been opposed to Dees's founding in 1980 of a new department within the SPLC called Klan-Watch. It investigated and sued the Klan and provided a central repository for information on hate groups. The lawyers had come to Montgomery to practice civil rights law, and as one of them, Dennis Blaske, wrote Dees about the founding of Klan-Watch, "Three of the four goals are not relevant to the practice of law." These young attorneys watched as Dees provoked the Klan to such an extent that their offices were burned and Dees needed a security team to protect him. Even Carroll received a death threat.

Dees favored the daring, the dangerous, and the provocative. That was fine sometimes, but the SPLC lawyers believed it was highly unlikely he would be successful winning a civil lawsuit suit against the Klan, and it was a monumental waste of resources.

The SPLC lawyers were shrewd enough to do little more than hint at their feelings. Dees knew he had a problem with the staff lawyers, but he was not about to do anything to placate them.

An Eye for an Eye

WHEN TWELVE MOBILE citizens sentenced Henry Hays to life imprisonment for the murder of Michael Donald, their sentence was only a recommendation. Henry still had to go before Judge Braxton L. Kittrell Jr., who could confirm the sentence, cut it, or impose the death penalty.

The judge was an elected official sensitive to political realities. In a racially tense community, it would be a strong symbol if, for the first time in over half a century, a white man died for murdering a black man. But in the early 1980s, it was almost unheard of to overrule a jury and send a man to his death.

As Henry sat in his cell in the Mobile jail, he spent much of his time thinking about Janet Deem, the older woman with whom he had fallen in love only a few days before his arrest. Henry wrote her letter after letter professing his love. "Darling, I'm really serious about asking you to marry me," he wrote her. "Being with you the time I have been is the greatest time in my life." He asserted his innocence and said he did not "believe in the death penalty or even life in an institution." As the day of the formal sentencing approached, the nightmares Henry had during the trial began again, and he awoke shivering in a cold sweat.

When the guards brought Henry into the courtroom for the first day of the two-day sentencing hearing, he saw Deem sitting near his family. He focused on her and not on what he considered "the circus of clowns" with their "outbursts in the court-room." "I really still feel like an outsider to this whole thing," he wrote Deem that evening. "The merry-go-round is going so fast I can't jump on."

The next day, as Henry was led into the courtroom for the sentencing, he was just as disengaged. When he heard Judge Kittrell's devastating, almost unprecedented words that he was sentenced to die in the electric chair, Henry did not flinch or cry, and showed not a glimmer of emotion or even recognition. When he shuffled out, his nod toward Deem was the only sign that he even recognized what had just happened.

The Donald family, including Mrs. Donald, had come to the courtroom to hear the sentencing. This morning she did not have to fear that the defense attorneys would cast aspersions on her son, and she sat quietly looking up at Judge Kittrell. When Mrs. Donald heard the sentence, she began to cry. Nothing would bring Michael back, and this execution was just more blood and pain. She wanted Henry to spend his life in prison where every day he would think about what he had done to her son. Most of the other family members, however, exalted at a sentence that they thought was justice.

Out in the corridor, Bennie fumed at the "liars and crimi-nals" who had sentenced his son in this "kangaroo court." "To get me, they got my son," he said. "I'm still a Klansman and will always be a religious man, with law and order as my concern. I had a nigger, I mean a black, come up to me in the courthouse and ask me why I wear a cover. He knew I was in the Klan; everyone in the hall knew I was in the Klan. I don't hide it. I've got nothing to be scared of."

Guards moved the condemned killer quickly to a seven-by-nine-foot cell on death row at Holman prison, an hour outside Mobile. Most of the other prisoners on death row were black, and in his first months, he was kept apart from them.

Henry fantasized that he would be getting out of prison and going off to live with his lover. He had a recurring dream that he was sleeping next to her in bed when he realized Deem was no longer next to him, and he screamed her name. That's when he woke up.

When Deem drove out to visit Henry along with his parents, the Hayses had little use for her, and Henry had little use for his parents. In the visitors' room, Henry cherished the time he sat alone with Deem, holding her hand and occasionally kissing her.

One day Henry told his father that Deem had a son whose father was a Filipino man living in the Philippines. Bennie said there was no way they would take such a child into their family. Henry was going to have to choose between his parents or this woman. The next week, his father stood up and waved his cane at Deem. "I'm not having no nigger in my family!" he told her.

The young Klansman had killed a man in part to gain his father's love and respect. But his father still disdained his youngest son and did not appear to wish him the best.

Henry told Deem that Bennie was an evil man. He began "dreading more than anything" his father's visits. When Henry's father came out to the prison, his son was so intimidated that he said almost nothing. "You said I was afraid of him, and he controlled me and always would," Henry wrote Deem. "Well, I've finally realized just how much power he has over me, and I am saying now Yes! I am afraid of him."

Only in letters could Henry pour out a measure of the truth. "Here I am 30 yrs old, and I'm still dependent on my mother and father for everything," he wrote Deem: that included even marrying his ex-wife. "When Ray [his brother] and Denise got divorced he [Bennie] really got me to keep her from getting the kids and stopping her from taking his money in alimony. So I even let him pick my family for me, but I will try to stand up to him. I really will."

Henry realized that his father was afraid of *him*. Henry had this horrible thought that to shut him up perhaps his father wanted him to die in the electric chair.

Henry's defense lawyer, Bubba Marsal, had done a good job

with an appeal, but Henry believed that "when things started to look like he might do something good for me, Dad started coming up with reasons to get rid of him. He was doing just what he was supposed to do. Dad wants to get rid of him. I think he's scared of me. Funny ain't it. I think he knows everything that happened, and he's afraid of me finding out."

The more Henry told Deem, the more he feared for her life. "I keep seeing you in danger," he wrote her. "If someone thinks you know too much he'll try to get rid of you. Please be careful. He's really a devil in disguise."

If Henry had implicated his father in the murder, he might not have been sentenced to death. Even now, if he spoke about Bennie's role, he might get off death row. But for all the boastful bromides that he would stand up to his father, Henry was so afraid of him that he did not dare to say anything.

Deem told Henry she was going to start going out with other men. Henry was desperate and despairing, but there was nothing he could do. Then Deem stopped writing and coming out to the prison. From then on, Henry was alone in the cell, his only diversion the visits of a mother he considered weak and a father he hated and feared.

A Clear and Powerful Message

MORRIS DEES WAS convinced that he could get up in a courtroom and persuade a jury that Shelton's UKA philosophy was crucial in motivating the murderers in the Donald case. But to win a civil lawsuit, Dees would have to show a *pattern of violence* involving the United Klans of America.

Many of the most vicious racists in America were members of the Klan. One of them, Mobile-born Joseph Paul Franklin, had been both a UKA member and a Nazi. Between 1977 and 1980, he traveled the country killing as many as twenty racially mixed couples and African Americans. The convicted murderer admitted he shot pornographer Larry Flynt in 1978 for publishing pictures of racially mixed couples in *Hustler,* leaving him crippled from the waist down. And two years later he said he got away with shooting another "race mixer," civil rights leader Vernon Jordan. As evil as these acts had been, to bring Franklin successfully into the courtroom, Dees would have to prove that a UKA official had conspired with him or given him assistance, and Dees could not begin to do that.

In the civil trial, Dees intended to bring up the 1965 murder of Viola Liuzzo because he believed he could link it to Shelton and the UKA philosophy. But since then, other than the lynching of Michael Donald, the lawyer could find no other instance of a crime that had Shelton's and the UKA's fingerprints all over a dastardly act.

Dees told Bill Stanton he was "going to have to find us something more recent." Through his work at KlanWatch, Stanton was becoming an expert on the Klan. The only thing he could find, however, was the 1979 conviction of thirteen UKA Klansmen for shooting into the homes of two NAACP officers in a small Alabama town. That was hardly a consistent pattern, but Dees grasped at it and decided, "This was the missing link we needed to file our lawsuit." To the more judicious staff lawyers, this was another example of his hyperbole.

If Dees could somehow get hold of all the Mobile investigatory files on the Donald murder, he believed he would have almost everything he needed to understand the crime. These files included documents from the Mobile police, the Alabama state investigators, and the FBI.

Dees called D.A. Chris Galanos, who said Dees could look at the files. When he started going through the papers in Mobile, he came upon a number of FBI FD-302 reports summarizing what the subjects had said.

For hours Dees stood at the copying machine, reproducing everything in the boxes. It was after midnight when he got back to his room at the Malaga Inn, but instead of going to bed, he started scouring the documents. As he worked his way through the papers, taking notes on a yellow legal pad, he read detailed evidence of the crime that the SPLC investigators would never have been able to compile. It was almost dawn when Dees finally finished and turned out the light.

Dees did not intend to argue that Shelton was directly involved with the murder. Instead he would allege that the Imperial Wizard headed an organization with a military structure whose custom, practice, and policy was to advance the goal of white supremacy through violence. Donald's murder was the natural consequence, and it was a UKA state officer, James Knowles, along with a Klavern officer, Henry Hays, directed probably by Shelton's top lieutenant in southern Alabama, Bennie Hays, who carried out the philosophy and violent dictates of the UKA in the killing of Michael Donald. There were others involved too, and Dees wasn't going to let them out of the case either.

On June 14, 1984, Dees filed an unprecedented $10 million lawsuit in Mobile's federal court against the United Klans of America and individual Klan members. The suit named Shelton in his capacity as the UKA leader, Bennie Hays, Henry Hays, James Knowles, Teddy Kyzar, and others yet to be named.

Given the financial resources of the UKA and the Klansmen, Mrs. Donald would never be able to collect more than a small fraction of the $10 million, if Dees were to win, and he doubted if any jury would agree to such an enormous sum. But he believed the large figure was a reasonable amount to ask the jury to assess, one that would send a clear and powerful message out to the Klan and other hate groups.

What mattered to Mrs. Donald was family and faith, not

the prospects of money, and she was grateful for the smallest of blessings. "We didn't meet until the trial, but Morris and I would talk on the phone," Mrs. Donald recalled. "He'd say, 'You still ready to go through with this?' And he did everything possible—he sent $35, $50 every few weeks. He helped when we needed it."

Natural Consequences

FOUR DAYS AFTER Dees filed his lawsuit, liberal talk-show host Alan Berg was shot to death as he drove his Volkswagen into the driveway of his Denver town house. In Montgomery, Dees and the staff at SPLC wondered if this was the start of an ominous new trend of domestic terrorism.

Dees could not give in to whatever fear he might have felt, and he carried his Beretta with him when he drove down to Mobile to begin a series of depositions. He was a hands-on attorney, and he did not even think of delegating much of the work on this case to other lawyers.

Dees's one great faith was in the law, and he was proud to be part of it. He loved the way it worked, with each side presenting its case as best it could, and then the jury or judge deciding who had told the truth or more of the truth. This was the most important case he had ever filed, and he expected that Shelton's lawyer, John Mays, would be dogging him at every step.

Dees made sure to inform Mays about the time and place of the depositions. The defense attorney attended only Shelton's deposition. It made it easier for Dees not to have the defense attorney poking into everything, but he nonetheless thought it was shoddy, lazy legal work. Mays said later that Shelton did not have the money to pay him to be there. The UKA could have mortgaged its headquarters, and clearly Shelton and Mays decided they did not need a major legal presence in what they considered an aggravating, foolish lawsuit.

Shelton attended a number of the depositions on his own. For the first one, the Imperial Wizard drove from Tuscaloosa and sat across from former UKA member Teddy Kyzar in a courtroom at the Mobile Federal Courthouse.

If Knowles and Henry had sufficiently trusted Kyzar he likely would have gone along when they murdered Michael Donald. But he had stayed home and because he had spoken to FBI agent Bodman about the blood on Tiger Knowles's clothes, Dees considered him a hero.

But Kyzar and his Klan colleagues gave almost no thought to what they did, and that made it even more frightening. The young man was good when others were good and bad when others were bad, but he had more fun being bad. He had gone out beating up African Americans and slashing their tires the way someone else might go bowling.

Whenever possible, Dees liked to take his depositions at federal courthouses. If there were no trials going on, a courtroom was generally made available. He thought the setting gave his questioning the gravitas of a grand jury.

As Kyzar sat in the witness chair, he told Dees how a few months after the murder, he had headed out with Henry and Denise Hays and William O'Connor to the Ramada Inn at the airport. On weekday evenings between eight and nine, for the one-dollar admission, you could drink as much as you wanted. When a black man had asked a white woman to dance, their little group looked on in disbelief.

"We were all mad," Kyzar told Dees. "I had done drank about sixty, seventy drinks. Henry wrote a note on a piece of paper and wanted me to give it to the girl: 'The Ku Klux Klan wants to know how you like blanking and loving with this nigger.' I followed the people out. I tapped on the window and said, 'Hey, this guy in here wanted me to give you this note.' She rolled down the window. She said, 'Thank you.' And when she rolled it up, I stepped up there and cut the front tire. Then I stepped back and cut the back tire."

The Klan was less a militant militia of white supremacist storm troopers than it was a motley, disparate assembly of marginal men. America had begun churning out a new breed of working-class man. For the most part, they were not connected to unions, churches, or social organizations. They didn't have much of a past to remember nor much of a future to anticipate. They were easily led. They had little to lose and little to gain. They gave scarcely any thought to what they were doing.

Shelton listened to Kyzar's testimony in disbelief. This was not the Klan he had spent decades building, but a bunch of drunken rowdies picking fights at a bar. When it was Shelton's opportunity to pose a question, he asked: "Have you ever heard anyone say that Robert Shelton advocates going out and hanging black people, burning crosses, tire slashing?"

"No, sir," said Kyzar.

"It's a pretty well-known policy of the Klan there's no drink; is that correct?"

"Yes, sir."

For Dees it was a sobering thought that there were men like Kyzar out there, looking for something to do and with little thought of the possible consequences. It was a reason to be cautious. Dees had not come bursting into Mobile shouting that he had arrived, but people knew he was there and what he was doing.

"When Morris Dees got to town and started speaking things as they were, we became afraid for him," says Donald's older sister Cynthia Donald Hamilton. "Our phone started to ring. We started getting death threats. When the ball got to rolling, they really began to put the pressure on."

A Book of Prophecy

SOON AFTER DEES got back to Montgomery one day in August 1984, a man showed up at the SPLC with a two-person camera crew saying he wanted to interview the SPLC cofounder. The visitor was Louis Beam, the Grand Dragon of the Texas Knights of the Ku Klux Klan, and a man who had threatened to kill Dees. The three men were shown out, but their intrusion showed just how vulnerable the SPLC's offices were.

Dees approved installing a security system, but he did not think much more of the incident until about a month later when he learned both from a Klan informant and the FBI that his life was seriously at risk. Although the FBI could not be more specific, the potential assassins were members of The Order, the right-wing terrorists who had killed the acerbic talk-show host Alan Berg.

The white supremacist group, formed in the state of Washington, had taken the right-wing dystopian novel *The Turner Diaries* as the literal truth. In its pages, the good white Christian people of America revolt against the Jewish-black tyranny by first assassinating the most malevolent of their oppressors. Turning prophecy into twisted reality, the militants of The Order had robbed several armored trucks, including one in California that netted $3.6 million, to finance their future operations.

The white nationalist terrorists felt they had done well in killing Berg and getting him off the air for good. Next on their target list was Morris Dees. In 1983, the civil rights lawyer had gone after Louis Beam, whose paramilitary force had been harassing Vietnamese-born fishermen in Galveston Bay. The SPLC lawsuit destroyed Beam's organization and drove him out of Texas, where he had connected with members of The Order and convinced them that Dees deserved to die.

The Order's leader, Robert Mathews, told his followers he was establishing a cell dedicated to taking out Dees. "We've gathered good intelligence on him," Mathews said. "We're going to kidnap him and then we'll torture him and get as much information out of him as we can, and when we have that, we'll kill him, and bury him and pour lye over him."

There was another potential threat that Dees would not learn about until later. At a monthly statewide UKA meeting, Robert Shelton said that Dees "was a type of guy we did not need." No court would indict Shelton for making such a vague statement, but in the euphemistic language of the Klan, he was suggesting to the impressionable that the SPLC cofounder should be eliminated.

Dees got on his motorcycle and went for a long ride on the country roads he had known since he was a boy. He hit eighty miles an hour, ninety miles an hour, a hundred miles an hour. As he drove back to Montgomery, he knew he wouldn't be enjoying this ride again for a while—at least not alone.

Dees, who treasured the privacy that allowed him to do his own thing his own way, reluctantly agreed that he would have to have a security team protecting him. There would be guards at his house, airtight security at the SPLC, and security around him wherever he went. It would cost about twenty thousand dollars a month and would be the SPLC's single largest expense.

A few weeks later Dees drove back to Mobile for the pretrial hearings in the civil lawsuit. As he stepped into an elevator with his security team at the Federal Courthouse Shelton and his lawyer, Mays, pushed in alongside them. Sitting in on the deposition with Kyzar, Shelton had seen what he considered a new, troubling Dees.

"I thought we were friends," said Shelton. He had talked to Dees as recently as a few months previously when Dees had asked his help in trying to destroy one of his Klan rivals. The Imperial Wizard had turned the lawyer down, but Shelton had been startled that Dees would attack him in a lawsuit.

"You know you really betrayed us," Shelton said. "Why did you want to do this? I thought you were with us."

Shelton had done what people often did with the gregarious lawyer, mistaking Dees's friendliness for friendship.

"I don't know where you got that idea, Bobby," Dees replied. "I did what I had to do, buddy. All I can say is good luck."

"You know you haven't got a chance against us," Mays said, his voice rising. "Why have you got us in this case?"

"Well, you know I represent the NAACP," Dees said. "I have to go with it and give it a shot. And you know, you may be right."

Dees seemed to be saying that he had included the UKA in the lawsuit to please his black patrons, but that he knew the case was likely going nowhere. That was just what Dees wanted Shelton and Mays to think, even further minimizing their concern about the civil lawsuit.

The courtroom was like most of those in which Dees had tried cases, largely empty of anyone but the principals and a few observers. A few rows away from the Donalds sat the Hays family. Bennie had drawn every one of them into this drama. His son Henry would not be sitting on death row if his father had not importuned him to join the Klan and then talked to him that evening after the Klavern meeting. Frank Cox would not be sitting in this courtroom as part of the civil lawsuit if he had not joined Klavern 900 to please Bennie. And Opal Hays would not have been criminally indicted for her alleged role in helping her husband burn down their house to get the money to pay Henry's defense lawyer.

Despite all that, Bennie felt that he was the one who had been abused. As he saw it, he might go to prison for the rest of his life for helping his son pay for his defense. And if those weren't enough bad things on his plate, he felt he had been dragged wrongly into this lawsuit.

Henry was no longer the only family member who realized how evil Bennie was. Gail and Frank Cox were also stunned at what his malevolence had done to their lives.

Although Dees thought of Bennie as a murderer, he saw no reason to turn the ex-Klan leader even further against him, so he put out a hand to the Klan leader, who refused to shake it. "Mr. Hays," Dees said, withdrawing his hand, "I'm sorry about your son being on death row. I've got problems with the death penalty. I've got kids of my own. I know how you must feel. It must really be hard on you folks."

Although he may have seemed unfriendly, Bennie was looking for some kind of signal that Dees wanted to do business with him, and the thwarted handshake served perfectly. He was infuriated at Shelton for not helping to fund his son's defense and the Klan's lawyer, John Mays, for refusing to represent him.

Mays had told Bennie it would be a conflict of interest to represent him here. The defense attorney had other reasons for avoiding the former Klan leader. Mays thought one of the biggest mistakes the Imperial Wizard had ever made was not throwing Bennie out of the UKA.

"Bennie was one of the most truly evil people that I've ever come across," says Mays. "Even in my criminal law practice, I've had few people I've represented who you could say basically were born without a conscience. Bennie Hays had no conscience. None."

Soon after Dees got back to Montgomery, he received a letter from Bennie. "You talked very nice to me and my wife," the former Klan leader wrote. "Much different than I expected after being told about you."

"I have a lot of helpful information," he told Dees. "I will be glad to work out any deal with you and get my life straigthen [sic] out."

Bennie included the original 1973 Klavern 900 charter signed by Shelton as "his lordship." This was a crucial document, since it proved that the Theodore Klavern operated under the authority and oversight of the national headquarters. By sending the document, Bennie made it clear to Dees that he wanted to harm Shelton and Mays, even if it meant breaking his Klan oath.

"As You Lie, You Forget"

AS DEES DROVE with Bill Stanton out to Bennie's home in Theodore, he left his security team behind, relying on the Beretta stuck beneath his coat. Bennie was about to go on trial in a federal courtroom charged with setting his house on fire for the insurance money. Dees figured he better get down to meet with the ex-Klan leader before he was likely sent off to prison.

Out in front of Bennie's place on a country road stood a twenty-five-foot-tall iron cross. Dees imagined what it must have looked like when on special occasions Klansmen wrapped the metal in diesel-fuel-soaked rags and set the cross on fire.

All that was left of Bennie's house were ashes and the foundation, surrounded by oak trees and Spanish moss. Dees pointed out to Stanton the tin shed where after a Klavern meeting the lynching had been conceived. It had hardly been used since the murder and appeared abandoned. Near the shed stood a single-wide mobile home that Bennie and Opal Hays now called home.

After Bennie greeted them with brisk familiarity and invited them inside, Dees asked to use the bathroom. He was worried that there might have been someone hidden away ready to come out and attack them, and he looked around quickly. Then he went into the bathroom, flushed the toilet with the door open so the sound reverberated through the trailer, and hurried out.

Everything in this trailer looked like it would fall apart in a few months. As he walked back into the kitchen, Dees started feeling sorry for Bennie and especially for Opal, his beleaguered wife. But then he caught himself remembering he was meeting with a man who probably directed his youngest son to lynch a black man.

When Dees reached the kitchen, he saw Bennie had placed a long cardboard box full of Klan documents on the Formica kitchen table. The former Klan leader wanted to bargain the contents in exchange for legal help for his son and also to get himself out of Dees's lawsuit.

Bennie said that Shelton had broken a promise to help in Henry's defense. As far as he knew, Knowles or the Communists had strangled Donald, but it wasn't Henry.

"Can you get my son out of this murder thing?" Bennie asked.

"Mr. Hays, you know I have no control over that because he's been convicted, and you got a lawyer, and you're going to appeal," Dees said.

"What would it take to let me out of your lawsuit?" Bennie asked, looking at the box of documents.

"I don't know, Mr. Hays. We'll have to talk some before I can answer that question."

Bennie let Dees spend a few minutes rummaging through the box. Dees knew that the Klan leader was violating his secret oath by letting him look through the many pages.

"Why don't you let me take it, make some copies, and get it back to you in a day?"

"No, sir," Bennie said, pulling the box away from him. "Can't have it unless you cut me a deal and guarantee me something here."

"Now don't you destroy them, Mr. Hays," Dees said. "They're gonna be real valuable and benefit you in this lawsuit."

Dees hoped that wasn't the truth. Instead, he wanted to use them against Bennie and his Klan colleagues in the civil lawsuit.

As Dees left, he made sure Bennie understood that he would have to make the next move.

"Call me if you want," he said.

TWO WEEKS AFTER his meeting, Dees drove back down to Mobile to take another series of depositions. In the days that Dees had been away from Mobile, Bennie and Opal had been convicted of arson in a federal courtroom. During the trial, even though his freedom was at stake, Bennie had not been able to control his overweening rage. At one point he had become so angry at Assistant U.S. Attorney E. T. Rolison's cross-examination that he said, "As you lie, you forget."

And that wasn't the end of his anger. When he left after hearing the verdict, Bennie became so incensed at reporters and cameramen who kept following him, asking questions, that he took his cane with both hands, raised it above his head, and struck away at the journalists, flailing at the air.

The court sentenced Bennie to three years in prison, revoked his bail, and ordered him to the Mobile County Metro Jail to await transportation to a federal prison. That was where Dees went to take his deposition.

Bennie sat on one end of his cot in his tiny cell, his steel cane next to him. Dees sat on the other end. Dees had been dreaming of this deposition since the day he had seen Bennie during his son's murder trial. He had watched him on the witness stand get angry over nothing, and the lawyer knew it was a fool's game to rev Bennie up. That was the easiest thing to do. The hard thing was to seem so empathic and understanding that the former Klan leader might say something useful.

At 2:00 P.M., Dees nodded to the court reporter who sat with them that they should begin the deposition.

"You own your home there [in Theodore]," Dees asked, as much a statement as a question.

"Hell, no," Bennie replied curtly.

"What do you mean by that?" Dees asked.

"What do I mean by that?" he shouted. "I'm having to give every goddamn thing I've got for lawyer fees. I can't even understand why in the hell this is going on!"

Despite beginning with the most benign and gentle of questions, Bennie was already fuming with rage. Dees decided he would try to bring down his anger by pretending he was ignorant and needed Bennie's expertise.

"When I wrote up the complaint in this case, I didn't know as much as I do today about the Klan."

"Well, that's because you've dealt with the goddamn liars and thieves out there that has finked on decent people, who has costed me every goddamn thing I got. . . . My God damn life history back yonder, I'm going to write a book, if I last long enough!"

Bennie said nothing that implicated him in any crime, and he did everything he could to destroy the reputations of those he considered his enemies.

Dees asked, "Did you make any comments when you saw the man hanging by the neck, 'That's a pretty sight'?"

"The one that told you it is a lying son of a bitch," Bennie stormed. "And I'd like to see him face-to-face."

When Dees ended the deposition, he did not tell the ex-Klan leader that he was hurrying off to depose his wife, who had been given probation for her role in the arson. A few days earlier, Stanton had knocked on Opal's door to hand her a subpoena for the documents Dees and Stanton had seen at their house trailer. In forcing her to give up the material, Dees was double-crossing Bennie, who considered the box of files his only leverage.

Dees worried that if Opal spoke to her husband, he would tell her to burn the box or bury it somewhere. That's why he included a note in the letter to Opal telling her that if she got rid of the documents, she would be guilty of a serious crime, destroying evidence in a federal case.

When Dees walked into Room 301 at the United States Courthouse at 3:35 P.M., he saw a tiny woman sitting next to a big box, and he was immensely relieved. He figured that Bennie's wife would have little to say about the murder. So after a few rudimentary questions, he moved on to ask Opal about each document, thereby entering it into the official court record.

The lawyer took out copies of the UKA monthly newspaper, *Fiery Cross*, but he also pulled out documents that no one outside the UKA had ever seen. These included *An Introduction to the United Klans of America*; *The Principals* [sic] *of the United Klan*; *The Miracle of the White Race*; *The Klan in Action Constitution*, and *The Seven Symbols of the Klan*, plus in a separate file Bennie's telephone records.

Dees went on to do another deposition in Mobile that day with Thaddeus Betancourt. Red knew he was no saint. He had been convicted for robbery a few years back. He had served some time, and he was fine with that, but as far as he was concerned, he wasn't a bad guy, and it was not right that he was being hauled into this mess. All he had done was to read an article at the Klavern meeting about the murder of a Birmingham police officer by a black bank robbery. He hadn't called out for the lynching of a black man, and he hadn't been with Tiger and Henry when they killed Michael Donald. Betancourt felt he had suffered enough. His wife had left him. He was out of work and living in his father's old place in the country. Joining the Klan was the worst thing that ever happened to him, and it wasn't going away.

"For what reason did you get out of the Klan?" Dees asked.

"Well, my reason for getting out was basically the fact that I got pulled into this. And I don't know anything about it. Somebody just dropped my name. And here I am. And I don't like that, me being implicated in something I don't know nothing about."

AS SOON AS Dees got back to Montgomery, he started going through the Klan documents. He didn't find anything specifically about Shelton, but the records provided the first crucial argument in the civil lawsuit. They showed indisputably that the UKA had a mock military structure in which each member took orders from his superior. There was the original charter for Klavern 900 and checks written by the Mobile Klavern to the national organization.

As Dees read through the pages, he felt he was reliving the earliest years of the Klan, which had been founded by six prominent Confederate veterans in 1865. To create mystery about the organization, they had invented quasi-mystical language and strange, unique rituals. Much of that old rhetoric remained in the UKA documents, but there was nothing that mentioned violence, the threat of violence, or retribution against black citizens.

Dees would not be able to invoke these documents to tell what he considered the true history of the United Klans of America. He would have to find witnesses who would say that Shelton fomented them to commit acts of violence, and the civil rights lawyer knew that would be extremely hard to do.

Intruders in the Night

ON THE NIGHT of December 3, 1984, Dees's perimeter guards came upon two men moving through the pasture grass on his 210-acre ranch. They ran off before being challenged. No one was sure who they were or what they wanted, but it was unsettling enough that many people would have moved into town to an apartment or gated community that was easier to patrol.

Thirteen days later, Dees was out at his rambling ranch-style home with his fourteen-year-old daughter, Ellie, preparing for Christmas. There may not have been any snow, but as far as he was concerned, there was nothing like an Alabama country Christmas. It wasn't the food or gifts from Santa Claus that mattered, but the family, and much of that was gone. He had buried his father and grandparents long ago. His uncles had always been there at Grandma's, but they were embarrassed that he carried their name and wanted nothing more to do with him. And that was not the worst reason he would have not much of a family Christmas.

In 1979, Maureene filed for divorce. Both her initial complaint and Dees's countercomplaint mentioned incompatibility, and the depositions contained stunning allegations of infidelity. Maureene's charges became public, starting a whispering campaign against her estranged husband that is still made much of today by Dees's critics. He had his own stories to tell about his wife and disputed much of what she said, but he never defended himself. He felt the divorce had hurt Ellie enough, and he wasn't about to make it any worse. He appeared not to give a damn what people thought. For a decade, half the people he met while walking the streets of Montgomery disdained him. What did it matter if a few more joined the club?

But Dees did care about giving Ellie the best Christmas he could, and trimming the Christmas tree that evening in December 1984, eleven days before the holiday, was the beginning. Only one other person besides his daughter was in his house, a security guard, E. T. Davis, who held a submachine gun as he wandered among the rooms. There had been yet another warning from the FBI, and Davis kept looking out into the darkness.

Unfazed, Dees went out and chopped down a cedar tree, dragged it into the living room, and set it up. Then he went and found the box of Christmas tree ornaments. As father and daughter sorted through the decorations, Ellie pulled out a white lace angel that had always graced the top of the family tree.

"Think you'll be able to get this on top?" she asked.

"Always have," he said. "If not—"

"Jesus Christ, there's someone out here!" said the outside guard on Davis's radio. *"Do you read me? There's someone on the property."*

"What are you saying?" Davis asked urgently.

"Two men in camouflage. Got AK-47s or some kind of assault rifles."

Dees grabbed his Beretta, and Ellie picked up the .22 pistol her father had taught her how to use. Then Davis pushed Dees and his daughter into the pantry, which served as a safe room, shut the door and stood outside, protecting them.

The pantry was scarcely larger than a closet. Ellie sat on the floor in her father's lap, holding on to him. They listened on the radio as the outside guard pursued the intruders, who managed to get away.

Dees felt his daughter trembling. "First, they burn down your law office, now they come after you," she said crying. "Why do you do the cases you do, Daddy? Why can't you practice law like anybody else?"

"Blood Will Flow"

DEES HAD BEEN relieved when on December 8, 1984, Robert Mathews, the founder of The Order, died in a shootout with police on Whidbey Island, Washington. In the following months police arrested the other known members of the neo-Nazi organization, and after conviction, the federal courts sentenced them to long terms in prison. No one ever discovered the identity of the intruders to Dees's farm, but the FBI found a camouflage cloth that the two men had probably dropped as they fled across the fields, and that was further evidence to Dees that he and his daughter could have been killed that night.

It disturbed Dees that when one of the terrorists, Gary Lee Yarbrough, was sentenced, he vowed that the fight would go on. "Blood will flow and it grieves me," he said. Yarbrough and his kind may have been a minuscule fringe, but all it took was one determined person to take him out. Dees, meanwhile, lived as normally as he could with a security person or two almost always around.

The security people were with Dees when he drove down to Mobile in March 1985 to attend the trial of Frank Cox. Due partly to the lawyer's prodding, District Attorney Chris Galanos had charged Cox with being part of a conspiracy in the death of Michael Donald. James Knowles was the crucial witness in the criminal trial, and while Knowles was in the city, Dees sat down with him for a deposition in the civil lawsuit.

Dees sought to have Knowles implicate Bennie Hays, Frank Cox, and the others in a murderous conspiracy. He was convinced that in previous testimony, Knowles had been protecting his fellow conspirators, but Dees believed there was no reason for the killer to do that any longer. He was hoping to bring Knowles to testify at the civil trial, but that was far from certain, and this deposition might prove his only occasion to take his testimony. Shelton was present, listening to every word.

Dees was only a few minutes into the deposition when he saw that on most crucial issues, Knowles was not moving beyond what he had testified to before. He said he had no recollections of Bennie directing the two young men to kill a black man or even being involved in a discussion of the crime. He spoke about the murder without emotion, as if this matter had nothing to do with him.

"Mr. Knowles, I assume it's not the general custom of—or maybe it is—of your Klan organization to just every once in a while to hang a black person?" he asked in a mocking tone.

"No," Knowles said.

"And it wasn't a discussion about handing lollipops out in a black neighborhood, was it?" Dees asked.

"No, it wasn't. A nigger was going to be hung that night, regardless, if he could be found and it was convenient."

As Dees grew frustrated with Knowles, he tried to push him to say what the lawyer wanted him to say, but he was up against a resolute witness. Despite his bland demeanor, Knowles was immovable and firm in his recollections. As he had tried unsuccessfully to save Henry from a death sentence, so was he trying to say nothing that would lead to more legal problems for Bennie or Cox.

When it was Shelton's turn to question the witness, he asked Knowles only about the few issues that concerned the Imperial Wizard. He had Knowles confirm that Shelton had never advocated violence and that the murder plot had been hatched *after* the Klavern meeting, not *during* the proceedings.

Dees attended most of the Cox trial. He was there the day Knowles walked into the courtroom accompanied by three federal marshals. Although the young convict held back in the way he had in the deposition, Dees felt the evidence was strong enough to convict Cox. But because D.A. Galanos had filed the complaint after the three-year statute of limitations, Cox walked out of court a free man.

The D.A. had royally messed up again, but it would not be double jeopardy to charge Cox directly with the murder, and Dees believed Bennie should be indicted along with him.

IN APRIL 1985, Dees and Bill Stanton, accompanied by the SPLC security chief Danny Welch, drove an hour north to Tuscaloosa to depose Shelton. As they reached downtown and walked into the UKA offices, Dees recalled as a college student being on this same street, selling ads to businesses; he had seen a sign above a drugstore for the upstairs office of the Alabama Ku Klux Klan. He was so intrigued that he walked upstairs. No one was there, but he could tell they were laying out the Klan newspaper. Dees walked back downstairs, thinking that in Tuscaloosa the Klan presence was as ordinary and accepted as a dentist's or insurance office.

All these years later, it seemed much the same. Dees greeted Shelton as an old acquaintance without any animus. Dees believed that Shelton was behind many of the most violent white supremacist actions of the time, and was an evil man, but Dees felt no personal hostility toward the Klan leader. Dees just was not a hater. He had a lawyer's way of shrugging off the worst kinds of human conduct and dealing with it as nothing notable of comment or disdain.

Shelton could take the Fifth Amendment rather than saying things that might result in criminal charges, but other than that he was legally obligated to answer Dees' questions. He had to be careful what he said for a deposition was as binding as sworn courtroom testimony.

Shelton and his lawyer, Mays, probably expected that Dees had come here to try to provoke the Klan leader into admitting he had exhorted the members into acts of fatal violence. Dees had, however, a narrow, specific agenda and wasn't going to squander his time grandstanding by asking Shelton a series of belligerent questions.

Dees spent most of his time using the documents that had been in Bennie's house to get Shelton to detail the structure and legal status of the UKA. Much of this would have fascinated only a forensic accountant, but Dees wasn't here to create a theatrical drama. He was gathering information that one day in a Mobile courtroom would help him win a victory for Mrs. Donald and her murdered son.

Shelton and Mays treated the deposition as if the whole tedious, unnecessary business was beneath them. Dees behaved as if everything mattered. He operated as if all he had to do was get the details right and the big things would come.

Dees and his colleagues worked obsessively over every detail of the lawsuit. The lawyer's associates had hunted down every document that might help them. Stanton had flown up to New York and gone through the files at the Anti-Defamation League. The Jewish organization closely monitored the Klan, and Stanton found year after year of the *Fiery Cross*, the official UKA monthly publication, on microfilm—which he printed and brought back to Montgomery. When Dees showed a pile of the papers to Shelton and Mays, they did not bother looking at them but agreed that they could be exhibits in the civil lawsuit. Dees gave no indication that by their refusing to look at the papers, he had placed a bomb that he would set off in the Mobile courtroom in front of Shelton.

When Dees finished with questions about the UKA structure, he asked Shelton about various Klan documents. Shelton replied, "I learned my lesson about that and I destroyed them."

Despite his full-time role as leader of the UKA, Shelton said he could not recall whether certain men who had been exposed as bombers, murderers, and violent provocateurs were members of the UKA, even though some of them had been among his closest Klan associates. Nor could he recollect ever having met James Knowles, although he had named the teenager a Klan state officer. Shelton said he wasn't sure if the three men convicted of violating civil rights in the murder of Viola Liuzzo were Klansmen, even though he had helped to raise several hundred thousand dollars to defend the UKA members.

Dees rankled Shelton by saying there was someone else who could give him the crucial information he was seeking. Referring to the FBI's undercover informant, Dees said, "We can take Mr. Rowe's deposition, if we can find him."

No one knew more about Shelton's role in UKA actions during the first half of the 1960s than did Gary Thomas Rowe Jr. The informer was in the Federal Witness Protection Program living under an assumed name in a secret location. Shelton and Mays thought it impossible that he would surface to testify in a deposition for Morris Dees.

"They won't even tell you where he is," Mays said, spitting the words out. "They won't even let you near him."

"I think we may have a little better luck," Dees said softly. He asked another question or two on inconsequential subjects to set the hook before returning to what truly mattered.

"The deposition of Mr. Gary Thomas Rowe is going to be held in Montgomery, Alabama, on the twenty-seventh at ten o'clock," Dees said pronouncing each detail with pleasure.

"I can't be there," Mays said. "I will be overseas."

Shelton and Mays rustled with uncertainty and apprehension. They saw Rowe as a turncoat and a pathological liar who had fired the bullet that killed Viola Liuzzo. They worried that he might say almost anything to implicate Shelton in the murder of Michael Donald or other violent actions. It was a frightening prospect, and it appeared there was nothing they could do to prevent it.

Shots in the Night

IN HIS KLAN days, Rowe had been handsome enough to have an easy time following the FBI dictates to sleep with Klan wives and see what he could learn from them. But when Rowe walked into the modest headquarters of the SPLC on April 27, 1985, his gut hung out of his brown khakis and he was a ringer for the country sheriff in *Smokey and the Bandit*.

During Dees's first phone call with Rowe, he realized he was talking to a man with an enormous ego. He played to Rowe's vanity, telling him how crucial he was to the case. "You're the only one who can do it, Tommy," Dees said, kneading Rowe's ego. "You'll be the star of the show."

Neither Shelton nor his lawyer was coming to the deposition. When Dees had called Mays offering to reschedule, the Klan lawyer said, "I won't sit in the same fucking room with that turncoat son of a bitch." Shelton's sentiments were similar.

Dees treated Rowe like a good ole boy with whom he could hang out drinking beer and playing pool, but he despised the informer. Lots of people believed Rowe had instigated many of the Klan acts of violence and then squealed on his comrades. In 1978, the political atmosphere in Alabama had changed so much that Rowe was indicted for the 1965 murder of Viola Liuzzo. He might well have been found guilty, but his lawyer successfully argued that the federal government had granted Rowe immunity from prosecution for testifying against his three Klan colleagues, and the case was thrown out.

Dees suspected that Rowe probably did pull the trigger, but he wasn't going to ask anything about that. For Dees's current purpose, it didn't matter if it was true or not, and to ask about it would only rile Rowe up. He had learned long ago that justice wasn't about a search for the whole truth, but only the truth that was useful at the time.

Dees had a narrow, focused agenda in deposing Rowe. He took him from event to event, getting Rowe to say that Shelton had given orders that led to various acts of violence. No one else had been there for all these meetings. It was unique material, and when Dees got all that he needed he ended the deposition. He flattered Rowe a little more, telling him once again that he would be the trial's star witness.

Despite what he said, Dees wasn't about to bring Rowe into the courtroom where Mays would probably have suggested that he had fired the shots that killed Liuzzo, and the trial would then become a circus of wild accusations. Rowe lived more than a hundred miles from the Mobile Federal Courthouse. That meant he could not be subpoenaed to appear at the trial. Dees would be able to read the deposition to the jury, and Mays would have to sit there, not able to do a thing about it.

Rowe's deposition was important because it would help Dees tell a story, and that was his specialty in the courtroom. He used the witnesses as building blocks, and not five witnesses tripping over each other's tales when one would do. In the end, he wanted to get up before that jury and tell a strong, simple, emotive story, and he felt he was on his way to doing just that.

AS PUMPED AS Dees was about the Rowe and Shelton depositions and the way the lawsuit was going, he was in an unsettled mood. The SPLC had just moved into its glistening new headquarters, an ultramodern glass and steel building that hovered above the Dexter Avenue Baptist Church and seemed an intruder in a neighborhood of more traditional buildings.

Dees had a sense of the growing national significance of the SPLC, and he wanted a new headquarters reflecting that reality. "The building design establishes a corporate image to reflect the national importance of the Southern Poverty Law Center" a brochure announced. That was why many on the legal staff were not happy. They saw him dumping them into an alienating new structure while at the same time he moved the SPLC away from its original emphasis on civil rights lawsuits and into a strange vendetta against the remnants of the Klan.

The legal team was angry that while they were working diligently on civil rights cases, Dees was devoting more and more energy and resources to what they considered his flamboyant, obsessive campaign against the Klan. They had come south to work at a public interest law firm and not at a virtual fortress manned by a well-trained security force quartered in a separate guardhouse.

They felt that the Klan was a dying force and the SPLC should focus on the less dramatic but more important work they were doing. They worried that Dees's obsession with the Klan was dangerous and destructive and would bring no good to him or the SPLC.

But Dees had every reason to believe the Klan and other white supremacist organizations were alive and dangerous. The SPLC offices had been firebombed, and likely assassins had come looking for him. There were not as many ultra-right-wing white supremicists as there had been during the 1960s, but it had never been about numbers. There were violent, dangerous men out there, and they were ready and able to act.

Dees was prepared to continue pursuing most of the cases that consumed his five-person legal staff, but he was not about to back off from fighting the Klan and other white supremacist groups. The SPLC was *his*. He had founded it. He had nurtured it. He had raised tens of millions of dollars to support it. He had the board on his side along with thousands of donors.

The young lawyers saw Dees as a martinet willfully driving the SPLC away from its noble original goals. He believed he had been a congenial, understanding leader, but the lawyers had pushed far beyond where they had any right to push and were dismissive of him and all he had done. There was no way they could continue working together. In the end, in a dramatic and telling moment, the entire legal team quit and left Montgomery for good.

Other fine young lawyers welcomed the opportunity to work at the SPLC, but there was no longer quite the same easy cama- raderie, trust, and openness there had been in the early years.

DEES PLUNGED BACK into the civil lawsuit with renewed energy. There was one enormous hole: he had no compelling evidence that demonstrated the Klan's consistent pattern of violence.

Randy Ward provided an opportunity to tell that part of the story. The twenty-one-year-old Ward had joined the UKA Klavern in Childersburg, Alabama, in 1978. He was named the Exalted Cyclops, the top leader of the Klavern. It was a high honor for a man of his youth who had so recently joined the Klavern. Ward envisioned himself one day becoming the Impe- rial Wizard, taking over when Shelton retired.

Ward led his Klan underlings into the night to shoot into the home of two local leaders of the NAACP who had been trying to get black men appointed to the police and fire departments and who were complaining about police brutality toward black citizens. When the FBI arrested the participants, Ward turned on the Klavern members he had once led into action.

Ward's testimony sent thirteen of them to prison, a staggering number for the small town and its surroundings in central Alabama. Almost everyone in Childersburg knew someone headed to a cell, and Ward was widely hated. The Feds led Ward out of town and put him in the Federal Witness Protection Program in a distant city.

To Dees it was a matter of little consequence that the key witnesses in a lawsuit to bring justice to Mrs. Donald were likely to be a convicted killer, James Knowles; a notorious informer, Thomas Rowe; and a Klan Klavern leader, Randy Ward, who bought his own freedom by selling out his former colleagues whom he had led to commit the very acts that had sent them away to prison. It was not the most inspiring scenario, but Dees gave it no regard.

Dees figured it would take six months to crack the federal bureaucracy and have a real shot at finding out where Ward was living, but the trial was coming up and he couldn't wait that long. Joe Roy led the team that provided security for the SPLC. Dees asked the former Montgomery police detective if he could track down Ward.

After spending several days going through newspaper and courthouse records in Childersburg, Roy failed to find any links to even one of Ward's relatives. He was about to give up when he ran into an old detective friend who knew Ward's parents and told him they had moved about as far away from Childersburg as they could get and still be living in Alabama.

When Roy drove over to the house and knocked on the door, the couple was astounded and distraught that the former police officer had discovered them. They finally settled down enough to tell Roy their great fear was not for their own safety, but that some livid Klansman would take out their son. They were so nervous about anyone tracking their son down that they walked a half-mile down the road and called Ward from a pay phone. And when they went to visit Ward, they met him in a town away from his new home.

Roy talked to the elderly couple about James Knowles, Henry Hays, and the lynching of Michael Donald, and even as he did so, he recognized a commonality between Knowles and their son Randy. They were both brash, precocious, working-class fellows who had taken a wrong pathway that had ended in tragedy. And now, Roy told them, out of this darkness could come a chance to end the organization that had brought young Randy such harm and to bring Mrs. Donald a modicum of justice.

Roy was a deeply religious Catholic. He asked the Wards if they would like to pray. They said yes, and they prayed for God's wisdom that Randy would do what was right. When Roy left that day, he felt he had done all he could do. A couple of weeks later, Ward called Roy, and the two talked for about twenty minutes.

"I redeemed myself testifying about the Klan," Ward declared.

"No, you didn't redeem yourself, Randy," Roy said. "You testified because you had to. This time you'll truly redeem yourself, and you'll help others from getting caught the way you did."

A few days later, Henry Froshin, the former assistant United States attorney who had convicted the Childersburg Klansmen largely on Ward's testimony, called Dees. Froshin said that Ward had agreed to meet with Dees in the former prosecutor's law office. Dees drove with Roy to Birmingham, where Froshin introduced him to Ward.

Ward wore work boots, jeans, and a flannel shirt. He had work-worn hands that looked as if they belonged on a far older man, and grease was embedded under his fingernails. Roy looked at those raw hands, the dirty nails, and the grimy pants and thought, this is a blue-collar man with a good job, a person who made one serious mistake and will not make another.

To try to give him added rapport with Ward, Dees loosened his tie, took off his jacket, and rolled up his sleeves. Pulling out photographs of the lynching scene where Donald's body was found, Dees showed them to the former Klansman.

"Did you realize this stuff was going on?" Dees asked.

"No, sir," Ward said. "But I guess with Bobby Shelton at the top I'm not surprised."

After a few minutes, Dees could tell that Ward would make a great witness.

"Randy, I'd like you to come to the trial and testify for us."

"I'm afraid," Ward said, his face turning white. Dees had never heard a Klansman express fear so openly.

"Son, most people live and do very little for their fellow man," Dees said. "This is between you and your God. I'll be praying for you to make the right decision."

Dees didn't believe in God any longer, but he felt that saying this was something Ward would respond to favorably.

"I'll have to think about it," Ward said.

Dees didn't know where Ward was living, but the Federal Witness Protection Program required that it be at least three hundred miles away from his former home. Ward had been planning to take a bus to visit his parents for the weekend, who lived about fifty miles from Birmingham. Dees offered to rent him a car that he could leave at the Birmingham airport before flying back to his home.

Ward thought it was a generous gesture, but the rental-car forms would also give them Ward's home address. That way if Ward turned them down, they could show up at his home. But Ward called back first, saying he would testify.

CHOOSING WITNESSES FOR a trial was in some measure like auditioning actors for a play. Dees wanted James Knowles to be the star witness at the trial. But Dees had sat in the courtroom during Henry's criminal trial and heard Knowles give details about the gruesome murder without any emotion. Such uninvolved testimony might alienate a jury. What's more, he had told many different versions of the story, and a good attorney could exploit his seeming contradictions.

Yet the more Dees communicated with Knowles, the more he believed that this was no longer the amoral teenager who had killed without remorse. The previous year, Knowles had written to Dees talking "of some sort of settlement for Mrs. Donald. . . . I'm not wealthy but would still like to offer assistance to Mrs. Donald if and when I am released from incarceration." With letters like that, Dees believed that the young man was ready to play a crucial role in the trial.

Dees did not know where Knowles was imprisoned, but he learned that he had passed his high school equivalency exam and was taking college courses. Knowles had been incarcerated for almost four years. He would be eligible for parole after serving ten years, but sitting in his cell, he had decided he had already served long enough to pay for his crime. He wanted to get out, study for his B.A. and a law degree, and then seek a pardon so he could practice law.

Knowles believed his testimony in the civil lawsuit would let him walk out of prison for good. Although Dees says he promised nothing, Knowles was convinced that if he spoke well in that Mobile courtroom, both the SPLC and Mrs. Donald would support his early release.

Dees was worried about Cox's lawyer interrupting the flow of the trial by getting up in the trial and making all kinds of arguments and objections. So at the same time that he was pushing to have Cox indicted for murder, he went to Cox's attorney and made an offer. He said that no matter what the jury decided in the civil trial, he would agree to take a maximum of $1,000 from Cox. Having no idea of Dees's real motive, the attorney pounced on the offer.

Even though Henry Hays would not even say his own name at his deposition, Dees wanted to bring him to the trial as a witness, but the court refused. As Henry sat on death row, he was an almost forgotten part of the civil lawsuit and the lives of most of those involved.

Henry had made a life for himself at Holman Prison. Until he entered prison, he had tried to avoid having anything to do with black people, but they were in the majority on death row. In his first months in custody, the authorities kept him isolated from the black prisoners. Henry struck up an acquaintanceship with several of the condemned men. The first time he was let out on the yard for exercise, one black prisoner fell in behind him, and another in front, to protect him from brothers who might want to harm him. That was the beginning of a number of friendships that enriched Henry's life immeasurably in his years on the death row tier.

In his first months in prison, Henry had been fed up having to talk to his parents on visitors' day when all he wanted to do was to sweet-talk Janet Deem and even manage a kiss or two. But his love was long gone, and Bennie was out in Missouri, serving three years in prison, and Henry did not know if he would ever see his father again. At least he had his mother.

Almost everyone had left Opal. Her friends. Her church. Her money. Her faith. During the winter, she only heated one room in her trailer so she would have the money to fly out to Missouri to visit her husband. When she was home, she wrote him a letter every day.

Almost every week, Opal drove the hour out to Holman Prison to visit Henry. It was always the same. Sitting together on stools at a Formica table. Smoking cigarettes. Drinking Cokes from the machine. Introducing Mom to his friends, most of them black.

On May 15, 1985, Opal had just gotten back from Missouri, and she was feeling a little tired. She had become ever more important to her son, Henry's one link to the outer world. As always, she stayed in the death row visitors' room as long as she could with Henry, saying good-bye at the last possible moment. When he got up with the other prisoners to be strip-searched before going back to his cell, she got up too. As Henry was leaving, his mother fell to the floor and died of a stroke.

The End of an Era

IN 1982, GEORGE Wallace was still so hungry to stay at the center of things that the sixty-three-year-old politician ran successfully for a fourth term. For most of the decade since the assassination attempt, Wallace had masked his pain and had been able to go on and live a public life, but it was impossible any longer to hide how much he had deteriorated. His hearing was so bad his aides had to stand behind him shouting names into his ears.

"For weeks now he has been unable to function more than marginally as governor," the *Montgomery Advertiser* editorialized in March 1983. "While he is disabled and still in office, there is no one constitutionally qualified to substitute for him." His aides spent much of their time trying to keep the public from accepting this image of a broken, troubled leader.

Wallace took 100 milligrams of the antidepressant Desyrel (trazodone hydrochloride) three times a day and 5 milligrams of methadone four times daily, a narcotic and pain reliever often used to wean addicts off heroin. And on occasion, he saw a psychiatrist to deal with his depression.

During his first two years in office, Wallace spent fifty-one days in the hospital, and on many other days, he was unable to perform his job. Meanwhile, the administration was run as a private fiefdom. A bond issue totaling $400 million was handed out to cohorts like party favors.

Wallace had risen to power on racial issues, and wherever he spoke on his presidential campaigns, his audiences were full of people who feared or mistrusted black people. Now in the last years of his political career, he played the race card again, but in a different way.

Thanks largely to the 1965 Voting Rights Act that Wallace had fought against, black Alabamans had won the right to vote, and the day was coming when it would be impossible for a Democrat to win an election without their support. The governor had not even wanted black Alabamans to attend his first inauguration. Yet now, when he needed them, he went to Tuscaloosa and crowned a black woman the University of Alabama homecoming queen, and he appointed black officials throughout his administration.

In 1974, Wallace won reelection as governor for the third time with 25 percent of the black vote. In his fourth and final gubernatorial campaign in 1982, he received around 35 percent of the black vote in his victory.

Wallace sent out one of his new black appointees, Delores Pickett, to campaign for him among her people. "Forgiveness is in our Christian upbringing," she told her black audiences. "It's something that Martin Luther King taught us."

Black Alabamans were for the most part churchgoing people who were taught that redemption comes from forgiveness. They wanted to believe the governor had changed, and if he of all people had changed, then the world had changed.

As he sat in his wheelchair filled with pain, Wallace said he had found Jesus. But that faith never led him to face up publically to his long-held beliefs. He claimed his actions were driven by a belief in states' rights and that he had never felt prejudice toward black people. He might have taken the lynching of Michael Donald and the conviction of the two murderers as a moment to talk about the wrongfulness of so much he had said and how words led to deeds, but he remained silent.

Despite the limitations of his public apologies, in private Wallace was beginning to grasp that he shared moral responsibility for so many reprehensible acts. One evening during his final full year in office in 1986, one of his aides, Kenneth Mullinax, was over at the governor's mansion. Cigar smoke wafted down from an upstairs bedroom, and Mullinax went up to chat with Wallace.

"I have a lot of regrets," Wallace said, "and I really worry about my soul."

"But you're born again, Governor," Mullinax said.

"I flew all them runs over Tokyo dropping bombs, but that don't worry me none. It's my words. They kilt a lot of people. That's why I'm worried I'm going to hell."

Wallace had spoken the most provocative rhetoric. Then he had stood back and taken no responsibility for what his words led people to do. Now after all these years, he had come to an understanding of what power he truly had possessed, how profound his impact had been, and how tragic the results.

After Wallace's retirement in January 1987, Birmingham-born *New York Times* writer Howell Raines provided an epitaph for Wallace's four terms as governor in the newspaper's magazine. Raines wrote that Wallace had arrived in Montgomery vowing to build a true people's government; he left office in a capital that had become so corrupt that "one can hear a person's profession described as that of 'hereditary bagman.'" He had arrived promising to boost the poor out of their circumstances; he left with more than 20 percent of Alabamans living below the poverty line, 4 percent having no running water, and the highest taxes on the poor in America.

Wallace was so outraged by the article he had his aide Elvin Stanton write a letter to the former governor's lawyer, Maury D. Smith, asking him if he felt "that legal action is appropriate." Wallace never sued.

After leaving office, Wallace took a position raising money for Troy State University and spent a few hours each weekday in his office on Dexter Avenue, looking out on the capitol. He was alone. His third wife, country singer Lisa Taylor, had left him. Like his second wife, Cornelia, the young woman had married him for what he seemed to be, and she was royally disappointed when she learned what he was.

Wallace's hearing had continued to deteriorate, and his staff had arranged for a special telephone system. His assistant was supposed to listen in and then type in the words spoken by a caller on a screen set before the former governor, and he could respond appropriately. But it was so difficult he largely gave up having telephone conversations.

Wallace preferred to sit in his big den chair wearing headphones, listening to country music laments. One guest found him playing a Hank Williams ballad at full volume. It was a tune both he and Lurleen had loved, and Wallace was crying.

Sending a Signal

MORRIS DEES WALKED into courtroom number one at the Mobile Federal Courthouse, just before 9:00 A.M. on Tuesday morning, February 10, 1987, giving off an aura of confidence. Robert Shelton and his lawyer, John Mays, arrived soon after with shrugs of reluctance and forbearance.

Shelton wore a conservative gray suit. The fifty-eight-year-old Imperial Wizard looked like a senior lawyer passing through the courthouse corridors on important business. He knew that he had never suggested that anyone in Klavern 900 kill a black man, and he believed the jury would find for the UKA in *Beulah Mae Donald, as Executor of the Estate of Michael Donald, Deceased v. United Klans of America, et al.*

To Shelton, the extent to which this absurd, vindictive lawsuit had gotten was a perfect indication of how far things had fallen in America. A quarter century ago, Shelton had stood at the right hand of George Wallace as the fiery governor promised to build a white supremacist nation. That dream was gone, and in the Imperial Wizard's mind, so much else had deteriorated along with it.

The *New York Times* and *Playboy* no longer courted his opinions. His grandchildren were taunted at school because they were his kin. In his only other time in an Alabama courtroom, in 1961, his co-defendants included the police chiefs of Montgomery and Birmingham, powerful, well-respected men. This morning he was sitting beside what he considered low-life defendants who, he believed, disgraced everything a Klansman was supposed to be.

The other Klan defendants—Betancourt, Cox, Hays, O'Connor, Knowles, and Kyzar—took no pleasure at being lumped in with Shelton, whose organization had caused them such grief. They were a befuddled and frazzled group trying to defend themselves without lawyers. They did not have the money to pay much of any judgment against them, and they worried they might incur financial burdens that would wreak havoc on the remainder of their lives.

Bennie Hays had just been released from federal prison in Lexington, Kentucky, and he walked into the courtroom cradling his ubiquitous metal cane. His son-in-law, Frank Cox, was a tall, hulking presence, and possessed a certain panache and a contemptuous manner toward these proceedings. He could indulge in such feelings because, thanks to his lawyer, no matter what happened here this week, it would cost him no more than a thousand dollars.

Mrs. Donald had decided to attend the trial, and she had arrived with several of her children and other relatives. Before her son died, neighbors liked to be around her, hoping a bit of her joyous sense might rub off on them. But she rarely smiled any longer. She walked the measured steps of an old woman, but those steps were resolute, and she came into the courtroom with purpose. Wherever she walked, she had a daughter or another relative at her side.

Dees sat next to Cathy "Cat" Bennett, the most prominent jury-and-trial consultant in America. Bennett and Dees had been romantically involved for many years when she was young and single, and today she was still his close friend.

In 1986, doctors had told Bennett she had breast cancer that had metastasized; they said she probably had only a few years to live. When Dees asked Bennett to come to Mobile to help select a jury for the trial, she said yes and insisted that she would not accept a fee.

Two decades earlier, when one of the murderers of Viola Liuzzo was found not guilty in an Alabama courtroom, it was almost impossible to find a jury in the Deep South that would dare to rule against the Klan. These days Shelton could not have paraded Knowles and Henry around as heroes as he had with Liuzzo's killers, and Dees believed that the plaintiff could now get a fair jury. As assured as he and his colleagues were, they still worried that one unrepentant racist might find his or her way onto the jury to nullify the results. It was Bennett's job to see that this did not happen.

It took no longer than two hours to select a six-person jury plus two alternates from the fifty-five-person jury list. John Mays used his challenges largely to get rid of the eleven black potential jurors and make it an all-white jury. Bennett had Dees use the plaintiff's challenges to ensure that the jury was almost all women.

The presiding judge, Alex T. Howard Jr., was new to the bench. He had specialized in maritime law, concerning ships and shipping, and he was still learning some of the procedures in a civil lawsuit. As the judge looked out on the courtroom, he saw it was largely full, and he knew that the trial was receiving more publicity than any other Mobile legal proceeding had in a long time.

The judge set out to let everyone know who was ruling the courtroom, and it wasn't Morris Dees. Even before the trial formally began, Judge Howard called the lawyers and defendants into chambers to discuss several important matters.

"I read your brief carefully, and you have not satisfied me as to just what you need to show to tie in the United Klans," the judge told Dees.

This was the essence of Dees's case. As the judge's lecture continued, Dees thought of the two former SPLC lawyers, John Carroll and Stephen Ellmann, and how they had warned him that a judge would likely say just this and Dees would get nowhere with the case.

Judge Howard even criticized Dees's preparation of the brief. "Now if you want to cite a case to me, either quote from the case or tell me what that case is," he said. "Don't say: 'See so and so.' My law clerks have a lot to do. You should have done that for the court."

Judge Howard returned to what Dees hoped to prove in the courtroom: "You're going to have to show that an authorized agent of the United Klans conspired in some way to cause the death of Michael Donald."

"We do not have to prove that the Imperial Wizard himself approved it," Dees countered. "We can show other line officials, high-ranking officials, approved this and carried that out."

"I do want you to understand," the judge said, "that you've got to prove that the United Klans conspired."

If Judge Howard thought Dees had brought them here on a ludicrously exaggerated charge, the plaintiff would have a long day in court. After the plaintiff presented their case, the judge could say that Dees had set forth so little evidence he was granting the defendants a directed verdict. Even if the judge let the case go on, he could instruct the jury in such a way that they would almost certainly find for the defendants.

Dees was troubled that Shelton was the only defendant represented by an attorney. He had a story he wanted to tell and had spent months preparing. He didn't want to have it interrupted and cluttered by assertions and questions no lawyer would ever make. He believed that if Judge Howard did not take control, the jurist might be presiding over a sideshow.

"I wish some of the defendants had employed counsel," Dees

said, even though he had personally orchestrated the absence of Frank Cox's lawyer. "I would ask the court to caution Mr. Hays when he gets up in front of the jury and comes up with reasons irrelevant as to the merits of this lawsuit. I think we would just have a circus in this case."

"I can't tell Mr. Hays at this point how to conduct his defense," Judge Howard said.

Judge Howard was perfectly aware of the dangers of these legal novices defending themselves against a formidable team of attorneys. On the plaintiff's side sat Dees; Richard Cohen, a Columbia University–educated SPLC attorney who had already shown the judge a strong measure of legal acumen; and Senator Michael Figures, a fine trial attorney in his own right and the most powerful black politician in the southern half of the state. On the defendants' side sat John Mays, representing Shelton and the UKA, and the other six defendants representing themselves. In a criminal proceedings, they would have been provided with court-appointed attorneys, but that was not offered in civil suits.

Judge Howard couldn't equalize the legal teams, but he could give the defendants unusual leeway in their presentations. Some judges are so embedded in the legal world and its jargon that they cannot speak in a manner comprehensible to people who know nothing about the law and the courtroom. Howard was not that kind of judge. He tried to make sure the defendants, the jury, and everyone else who was present understood the proceedings.

The plaintiff's lawyers had debated whether they should reduce their team. But each had a crucial duty. Dees's task was to convince the jury. The thirty-two-year-old Cohen was newly arrived at SPLC. His job was to watch over Judge Howard to make sure he did not make any reversible errors that would destroy the verdict. As for Michael Figures, the legal team needed to have local counsel sitting there. The black attorney's crucial task was to make the final closing argument.

Dees and his colleagues were facing an all-white jury in the heart of the South in a case that sought to decimate the largest

Klan organization in America. The jurors were being asked to send a message that there was no room in the new South for purveyors of racial violence, even if their only contact with the act were words spoken with innuendo.

Dees had named the six Klansmen in the complaint largely because he wanted their stories out there in the courtroom, and the jury to see what these men were like. But they were pawns to be wiped off the board with a flip of his hand. Only Shelton and the UKA mattered. The breaking of the Imperial Wizard and his organization was the measure of victory.

Dees feared the jury might come up with a split, Solomon-like decision, finding against the six Klansmen while deciding that Shelton and the UKA had been unfairly brought into the lawsuit. Cohen had a different worry. He felt that Judge Howard was so out of his depth that he might make mistakes so egregious that the case would have to be tried all over again.

Dees saw this as the most important case of his life, and he brought his seventeen-year-old daughter, Ellie, to the courtroom. It had been almost three years since two intruders had terrified Ellie. Dees had vowed he would show her what he did and how he did it and why it mattered. Ellie sat in a prominent seat in the front row between the SPLC security chief Danny Welch and one of Michael Donald's cousins.

At the beginning of the trial, Bennie and Cox asked the judge to remove two exhibits: the picture of Donald strapped to a tree and the rope Henry and Knowles had used to hang him. Cox had spent enough time in courtrooms to learn something about the law. He knew that defense lawyers had tried that objection unsuccessfully in previous trials, but that was no reason for Cox not to try again.

"I do want to object to the photograph of Mr. Michael Donald hanging from that rope," Cox said with the jury outside the courtroom. "It does nothing but make the jury mad."

Dees made Cox pay a price for what the lawyer considered his insolent attempt to sanitize the case. "This exhibit of this person lynched and how he was lynched is highly important and relevant to proving this lawsuit," Dees said. "I had this picture enlarged because I'm going to have a witness [Knowles] say this was a nylon rope; he burned it in the presence of Mr. Cox right here. And that's part of the conspiracy taking place."

"I'm going to admit the picture into evidence," Judge Howard said.

Dees had gotten what he wanted, but he almost always pushed matters to the furthest reaches of the permissible and sometimes beyond.

"There's one other thing I would—" Dees began.

"You're taking chances," Judge Howard said, tiring of Dees's aggressiveness.

"One other thing I want to put in the record, Your Honor," Dees said. "One of these defendants put a boot on this fellow's head to tighten the rope."

"I *said* I would admit it," Judge Howard said.

Dees didn't care that his courtroom opponents were rank amateurs, most of whom probably knew less about the law than the average citizen. He went at them as fiercely as if he faced Clarence Darrow across the courtroom. And as the trial began, he was convinced the judge was dead-set against him.

Curveballs

DEES HAD BEEN anticipating his opening statement for two years. He could have shouted out in fury at the magnitude of the injustice, but he knew it was best to leave the high emotions until later in the trial. Instead, in a simple, largely dispassionate way, he laid out an outline of the story he would tell and the witnesses he would call, hoping the jury would anticipate with relish what they would hear later in detail.

Dees pointed out the various players, so the jury could begin to connect the grizzly act with the assembled players. There was Bennie Jack Hays. "He's the gentleman sitting right here, white hair. He's got a title called a 'Titan.' That's a very important official of the United Klans of America." And there was James Knowles, who attended most of the trial. Knowles was "the fastest rising official of the United Klans and the second highest official of this corporation in Alabama."

"I want you to wait and hear from Tiger Knowles about this murder because I have a hard time talking about it," Dees said. He was not going to spoil the drama by foreshadowing what was to come.

Then there was Frank Cox, who had already spoken in the courtroom. He looked like a decent enough fellow, but he had procured the rope that was used in the killing, and when the deed was done, "Mr. Frank Cox went out and looked at him [the body] in the trunk of the car: 'Good deed, fellows.'"

And everything began and ended with the United Klans of America. "Officials of the United Klans were part of this conspiracy and made this thing happen and used some of these people here to get it done," Dees said. "We have a piece of evidence, I think, that's going to convince you that this national organization did more than just espouse a racial philosophy; they actually encouraged their members to kill and lynch black people."

Dees had both the case and the defendants he had labored so steadfastly to litigate. "We're going to be asking you at the end to return a very large judgment—very large judgment," he repeated. "We believe that only a large verdict in this case will set the kind of example that will ring out from the top of this courthouse, around this state, and around this nation, that good people will not tolerate this kind of conduct."

Dees thought Shelton belonged in prison along with several of the defendants, but this was a civil lawsuit, not criminal proceedings, and nothing that happened here would send them there. Justice would be doled out in dollars, but Dees hoped the amount would be so large that it would dramatically announce that the Klan could no longer commit violent acts against black people. He also thought that the trial might focus so devastatingly on several of the defendants that the D.A. would have little choice but to criminally indict them.

When John Mays got up to make his opening statement, he did his best to distance Shelton from the other defendants. "You will hear no evidence that Robert Shelton or any other national officer in the United Klans of America, was involved in the atrocity that was committed," the Klan lawyer told the jury.

Mays had heard what Judge Howard had said about Dees's dubious legal theory. The defense lawyer's short presentation played to that. "In order for him to recover, he will have to prove that the United Klans of America conspired, endorsed, encouraged, assisted in some way in this atrocity," Mays said. "I don't believe he can prove that."

Bennie Hays was the only one of the other defendants who chose to make an opening statement. His rambling soliloquy jumped from subject to subject with manic haste. It was precisely the digressive sideshow Dees had feared.

"Everything that happened to that fellow was one of the awfulest things I ever saw," Bennie said. "Now, my son has a death sentence on that. If he's guilty, well, blame the Lord for it. This Tiger Knowles, the man that brought this to us, is nothing. Knowles is a liar, a cheat. He's just no good. I believe Knowles was in on it. But I don't know that I can prove it. I absolutely do. Because he told me. But the others, I cannot in no way. Like my son, I don't know whether he was or not."

The judge let Bennie continue until he petered out. Dees then called Shelton as his first witness and began by using the UKA constitution and other Klan materials to show the

military-like structure of the organization. These were secret
Klan documents, and Dees believed this was the first time they
had ever been used in a courtroom. He played upon that as he
forced Shelton to divulge matters he had sworn never to discuss
with "aliens."

"What is the attorney for the Klan called?" Dees asked.

"It's according to whatever the Klonvokation or Imperial
Wizard wants to place on him," Shelton replied.

"Well, have you in fact referred to your official document
as a Klonsel, spelled with a *K*? And has Mr. Mays, the attorney
with you today, served—"

"Object!" Mays shouted, rising angrily. "Excuse me, Your
Honor."

"In the past—" Dees continued, ignoring Mays.

"May we approach the bench?" Mays asked.

"All right," Judge Howard said.

The lawyers and the defendants came forward and stood beneath the judge, outside the hearing of the jury. "[Dees] is attempting to get before the jury the suggestion that I myself am a
member of the Klan," Mays said fiercely. "I am not."

"What's your position, *sir*?" Judge Howard asked Dees.

"I'm going to show that Mr. Mays, as counsel of this organization, was part of the cover-up of this murder of Michael Donald," Dees said. "Mr. Mays telephoned Tiger Knowles and told
him not to rat on any of our members. Bennie Hays is going to
testify that Mr. Mays said 'Tiger Knowles ought to put a gun in
his mouth and blow his brains out; if he didn't somebody would
do it for him.' And secondly, I intend to put on many witnesses
to say this man was a member. That's part of my conspiracy."

Dees had played friendly with Mays for months, trying to
lull him into thinking this trial was of little consequence. But
this morning, he had pulled off the camouflage. These were
explosive allegations. If proven, they were more than enough to
disbar Mays and perhaps lead to a criminal indictment, but no
one ever followed up on the charges.

"You had every opportunity to bring this up ahead of time," Judge Howard said. "I resent the fact that you bring it up at a later hour."

"Your Honor—" Dees began, his voice taking on a pleading tone.

"You're trying to throw a curveball to the court," Judge Howard continued, his voice rolling over Dees's.

"Your Honor, I didn't intend to throw it as a curveball," Dees insisted.

"We are not going to have trial by ambush in this court-room," Judge Howard said emphatically. "You are not going to testify about any other lawyers. That's entirely improper on your part. You ought to be reprimanded. Let's don't have any more tricks like this."

"I didn't mean it as a trick."

"That's what it is."

As rattled as Dees was, he had no choice but to jump back into his questioning of Shelton. He was able to use this moment to set off the legal bomb he had set in place during Shelton's deposition. Then the Imperial Wizard and his lawyer had not taken the time to read the copies of the Klan newspaper, *Fiery Cross,* that Dees had handed them as potential exhibits in the trial.

Dees approached Shelton with a copy of issue number fifteen from 1979. "If you would turn to page three," he instructed. "I want you to read to the jury what it says right below this picture. And what is this a picture of?"

Shelton looked at the paper through his wire-rim glasses and then up at Dees.

"It's a picture of an individual looking out," Shelton said. "Apparently, it's a white man."

"And what does it say?" Dees asked.

"'It's terrible the way blacks are being treated. All whites should work to give the blacks what they deserve.' It says, 'turn page' with an arrow."

"What do you see on the other page?" Dees asked and held up a three-by-three-foot blowup of an illustration from the Klan's newspaper of a black man hanging by a noose.

"It is a black man with a rope on it," Shelton said, hurrying toward his larger point. "This was printed in Louisiana. When it came out, I called with concern about it. I was told that it was used as a fill-in. And I was assured it would never happen again."

Shelton was paying the price for his lax disregard during his deposition.

"I took your deposition, and I showed you this newspaper," Dees said. "Did you say anything to me then about the fact that you tried to make sure nothing like this ever got published, and you jumped on anybody? Is there anything in your deposition about that?"

"I don't remember exactly," Shelton said.

For Dees this was a perfect ending to the questioning. When the jury passed around the newspaper copy, they looked at the two pages with what appeared to be fascination and disbelief. The cartoon of the black man was a thick-lipped caricature.

"Nice Job, Daddy"

AS MAYS TRIED to minimize the damage from the racist cartoon, Cohen handed Dees a note from his daughter: "Nice job, Daddy." During the lunch recess, Ellie sat with the legal team and asked question after question. Listening to her, Dees was convinced his daughter had the makings of a fine attorney. He would have been proud if his daughter decided to study law, but he felt he shouldn't push her. At least he could ask her to sit by his side during the remainder of the trial, where she could pass notes to her father without an intermediary.

After lunch, Dees called Thaddeus Betancourt. The former Klansmen sat slumped on the witness stand like a man bewildered that he had been brought here to a place where he believed he did not belong. As far as he was concerned, his only mistake was joining the Klan. He wanted nothing to do with his memories of his years in his Klan. He had no money, and it was a cruel joke that he could be hit upon to give money to Mrs. Donald.

Dees had been his genial, empathetic self taking Betancourt's deposition, even offering to pay for a copy of the interview for the impecunious former Klansman. But in the courtroom, as Betancourt exhibited a fortuitous memory loss, the lawyer pounced on him, reading his deposition words back to him like biblical text.

"Now I went on and asked you the question," Dees said, standing in front of Betancourt and reading from the deposition. "I said, 'Right in the middle of your reading didn't Bill O'Connor raise his hand to be recognized and said, "Well, if that nigger gets away with killing that police officer, then somebody out to hang a nigger."' What was your answer?"

"I don't remember Bill saying exactly that," Betancourt said though the deposition refuted his very words.

Time and again, Dees came back to the deposition exposing Betancourt as a dissembler or a victim of youthful dementia. He walked off the witness stand defeated and embarrassed.

Dees then called Knowles, his most important witness. The safest thing would have been to read the convicted killer's deposition, a procedure generally required for inmate witnesses in civil cases. But Dees almost always opted for drama inside the courtroom as well as he did outside of it. Dees had talked to the twenty-three-year-old at the Mobile City Jail the previous evening where he had been transported from federal prison. That conversation gave the lawyer confidence that Knowles would tell his story the way Dees wanted it told.

No one in the courtroom knew that Knowles was serving his time at Sandstone Federal Correctional Institution, a low-security facility in northern Minnesota. He had lost more than twenty pounds, shaved his mustache, trimmed his mop of hair, and he looked lean and fit.

Dees stepped back and let the witness tell the tale in all its excruciating detail. "Just tell the jury," he said. "And I won't interrupt you. Just tell them in your own words what happened and just keep telling the story."

As he had many times before, Knowles talked about Donald fighting "like a crazed animal" when he had actually been fighting for his life. "And finally Donald just fell," he said. "And then Henry rushed over to the other end of the rope. And grabbed the rope and started pulling it. And it was like he was enjoying this. And then he was pulling it and then finally I said, 'He's dead.' And so we got him and we put him in the trunk of Henry's car. And then Henry took a razor knife and cut his throat. And I asked him what for. He said to make sure he was dead."

Knowles was for the most part a credible witness. He was publically confessing his role in the murder in detail while also implicating others, but he did so with no more emotion than a coroner dictating an autopsy report. But the jury was not sitting in judgment on the authenticity of his remorse, only on the veracity of his words.

As Dees continued to question Knowles, he had an agenda in this courtroom not only to bring Shelton and the UKA to justice, but also to do whatever he could to implicate Bennie and Cox in the conspiracy in such a way that D.A. Galanos would be forced to indict them.

Knowles went on to say that Cox had been in the car when the murderer had tied a hangman's knot and burned the ends of the rope so they would not unravel. And Cox had been there after the crime as well.

"Did he [Cox] stand at the trunk of the car and look at the body?" Dees asked.

"Yes, sir," Knowles said.

Dees brought forth the 1979 issue of the *Fiery Cross* with its racist cartoon and got Knowles to say that he had seen that issue of the Klan newspaper.

"Now, when you saw this piece of information, how did you interpret that coming from Robert Shelton, editor in chief, as a Klan official?" Dees asked.

"That that's what blacks deserve, to be hung, and that we should go out and, that's what we should do, go out and hang people, black people," Knowles said.

Knowles was a compelling witness, but he had told so many different stories over the years that a cross-examination should have been a feast for a defense attorney. Knowles had never previously publically claimed that Cox had seen him tying the rope. Then there was the question of whether a seventeen-year-old had truly read and remembered that cartoon in the *Fiery Cross*.

A defense attorney could have challenged Knowles's truthfulness and likely put some doubts into the jurors' minds. But John Mays cared only about narrowly protecting his client's reputation. He focused his questions on getting Knowles to admit that he had seen a racist cartoon in only one issue of the *Fiery Cross* and to confirm that he had never heard Shelton promoting violence. In limiting himself so profoundly in his questions, it was clear that Mays found it supremely unlikely that his client would join the six Klansmen in being found culpable.

But in seeking to distance Shelton from the murder, Mays provoked Knowles into making one of the most important admissions in the trial.

"Who ordered you to kill Michael Donald?" Mays asked.

"It was an act from Mr. Hays," Knowles said. "It was a suggestion from Mr. Hays to Henry Hays and myself."

"Do you recall what your response to that was?" Mays asked.

"I said, 'I wonder what someone would think if they found a nigger hanging out on Herndon Avenue.' And then Mr. Hays said, 'Well, we don't want to do anything until after Friday until I close the deal on the houses.'"

These were the most serious allegations ever against Bennie Hays by a credible witness. When Bennie got up to cross-examine the witness, it seemed obvious that he would attempt to cast doubt on charges that could send him to the electric chair. But even with all his days in courtrooms, Bennie apparently had picked up little knowledge of how to defend himself. He squandered his time telling the jury that there was no such thing as the Junior Klan (though there was) and that Knowles had borrowed money from him.

Frank Cox was the last of the defendants to confront the witness. He was an articulate, intelligent young man who sensed in Knowles's words real danger to his freedom. He had tried everything to distance himself from the killing, pretending he had not given Knowles the lynching rope or had even been on Herndon Avenue the evening of the murder. But in the past three years, witness after witness had linked him to having been on the street.

"Me and you both know you've told this story so many times, and each time, you've lied and said you've told the truth," Cox said. "And Mr. Dees was nice enough to point out that you're coming clean. But how dirty are you that you're going to keep coming clean every time?"

"I have told, beginning in June of '83, when I came clean," Knowles said.

"Well, that's between you and your conscience. That's all, Your Honor."

LATE ON THE afternoon of the first day of the trial, Dees called a series of witnesses who could add vital details to the story. The first to testify was Donald's twenty-nine-year-old niece, Vanessa Wyatt, who had been with Michael the evening he left the Orange Grove apartment. Michael Figures questioned her.

Wyatt described how late on the evening of the murder, the dutiful son left to buy cigarettes for his aunt. She talked too of how she had learned of his death. Saturday morning Wyatt was in the kitchen of her mother's house where she was baking a cake for a relative who had suffered a stroke. That's when the phone rang.

"I heard my mother cry out," Wyatt said. "And I think at that particular time, I knew something had happened to Michael, because it wasn't like him to stay out all night long. You know, we had been worried about him practically all night, because he was supposed to come right back."

None of the defendants asked Donald's niece any questions. Nor did they query the next witness, Dr. Leroy Riddick, the Mobile County coroner. Then Dees called Frank Cox to the witness stand.

Cox had joined the UKA largely to become closer to his father-in-law and a more intimate part of the family. It had become natural to him to mouth racist sentiments, but he believed that he was not a murderer, not even close, and he felt he had been wrongly inveighed into this tragic morass.

"Were you in the car with—" Dees started to ask.

"Mr. Dees, I take the right to the Fifth Amendment," Cox said.

"May I finish my question?" Dees asked.

"Well, you know what you're going to get," Cox said.

Dees asked his questions again and again, and each time Cox said the same thing. The lawyer wanted it remembered that this witness spoke when he wanted to speak, and sealed his lips when he might be legally threatened.

"Were you a part of the conspiracy to kill Michael Donald?" Dees asked as his final question.

"I plead my right to the Fifth Amendment."

Dees could be magnanimously forgiving to those like James Knowles who helped the lawyer, but not those who stood against him. For his next witness, Dees called Cox's mother, Sarah Cox.

"Did your son that night [of the murder] come out to your house and ask you anything?" he asked.

"Yes," Mrs. Cox said. "He came to borrow a rope."

That was the truth, and it could send Frank Cox to prison for life or even to the electric chair.

Then Dees asked his final question of Mrs. Cox. "Did you ever ask your son what happened to that rope you lent him?"

"He said that they used it to tow a car and that it broke into so many pieces that there wasn't anything left to return."

Dees called the last witness for the day, Henry's ex-wife, Denise. On the morning of the lynching, Teddy Kyzar had knocked on her door at dawn and told her a black man was hanging across the street. A little later she overheard her husband calling his father and a television station, alerting them to the crime. Months later she overheard him telling a friend he had killed Michael Donald. She had little more than that to say, and she left the witness stand and the courtroom to return to her broken life.

Purity of the Race

AS DEES AND Ellie left the courtroom that evening, she saw Kyzar standing on the street corner. He was a plump little man wearing a cowboy hat fit for someone twice his size, and he looked like he might keel over. She felt even sorrier for him when he told her he would be waiting on the corner until 9:00 P.M. for his mother to come by to get him.

Ellie wanted to do something for Kyzar. A beginning was to ask Joe Roy to drive him home. On the ride out to Prichard, Kyzar told Ellie that he'd had only one date in his life, and as he arrived with flowers, the young woman had stood him up.

When Ellie got back that evening, she burst into her father's room at the Sheraton Hotel where the SPLC security team watched over the lawyers. She told her father she had read Kyzar's deposition and she believed he should be cut from the case. If it hadn't been his daughter making the plea, Dees would not have considered doing so. As it was, he told her he would decide only after he heard Kyzar on the witness stand.

Dees believed the first day had gone well. He felt he had proven a broad conspiracy involving all six of the Klavern members, each one leaving an imprint on the murder in a different way. That was only the beginning, for he knew that in the morning he must show that the UKA had propagated a philosophy and pattern of violence instigated by prominent officials in the hierarchy. If he didn't do that, the jury would rightfully find for Shelton and the UKA.

During the morning of the second day of trial, Dees called William O'Connor, whose former Klan colleagues had sworn that at the Klavern meeting prior to the lynching, O'Connor had stated that a black man should die. O'Connor denied having said any such thing. He claimed that his Klan accusers were all liars. He recalled how on the morning the body was discovered, he stood on Herndon Avenue and heard Bennie say as he looked across the street, "It was a pretty sight."

Bennie got up to rebut O'Connor's statement. As soon as Bennie finished lashing out at this former colleague, Dees called him forward as the next witness. He had collected the sworn testimony of those who challenged Bennie's statements, and time and again he confronted the former Klan leader. Dees even read letters Bennie had written and signed that now he attempted to disavow.

"Didn't you come up with a plan for several members of your Klan to go out and slash tires parked along the Mardi Gras route here in Mobile [during] a parade of blacks?" Dees asked.

"No, I did not."

"Well, didn't you with knife in hand go out and rip those tires yourself along that parade route when the bands were playing?"

"No, I did not," Bennie said.

"And if Teddy Kyzar says you did that, he's lying, isn't he?"

"Worse than that."

"Didn't when your daughter-in-law was threatening to tell what was going on that he [Henry] slammed her up against the wall three times and threatened her if she talked?" Dees asked.

"I never heard such," Bennie said.

"Did he [Henry] tell you that shortly after this, because of his violent attacks on her, that she got a divorce from him?"

"All of that, where it comes from, I don't know," Bennie said angrily. "But it was a lie."

Mays got up to try to distance Shelton as far from this as he could. He asked only one question: Had Bennie ever heard Shelton "make any suggestion that anybody should commit an act of violence?" When Bennie said, "Never," Mays sat down.

Dees called the next witness, Teddy Kyzar, knowing he would have to decide if he was going to follow his daughter's plea and drop Kyzar from the case. Kyzar had much in common with the other Klan defendants. They seemed to be not monumentally evil but mundane, ordinary men who had committed their acts with little forethought or comprehension. They were a motley, dispirited underclass that wanted black people held down in part because they needed someone to look down upon, as most of the white world looked down on them.

As Dees finished his last question, he saw a note before him from his daughter: "You heard him, Daddy. Please drop him." In the end, he decided to defer to his daughter's judgment and remove Kyzar from the case.

"Mr. Kyzar, you're free to go," Judge Howard said.

"Home?" asked a bewildered Kyzar, unsure what was happening.

"Yes, sir," Judge Howard said. "Wherever you want to go."

"Okay, thank you, sir."

Kyzar got up and walked slowly out of the courtroom, never turning to look back. Dees's daughter had to leave to go back to college, but Ellie was happy that her father had made this gesture.

AFTER LUNCH, DEES called his next witness, former undercover agent Gary Thomas Rowe, who was not physically present. Dees asked his security chief, Danny Welch, to read Rowe's words from his deposition, which he did while Dees read the questions.

Shelton's prized subordinate had been present when the Imperial Wizard made many crucial decisions. When young black men and women staged a sit-in at the lunch counter at the Birmingham Woolworth's, Rowe heard Shelton say "that they needed to get the boys together and do something with that; it was getting out of hand." After that, the Klansmen "beat up demonstrators that were sitting in and trying to obtain service."

In May 1961 when Freedom Riders were beaten unconscious at the Birmingham Trailways Station, "Shelton was totally in charge." Rowe testified that four years later at the time of the Selma march, Rowe had been present at a discussion with Shelton and others "about how they had acquired some land mines, and how it would be feasible to disrupt them [the marchers]." And when the actual march was protected by the authorities, Shelton said "damn it, we had to go down there and get that shit taken care of."

The next day Rowe and three other Klansmen drove to Selma where at a traffic light they saw a white woman and her passenger, a black man. The UKA members chased after the other car until the pursuing vehicle pulled up alongside. "The lady just turned her head solid all around and looked at us like I will never forget it, and her mouth flew open, she was saying 'Oh, God,' or something like that," Rowe said. "At that point, [Collie Leroy] Wilkins fired a shot. And he fired three or four more shots. It looked to be like blood running down the side of the lady's face. She just kind of fell right down toward the wheel, and the car just very casually went and ran off the road into some bushes."

In all the passages from the deposition that Dees read to the jury, never once did Shelton explicitly tell the Klansmen to murder anyone or commit other acts of violence. But his subordinates carried out his vague suggestions as if they were direct orders.

Dees's final crucial witness, Randy Ward, extended Rowe's portrait of a violent UKA forward to late 1978. Ward was afraid he would be killed for testifying, and even a few days before the trial, it was uncertain that he would show up.

To ease Ward's worries, the SPLC security team flew him into another city and drove him to Mobile. They booked him in a hotel under his own name and hid him away in another hotel under an assumed name protected by members of the team. In the courtroom, they left matchbooks from the hotel where Ward was not staying to throw off potential assassins.

As Ward began his testimony, it was clear he had found in the UKA a kind of excitement and promise unlike anything else in his circumscribed, pedestrian life. Ward was named Exalted Cyclops or president of Unit 1015. His immediate superior in the northern half of Alabama was Great Titan Les Suttle, the same role Bennie played in the southern portion of the state. Suttle was all for action and what he called "intimidation." He believed "that was the best policy, to put the fear of God in the people."

Suttle wasn't the only Klan leader who helped give Ward direction and purpose to his life. Shelton had come to the Klavern meeting one evening to impart his Klan philosophy based on three decades leading the UKA.

"Did [Shelton] give you any examples of violence that the Klan had used in the past to keep blacks from having rights?" Dees asked.

"Yeah, he talked about during the Freedom Rides the Klan was there to keep the people on the buses and not let them come into Birmingham and that he was standing there, more or less, directing the people that were there. He said they used pick handles, axes, axe handles, and pipes, and clubs, and things like that."

"Did he talk about white supremacy and purity of the white race?" Dees asked.

"Yes, he did," Ward said, looking at the Imperial Wizard.

"How did you interpret this example he was giving you about what he had done as to what you should do as an official of the local unit of the UKA?" Dees asked.

"To use any means necessary to carry out this to maintain the white race," Ward said.

"Did it fire you up?" Dees asked.

"Everybody was fired up," Ward said. "When Mr. Shelton came around, people would follow him through hell if it came to it."

Shelton had not advocated violence in public for decades, but he was a different man sitting with the Klan inner circle. Ward had been there, had listened closely, and had remembered well. When Dees went on to ask Ward about what he had done when "fired up" by the Imperial Wizard and the Great Titan, the finger of guilt pointed not just at Ward and his fellow Klansmen in Childersburg, but also at Shelton and Suttle, who had inspired the actions.

The Childersburg Klansmen tried to catch a local white woman with one of the black men she was dating, but when that failed, they settled for driving past her home and shooting out her windows. They also went after Charles Woods, president of the local chapter of the NAACP, who was promoting the hiring of black police officers and firefighters. They slashed his tires and drove past his house, firing away. Worried that the black activist may have contacted the FBI, they broke into his house and took any letters and other documents they could find.

From Dees's perspective, Ward was a superb witness detailing how the UKA's violence was not a thing of the past, and Shelton was the leader who provoked the Klansmen into present-day criminal acts.

When John Mays got up to cross-examine Ward, he had every reason to challenge Ward on whether or not Shelton had actually called for violence. It was absolutely crucial to Dees's case that he show a pattern of violence within the UKA, and Mays could have attempted to undermine Ward's testimony and to argue otherwise. But Mays was so upset at the turncoat Ward that he spent his time condemning Ward's conduct. Ward had helped to send thirteen of his fellow Klavern members to federal prison. Mays felt Ward was very much like Rowe, an incendiary who pushed others into actions.

"Even though you did the shooting and the planning on every one of them, other people went to prison and you received probation," Mays said.

"I guess, yes," Ward said.

Standing back up, Dees got Ward to say that his superior, the Great Titan, had approved the plan to go after the black men.

With that, Dees rested the case.

A Jury of One's Peers

AFTER THE JURY filed out for an extended break, Judge Howard invited all the defendants and lawyers into his chambers. This was the point in the trial where the defendant usually argued that the plaintiff had not come close to proving the case, and the defendant should be allowed to walk out of the courtroom for good. But the six Klan defendants didn't know they had the right to ask that.

"Let me put it this way," Judge Howard said. "Do any of you feel that there's nothing that has been said that can tie you into this matter?"

One by one the six Klansmen said they had heard nothing in the courtroom to link them to the death of Michael Donald. And each time they did so, Dees pointed out witness statements that tied the defendant to the conspiracy. And every time, Judge Howard said the evidence was sufficient to go to the jury.

On day one of the trial, Judge Howard had told the lawyers and defendants that the plaintiff's case against the UKA seemed weak. The judge appeared to be signaling to Mays that he might throw out the part of the case against the UKA.

Despite the judge's words, in a gesture that was either astoundingly self-confident or dismissive of the court system, John Mays did not ask for a directed verdict, in which Judge Howard would rule that the plaintiff had presented such a weak case that the UKA deserved to be severed from the proceedings. Dees was astounded. It was yet another illustration of what a poor job, in Dees's judgment, Mays did in defending his client, or else how confident the defense attorney was that his client would not be found guilty.

And then without calling a single witness or presenting any evidence in their defense, Mays rested the UKA case. This might have been a reasonable decision if Dees had presented only the most insubstantial, dubious evidence, but that was not what had happened in this courtroom.

Mays apparently believed he did not have to worry, because no one was claiming that Shelton had ordered the lynching. Dees was convinced that Mays and Shelton had not really been listening to what was going on in the courtroom and did not understand how vulnerable the UKA was.

The other defendants had the right to present their cases. But by calling the defendants as *his* witnesses, Dees had gotten them to lay out most of their defense. They had almost nothing left to say and no witnesses to call.

"Let me state that I am surprised by the fact that the defendants didn't put on any evidence," said Judge Howard once he had both sides back in his chambers. "That's their business. They are entitled to do that. But I anticipated that we would be spending the rest of the day putting on testimony."

That wasn't the way the system of justice was supposed to work, and Judge Howard was upset.

Trading Places

THE COURTROOM HAD a restless energy on the final morning of the trial, Thursday, February 12, 1987. Everyone present knew a verdict would likely come down today. All that was left were the closing statements and Judge Howard's charge to the jury before the six citizens began their deliberations.

The judge gave the defense and the plaintiff two hours apiece for their closing statements. The plaintiff's time was broken in two, and they spoke both first and last.

A bored jury was not a happy jury, and Dees knew that he and Michael Figures probably would use no more than half the allotted time. "It won't be a show for you to get all excited and emotional," Dees said as he began. He would leave that task to Figures.

Dees scoured up every bit of the important evidence that had been presented against each defendant and laid it out as clearly and simply as he could. In the end, he focused on the UKA and the role of its leaders in the lynching. The attorney made the point that Shelton was not on trial personally, but only as the head of "a very complex, very organized, highly financed organization with a goal that operates like a military unit." He told the jury "their belief is simple but tragic. White supremacy. God-given white supremacy."

Dees said: "I want to make it real clear to the jury, I do not want you to come back with a verdict against the United Klans if you decide so just because they are an unpopular group. Don't do that at all. Because in this country you have the right to have unpopular groups just as long as you don't take those beliefs and translate them into violent actions that interfere with somebody else's rights."

The jurors had intense, serious looks on their faces. Dees took that as a good sign.

"I hope at the end of this case, that you send them a message back that will be heard all over Alabama and all over the United States," Dees concluded. "And Michael Donald will go down in history. Viola Liuzzo went down in history. Dr. Martin Luther King. Reverend James Reeb, who was killed in Selma. They won't know Michael Donald as a famous person, because he didn't do anything to die. He died because the Klan killed him. But he'll go down in history in the civil rights movement, a struggle of black people for their rights. And I hope that your verdict goes down in history right on that side."

Once Dees sat down, the defendants made their closing arguments. O'Connor knew that four individuals had given sworn testimony that the former Klansman had said that if a black man got off for killing a white police officer, another black man should die. After denying he ever said such a thing, O'Connor sought mercy from the jury simply because he felt he had suffered enough.

"I haven't done nothing to hurt anybody," O'Connor said. "Onliest thing I ever done in the Klan to hurt somebody was for myself. That only. God as my witness, the only person I've hurt was myself and my family. My wife divorced me over this thing. But before I found out, it was too late. It done slid too far. I haven't hurt nobody. That's all I've got to say."

When Cox got up for his closing argument, he had the same problem as O'Connor. Witnesses said he had borrowed the lynching rope from his mother and had known its purpose, had seen Donald's corpse in Henry's trunk, and had burned a cross on the courthouse lawn after the murder. Cox criticized those who had given what he considered false testimony, and then he too turned himself to the mercy of the jury.

"I'm not a lawyer and don't have the knowledge of the law, as these gentleman around the table," Cox said. "So I appreciate your patience and your attentiveness. And, simply, may God be with you during your deliberations."

Next Bennie walked forward using his cane, and he used this moment not in his own defense but to attack others. "I want to talk about Tiger Knowles first, as Tiger Knowles sat right there on that stand before you people and acknowledged what a liar he has been. A liar is a liar as a thief is a thief. And that's the only way I can look at it. I know you people feel the same way.

"Now we're going to talk about the fellow that walked out here, Teddy Kyzar, and all that stuff about killing in eight or twenty-four hours. He's not dead. And he sung like a bird. So evidently, he lied again. So as far as I saw it, them two people is professional liars. And a liar is a liar.

"Now we get to Denise Hays, who was married to my son. After she separated, she turned and she had a story. With Bill O'Connor, I disliked him very much because of his big mouth. This Tiger Knowles, Teddy Kyzar, Bill O'Connor, lied. These others is professionals and they have told a number of them up here. Quite a few. And I hope and pray that when you go out of here, you keep that in mind."

After Bennie finished, Judge Howard called a noontime break.

DURING LUNCHTIME, A U.S. marshal came to Dees and told him that James Knowles was in the daytime holding cell and wanted to talk to the lawyer. In the morning, Knowles had been in the courtroom listening as Bennie condemned him in the fiercest terms as a liar.

For the first time in his life, Knowles had told in full, uncompromising detail what had happened that terrible night, and he believed it was unthinkable and unspeakable that for doing that, he should be called a liar. He had felt cleansed in speaking out and knowing that his words might help to bring an end to Shelton's UKA. And now Bennie was trying to sully one of the few acts in his life that could help to do a great deal of good. Knowles did not want to let things rest there. He had decided that he should make his own closing argument, but only if Dees agreed.

Although Dees believed Knowles was genuinely sorry, unplanned moments were dangerous in a trial. Dees could have told him that it was probably best if he did not speak again. And if he wanted him to speak, Dees could have limited the risk by prepping Knowles, outlining exactly what he should say. But he told Knowles the decision whether to speak and what to say were up to him. And so when he stood up in the courtroom that afternoon, no one knew what he would say.

Alone in that cell in Minnesota, Knowles had in some measure come to terms with what had happened. As he looked back, it was as if a perverse appendage had attached itself to his body. That appendage was gone now, and he felt terribly sorry for what he had done and how he had ruined so many lives. If he wailed and pounded his fists on the ground in remorse people might say he was truly sorry. But that wasn't him, and he wasn't going to fake it, and that was part of telling the truth. But he was sorry, and he was telling the truth. That's why he was outraged when Bennie mocked him as a pathetic liar.

This afternoon Knowles spoke with a poignant emotive tone. Listening to him, it was hard to believe this young man was the same person who two days ago had testified so bloodlessly.

"I know that people's tried to discredit my testimony," Knowles said. "But I want you to know that everything I said is true. And I hope that people learn from my mistake. And whatever judgment you decide, I do hope you decide a judgment against me and everyone else involved. Because you people need to understand this can't happen."

Knowles began to cry. "I can't bring your son back," he said, looking at Mrs. Donald. For the first time in the trial, she came out of herself and seemed on the verge of tears.

"And God knows if I could trade places with him, I would," Knowles said, shaking his head and continuing to gazed directly at Mrs. Donald as he offered to pay her compensation for the evil act he had committed. "Whatever it takes, I have nothing, but I will do it. And if it takes me the rest of my life to pay it, any comfort it may bring, I hope it will. I will."

People in the gallery were crying, and even Judge Howard's eyes appeared moist. For the jury, as for everyone else, it seemed not to be a trial any longer, but a moment of profound human catharsis.

"I want you to understand that it is true what happened, and I'm just sorry that it happened," Knowles said, his words almost lost in the sobs.

And then in a voice that was little more than a whisper, but still carried throughout the courtroom, Mrs. Donald said, "I forgive you. From the day I found out who you all was, I asked God to take care of y'all, and He has."

James Knowles again looked directly at Mrs. Donald and then at the jury. "My life has been ruined," he said. "So has Mrs. Donald's and her family's and a lot of other lives. I do hope that you find a judgment against me and everyone involved. Because we are guilty."

"That's My Mom"

WHEN JOHN MAYS prepared his closing arguments for Shelton and the United Klans of America, he had planned to begin by condemning James Knowles's emotionless confession. But after the drama that had just taken place in the courtroom, that made no sense, yet the lawyer went ahead anyway, condemning Knowles for his previous testimony.

"I could not help but be moved by what Tiger Knowles had to say just a few minutes ago," Mays said. "I want to take you back just a minute. When he testified in this case, he sat in that chair and gave the details of an atrocious murder like he was off ordering a cup of coffee and a doughnut for breakfast. How much emotion did you see when he took you through the details of that atrocity? How many tears did he shed on that witness stand? How much emotion did you hear in this voice when he testified in that chair?"

Although he didn't mean to do so, Mays highlighted for the jury how extraordinary Knowles's testimony had been. The attorney then quickly started condemning Gary Thomas Rowe and Randy Ward, the two witnesses to UKA violence. Then he began talking about the plaintiff's attempt to link the UKA to the Donald murder. Mays did this in a series of vivid analogies. For the first time in the three-day trial, he seemed to connect with the jury. Dees had made a compelling case for the plaintiff, but Mays cast strong doubts on Dees's arguments.

"Suppose we form a society, Mobile Citizens Against Gay Rights, and we talk about how horrible homosexuality is and two or three people that hear these talks, they go out to a gay bar, physically attack two or three individuals that I guess we would call transvestites, and suppose one of them is killed. Is that attributable to the entire organization? No, it is not."

Mays used a couple of other homespun examples, making the same argument several times. "It is a dangerous thing if in the case of a corporation—not a business corporation, not Burger King, not McDonald's—but an organization political in character like the United Klans of America, the Black Panthers, the Right to Life Committee, and other political organizations which have strong views about certain things, when their members go out and commit acts of violence. Those people should be prosecuted to the fullest extent of the law. But in this country we don't punish organizations. We don't punish thought. It would be bad if we did."

If jurors were looking for a way to come back finding for the UKA, Mays had given it to them.

Senator Michael Figures made the plaintiff's final arguments. He had been there on Herndon Street the morning of the lynching, and he had seen Donald's body hanging from a tree. He had been with Mrs. Donald many times to succor her.

Figures stood before the jury and spoke with the passion and rhetoric heard from preachers every Sunday in black churches across the South. Figures dominated the room, speaking slowly, savoring each syllable, building always to an emotional climax.

"I'm impressed with Mr. Mays's argument," Figures said. "It could be persuasive if we were talking about pornography, gay rights, prayer in the public schools, or abortion. But we aren't talking about that. We're talking about a murder and we're talking about a conspiracy to commit murder.

"The court will give you certain instructions. It will tell you that it was not necessary for the United Klans of America to vote to go to Mobile and pick some black person at random and to take that person to the woods of Baldwin County at gunpoint and beat him to death and then strangle him with a rope with a hangman's noose in it. They didn't have to vote to do that."

Figures was angry, and he told the jury why. He was upset at Mays's lawyering. He pointed out how the defense attorney had not attended Rowe's deposition where he could have cross-examined him—nor had Mays truly cross-examined Ward in the courtroom. Yet in his closing argument, Mays had vilified the two former Klansmen as liars. Figures was also angry with the defendants, whom he said accused others of lying and tried to hide their own deceit.

"There's been talk about the fact that some of the defendants don't have lawyers," Figures said. "Michael didn't have anything that night to help defend himself. No weapon. But he's confronted by two men with a pistol, a rope, and a razor knife—and they kill him.

"One of them comes in here and expresses regret. And that's honorable. Mr. Mays would have you believe that's he lying now, as he lied in the past. Well, I submit to you that the only difference in Tiger Knowles lying and the other lies you've heard in this courtroom, especially from Bennie Hays, is that Tiger Knowles has repented at an early age and Bennie Hays is still lying in his old age.

"Oh, yes, it was Michael Donald on March 20, 1981," Figures said. "But who will it be tomorrow unless you speak very loudly and very clearly to send that message throughout the country? Who will it be tomorrow? It has to be loud and clear, because they came for Michael on March 20, 1981. It could have been me. It could have been anybody who happens to be black."

And then this black Alabama politician moved this most racial of cases beyond race. "The fact is, we're all involved in this together," Figures said. "And it reinforces my belief that was expressed in the sixteenth century by John Donne. 'No man is an island entire of himself; every man is a piece of the continent, a part of the main.'

"Donne goes on and talks about some other things and closes: 'Any man's death diminishes me, Because I am involved in mankind, And therefore never send to know for whom the bell tolls; it tolls for thee.' It tolls for Mrs. Donald right now. But one day, it may toll for thee. Thank you."

AS SOON AS Figures sat down, Judge Howard began reading the lengthy jury instructions. The judge laid out for the six jurors the specific steps they would have to go through to determine if there had truly been a conspiracy. If they were going to include the UKA, they would have to conclude "by a preponderance of the evidence that such corporation, through its duly authorized officers or agents acting within the line and scope of their authority, conspired to deprive black persons of the equal protection of the laws."

The judge set a complicated task before the jury, and although Alabama juries have a reputation for quick verdicts, there was no telling how long they would be out. This was only Richard Cohen's second case at the SPLC, and he was especially nervous. He had no illusion that he could read the minds of the jurors. He believed that all it would take was one juror who didn't understand the case or who was secretly sympathetic to the Klan, and they might be doing this all over again. Instead of merely sitting and contemplating various outcomes, Cohen busied himself preparing for a triumphant postverdict press conference. As he did so, he looked over at his boss, realizing he had never met anyone like Morris Seligman Dees Jr.

While Dees was waiting for the verdict in the most important case in his life, he was whiling away the time with a beautiful television reporter covering the trial. In 1985, he had married a young nurse, Mary Farmer. He thought that he had finally found a woman for a lifetime, but after a few years, the relationship slowly sank. He was back on the prowl, and he was intrigued enough with the young journalist that he ended up dating her.

Dees was perfectly capable of thinking about two things at the same time, and he didn't care what kind of impression he made on the lawyers and others sitting around waiting for the verdict. Dees was a little worried, though no one would have guessed that as he continued to play the irresistible Morris Dees to the fascinated TV reporter.

Dees usually had an instinct about jury deliberations, but this time he didn't know what to expect. He hadn't liked some of what Judge Howard put in his charges, and he worried that the judge might have said things that would push the jury to decide for the defendants. That apprehension grew when after an hour and a half the jury asked for a copy of the judge's charges. That got Dees guessing that at least one juror was playing lawyer. He didn't like it when juries started focusing on the law instead of the facts. If they lost, he told himself, it would be largely to non-lawyers, and that would be laughable, a story his enemies would spread with pleasure.

Once the jury returned to their deliberations, the judge asked the defendants and their counsels to stay nearby in case they were called back into the courtroom. At 7:10 P.M., after a little more than four hours, the jury returned with its verdict.

For the three days of the trial, Mrs. Donald had sat among the spectators with her family. Without her, there would have been no civil suit, and it was only fitting that to hear the verdict, she sat up front between Dees and Figures. She displayed none of the restless nervousness of Dees as she awaited words that she hoped would give her son's life new meaning and add his name to the pantheon of civil rights heroes.

The clerk read in an emotionless voice, "We the jury find for the plaintiff and against defendant United Klans of America. . . . We the jury find for the plaintiff and against the defendant Bennie Hays." The clerk droned on, calling out the names of defendant after defendant with the same result. And when he finished calling out the names of the six defendants, in that same subdued voice, he read, "We fix plaintiff's damages at seven million dollars."

The amount was so staggering that there were gasps across the courtroom. Mrs. Donald reached out and grabbed Dees's and Figures's hands. Shelton and Mays jumped up and with downcast eyes hurried out of the courtroom.

The jury had spoken narrow, specific words in their verdict, but those in the courtroom heard far more than that. The jurors were surrogates for the people of Alabama, and the people of Alabama had said enough is enough. No longer could a man espouse violence against the black race and then stand back watching the bloody results with the benign smile of the innocent. Alabama-born congressman John Lewis grasped immediately the significance of the verdict. It is "the strongest thing in modern times . . . for an all-white jury in Alabama to send such a message."

To Mrs. Donald the attentions and demands of winning justice for her son were almost overwhelming, but she had never faltered. The jurors came forward one by one and shook her hand and said they felt for her, and she was sure they did, and she was amazed that these white folks had voted as they had. The jurors needed to touch Mrs. Donald's hand and hug her and feel they had done something worthwhile. When a reporter asked her what Michael would have said, a trace of a smile crossed her lips. "He would say, 'That's my mom.'"

Dees saw Betancourt and O'Conner standing aside from their former Klan colleagues, staggered that they would be yoked to this financial burden for the rest of their lives. The lawyer walked over to them and put his arms on their shoulders. "Hey, don't worry," he said. "We're after the Klan and Bennie, not you guys." Up until then, Betancourt had despised Dees for putting him through all this, but he decided the civil rights lawyer was okay.

As Mrs. Donald walked out of the courtroom to the press conference, she stood between Figures and Dees. "I don't want no other mother to go through what I did," she told the reporters. "I just hope it helps someone else with children. It could have been somebody else's child, just like it was mine."

When Mrs. Donald thought about the money, it was about what she could do for others. "What is a dream to me is that money comes out of this," she said. "I don't need it. I live day to day, like always. But there's some sad people in the world who don't have food to eat or a decent place to stay. I've been there. I know what it means to have nothing. If the Klan don't give me a penny, that's okay. But if they do, I'm going to help a lot of people who don't have none."

As Dees listened to Mrs. Donald, he was both ecstatic and relieved. He knew that the defendants had nowhere near $7 million in assets. The jury knew that too, but the jury wanted to shout out a message to Shelton and his kind, and they had done so.

When the Donald family and the reporters left, Dees phoned his daughter, Ellie. It was the last important act of a monumental day. "I'm really proud of you," Ellie said. "I understand why you do what you do, Daddy."

Remembrance

MRS. DONALD'S $7 million victory over the UKA was a big story across the United States, and she received all kinds of attention. It was never supposed to have been about *her*, and she cringed at all the interest she was getting: a cover story in *The New York Times Magazine* about "The Woman Who Beat the Klan"; named as one of *Ms.* magazine's 1987 "Women of the Year"; and a mailbox filled with letters from adoring people from across the United States. It was all too much, and she asked that the letters be returned unopened.

That fall of 1987, the Alabama NAACP honored Mrs. Donald and Morris Dees at their annual convention in Mobile. For Mrs. Donald this was about Michael as much as it was about her, and she was being celebrated by an organization that she revered, and so she was willing to sit on the dais.

In his speech to the assembly, Dees evoked the names of civil rights martyrs. Afterward, a young black man came up to Dees and asked him, "Who were Medgar Evers, Viola Liuzzo, and Emmett Till?" He told the teenager about their acts that had made them heroes.

Driving home later that night, Dees lamented that young black people born after the end of the civil rights era knew almost nothing about those who had died so they could live freer lives. And those of the white race knew even less about one of the most important social and political movements in American history. Dees decided the SPLC should build a civil rights memorial emblazoned with the names of those murdered during the civil rights movement.

To design the Civil Rights Memorial, Dees sought out Maya Lin, who had designed the Vietnam Veterans Memorial in Washington and had become the most celebrated young architect in America. Flying down to Montgomery for the first time, she read Reverend King's "I Have a Dream" speech and sketched on a Delta Airlines napkin her vision for the memorial.

To honor the martyrs of the civil rights era, Lin designed a simple, understated memorial. The centerpiece is a black granite circle on which are inscribed the names of forty men and women murdered, from 1955 to 1968, because of their role in the civil rights movement or simply because of their color. At least six of them were the victims of UKA members. A constant stream of water flows over the names, evoking Reverend King's words at the Lincoln Memorial: "We are not satisfied and will not be satisfied until justice rolls down like water and righteousness like a mighty stream."

AFTER THE VERDICT in the Donald case, Dees should have been celebrated and almost universally admired for winning one of the most important civil rights lawsuits of the decade, but he could do nothing without provoking controversy. He was, as Richard Cohen said, "one of the most notorious characters in Montgomery."

Much of the rancor directed at him came from his wealth and the way he used it. He lived with his now fourth wife, stockbroker Liz Breen, in a large house on a property with a tennis court, a pond, and a barn for his two horses. Their marriage lasted only four years and was viewed by Dees's enemies as yet another example of his profligate ways. His friends knew Morris as a romantic idealistic who went willy-nilly into relationships that anyone else could have told him would last as long as a snow cone on an Alabama August afternoon.

It appeared to upset people that Dees had the audacity to live an upscale lifestyle while advancing the cause of civil rights and, despite his fortune, paying himself a six-figure salary to boot. It did not help that he was still this blue-jean-wearing, motorcycle-riding guy who didn't kowtow to anyone, not the country club set, not Montgomery's insular liberal community, not even the grandees of the civil rights movement.

"That this white southerner would become a champion of civil rights is upsetting to other champions of civil rights," said SPLC president Julian Bond. "And when you probe, it's because he has all this money." Some of that irritation may have had to do with Dees's phenomenal fund-raising ability. The SPLC was pulling in more than $4 million a year, and socking almost a third of it away in a large endowment, while some other groups begged to raise enough money to pay staff salaries that were half of what people were earning at the SPLC.

Dees had thought the Klan headquarters was worth more than $200,000, but it sold for a net amount of $50,575, less than one percent of the $7 million judgment against the UKA. It was not much money, but it was more than enough to buy Mrs. Donald the first house she had ever owned. Her new home was located just a few blocks from her apartment in Orange Grove. She would have been content to stay in the projects, but the money made her no longer eligible to live there.

Mrs. Donald died in September 1988, only a few months after moving into her new home and before she had much opportunity to do the good things she wanted to do with the money that remained. There was no fatal illness, only the exhaustion of endless grieving.

Everywhere Robert Shelton looked, he saw the world was different, even within his own home. His granddaughter Amanda talked about her admiration for Martin Luther King Jr., and outside on the streets of Tuscaloosa, some of those who had once embraced Shelton now shunned him. He could have found some way to continue with his Klan work, but he had burned his Klan robes and documents, and his once resolute will to fight had been destroyed as well.

Shelton had a heart condition, and he spent most of his time tinkering around the house, conserving his energy. He became reclusive and rarely spoke to his old Klan friends. "The Klan is my belief, my religion," Shelton told the Associated Press. "But it won't work anymore. The Klan is gone. Forever."

When Shelton's sixteen-year-old grandson Jason rebuilt a Camaro Z/28, he spent hours on the driveway with the youth working on the car. Jason loved his grandfather, but he feared him too, for if the teenager misspoke or acted improperly, Shelton roughly cuffed him on the ear. On weekends, Shelton often took the family to Krispy Kreme for chocolate-filled doughnuts, and no one imagined that the kindly old man was the once-feared Imperial Wizard of the United Klans of America.

The only former Klansman Dees kept in contact with was James "Tiger" Knowles. He was convinced that Tiger was a different person from the unfeeling killer who had strangled Michael Donald in 1981. But he was still an impetuous young man, and when he wasn't released when he thought he should be, in May 1988, he attempted to escape from Sandstone Federal Correctional Institution in northern Minnesota. He didn't get any farther than over the first fence and was brought back and placed in solitary confinement.

WHEN THE CIVIL Rights Memorial was completed, Dees wanted its dedication in November 1989 to receive fitting attention, and the SPLC paid for close to six hundred of the victims' family members to attend the dedication. Most of them had never met each other, and for that reason alone, it was an extraordinary gathering.

George Wallace had been invited, but no one expected him to attend. Since he left office in January 1987, he was alone most of the time, lost in the murky past and consumed with what was and what might have been.

The George Wallace who had stood in the schoolhouse door would have considered it unthinkable that a civil rights memorial could be constructed down the street from the capitol still flying the Confederate flag, but the four-time governor knew that Alabama was changing. On the evening before the dedication, Dees received an unexpected phone call from the former governor.

"Morris, I'm not going to be able to come," Wallace said in a weak voice. "I have to go into the hospital tomorrow. But tell everybody I wish I could be there and that I'm with you all in spirit. I think the memorial is a wonderful idea."

More than five thousand people stood in the street for the dedication of the Civil Rights Memorial. Dees thought that he did not belong on the podium alongside heroes of the civil rights movement, including the eloquent Julian Bond and the courageous Rosa Parks, whose refusal to give up her seat on a bus to a white person signaled the beginning of the Montgomery bus boycott. Instead he sat across the street in an old house, watching the ceremony from afar.

As Dees listened, he knew he was right that it was important to witness the sacrifices that had been made so that others could go on and build anew. Myrlie Evers stood before the thousands and told how in Jackson, Mississippi, her activist husband Medgar had been shot and killed. Chris McNair talked about how his eleven-year-old daughter, Denise, had been killed in Birmingham's 16th Street Baptist Church bombing. And Mamie Till Mobley told how her fourteen-year-old son, Emmett, was murdered on a visit to Mississippi.

"Now the world will remember," Mrs. Mobley said.

A Question of Justice

LATE IN 1987, Bennie Hays was plucked off the street in Wilmer, Alabama, and locked up in a cell at the Mobile County Jail. Chris Galanos had indicted the former Klan leader along with Frank Cox as accomplices in the murder of Michael Donald. More than ever, Galanos needed black votes, and that likely had something to do with the indictments.

In 1985, Mobile's voters had decided upon a new mayor-council form of government, and that fall the three newly elected black council members were the first representatives of their race ever to be part of Mobile's government. There was a rising number of black officials in city government, culminating in the election of Samuel Jones as mayor in 1995 with the wide support of business leaders of both races.

Michael's sister Cynthia was a corrections supervisor at the jail. One of her tasks was to walk through the cell block. As she did so, she was used to hearing the grossest profanity and insults beyond measure, but one day she heard screams so loud, curses so foul, and demands so insistent, that even she was shocked. It was Bennie Hays.

"He was being a beast," says Cynthia Donald Hamilton. "Nothing was good for him, the food, the water, nothing, and he had that evil look on his face." When Bennie paid his bail and was released, he turned toward reporters who asked for a comment and said, "Go to hell."

Mrs. Donald decided that she could bear sitting through Bennie's February 1988 trial, and she and a daughter or another relative were there every day. The key witness Knowles had grown long hair and a beard, and Cox thought he looked like Jesus. This was not the tearful, contrite young man Mrs. Donald had seen in the courtroom during the civil trial. This Knowles spoke with the same disembodied voice he had employed in Henry's murder trial.

Defense attorney Neil Hanley ripped away at Knowles, mocking his assertion that he was telling the truth when he had changed his story so many times. Point after point, claim after claim, Hanley attempted to shred Knowles's credibility. Bennie listened to this with mounting anger, his face growing red. He grew more and more tense until it seemed he was only seconds away from getting up and flailing away at Knowles. Then as the young convict described how he and Henry had made the hangman's noose, Bennie rose and then teetered, grabbing his walker. The defense attorney interrupted and asked for a short break.

Bennie's son Raymond rushed forward and helped his father move slowly across the courtroom toward the door. As he did so, Bennie fell to the ground directly in front of the jurors. He was taken away on a stretcher with an apparent heart attack, and the judge declared a mistrial.

A year later Cox was tried alone, again in the same Mobile Courthouse. The truck driver had gained so much weight that he had a double chin and jowls so thick that they disguised the emotions on his face. He had a loving wife who stood with him and a mother and father who were always in the courtroom.

Since the two men who had strangled Donald to death had been convicted, Cox could not understand why the prosecutor did not leave him alone. As he saw it, he was no murderer. The worse thing he had done, though he denied this, was to have knowingly given Knowles and Henry the lynching rope and after the murder looked at the body in the trunk of Henry's car.

Defense attorney Neil Hanley believed that he had been well on his way to shattering Knowles's credibility when Bennie's apparent stroke or heart attack ended the previous trial. Hanley decided in his opening statement to pick up precisely where he had left off in his vivisection. Galanos listened with increasing dismay as Hanley attempted to make this a trial about Knowles's character, and not about Cox's acts.

The D.A. decided that he would destroy Hanley's case if Galanos did not call Knowles as a witness. An angry, frustrated Hanley decided that he would defeat the D.A.'s ploy by calling Knowles as a defense witness, but Knowles said that if Hanley did so, he would take the Fifth Amendment. So the defense attorney had to hobble on, jerry-building a new strategy, but without Knowles's testimony, the prosecution's case was weak.

Many in Mobile believed that the only way to expunge the shame of the lynching from the soul of the city was to bring anyone who touched the murder to harsh, certain justice. That thinking may have been at work to some degree when the jury returned a guilty verdict.

"It was Frank Cox who was found guilty, but it was not Frank Cox who was on trial," says Cox. "It was the Klan."

When it came time for sentencing, Hanley argued that Cox was a good man who had been led astray, a good man who had suffered much already, a good man who should be given probation. Galanos argued the law: there was no difference legally between Cox, who had provided the rope, and Henry and Knowles, who had strangled Donald—and Cox deserved to be sentenced to the furthest extent of the law.

As Judge Michael Zoghby looked down upon Cox, he was not just sentencing the twenty-seven-year-old defendant. "Punishing a person for the crime is only one reason for punishment," Judge Zoghby said. "There is another reason. And that is to deter others from committing the wrong again in the future. The message that should go out of this court is that civilized society will not tolerate this kind of conduct. Those who are convicted of aiding and abetting in the commission of a crime of this nature should be severely punished.

"Benjamin F. Cox, it is the judgment of this court that you shall be sentenced to the State Penitentiary for a period of ninety-nine years."

Before Cox was taken away in handcuffs by sheriff's deputies, he turned to his wife Sarah and said, "I love you." Sarah had been unfailingly true to her husband during the anguish of the past half-decade, but she believed Frank was gone for good, and she had two children and a life to lead. She started returning his letters and eventually built a new life with a new husband who happened to be one of Knowles's cousins.

After successfully convicting Cox, Chris Galanos set out to bring Bennie Hays, the man who may have ordered the murder, to some measure of justice. The former Great Titan had deteriorated mightily after the conviction of his son and his son-in-law and the death of his wife. He had moved to Ohio to live with his son Raymond.

Many were angry that Bennie should live out his last years without being brought to justice. No one spoke out more strongly than Michael Donald's brother Stanley, who could not understand why Bennie had been allowed to leave Alabama. "If I had been charged with murder and left the state, they'd bring me back," said Stanley Donald.

The Mobile D.A. wanted to bring him back for trial, but every time Galanos tried, Bennie's lawyer claimed health issues so extenuating that bringing him to court would have been a death sentence. In July 1992, Bennie was admitted to Mary Rutan Hospital in Bellefontaine, Ohio, with angina. He was diagnosed with cardiac artery disease and chronic depression.

The D.A. grew tired of these endless medical laments and in September 1992 had Bennie arrested at the nursing home where he was residing and jailed in Morgan County, Ohio. Bennie had hardly arrived when he complained of chest pains and was rushed to the intensive care ward of a local hospital, where he slowly recovered.

After nine months, seventy-six–year-old Bennie gave up

fighting extradition and was flown back to Alabama in a private plane rented by Mobile authorities. He was taken off the plane wearing a prisoner's orange jumpsuit, pushing a walker, and was taken to the infirmary at the Mobile County Jail. He was suffering from coronary artery problems and Alzheimer's disease. Two months later, Bennie was moved to the Veterans Administration Hospital in Biloxi, Mississippi. He died there a week later, in August 1993.

Stanley Donald was upset that Bennie had died without a trial, but he looked forward to seeing Bennie's son executed. Mrs. Donald had wanted Henry's death sentence to be commuted, but Stanley was not so easily assuaged. He didn't use words like *closure* to justify his feelings. He just wanted his brother's killer to die. "I want to see his reaction when he dies," Stanley Donald said. "The reaction might not be the same as what happened to my brother, but I want to see the person who did it fade away right in front of my eyes."

Dees was opposed to the death penalty as much as ever. He wanted to write a letter asking that Henry be spared, but Richard Cohen convinced him to be silent because several members of the Donald family wanted Henry to die.

In his cell on death row, Henry had a worn copy of his favorite book, *Wild Freedom*, by the old-time western author Max Brand. Today the book would be called young adult fiction, and Henry read it endless times. It is the story of Tom, a twelve-year-old boy whose impetuous, unprepared father leads his son over a mountain pass where the father disappears, leaving his son to fend for himself in the wilderness. The youth has a magical way with animals and rides through the primeval forests on a grizzly bear. Tom grows into a lean, tall young man. He is fearless and bold.

Henry read *Wild Freedom* as his story. He was Tom. His father had led him into the Klan, but Henry had grown beyond the hatred and the racism and had many black friends on death row.

As Henry read and reread *Wild Freedom*, in its pages was a tale that resonated with his life with Bennie, but Henry never talked about this part of the book. The young hero builds himself a good, simple life. One day a great, black-bearded, rough-hewn fugitive shows up wearing rags and carrying an arsenal of weapons. He strikes the boy, knocking him to the ground. The man sets out to subjugate Tom, turning him into his virtual slave.

Tom is a gentle boy, but he knows that to live he must strike back, and after a brutal struggle, the boy falls upon a pistol and kills the man. And with this death, the boy becomes a man: "That crease of pain and thoughtfulness which had been cleft in the center of his forehead had never departed, and there was a resolution, an independence of a grown man in his face."

Henry did not have to kill his father. He only had to speak the truth. But in his thirteen years and four months on death row, he had not been able to do that. He could not do that when his father was alive, and he dreaded his weekly visits and believed his father wanted to continue controlling him or even to have him die with his secrets unspoken. And he could not do it after his father passed on, even if it might save his own life. He was cowed, fearful, and impotent.

In the last weeks of his life, Henry gave any number of media interviews. He had no supposed wisdom to impart, no warnings to young people, no apologies for his life in the Klan. He just wanted to be liked. "You'll remember a smile we shared together," Henry told Michael Wilson of the *Mobile Press-Register*, "and say, 'Maybe he didn't do it. And if he did, he wasn't such a bad guy.'"

Henry's black buddies came through in those last days with drugs smuggled into Holman, and Henry was seemingly stoned much of the time. The evening before the scheduled execution, Henry met with Bob Smith, a black minister. That Henry was willing to meet with the African American preacher, who was the president of the Mobile chapter of the NAACP, suggested how much his racial attitudes had changed. Reverend Smith was a burly, charismatic man with a voice that sounded as if he was a direct emissary from God.

When Henry walked down the corridor at Holman Prison to the electric chair just before midnight on June 5, 1997, he was on a pathway taken by far more black men than white. Since 1930, the state had executed 118 black prisoners and only 32 white prisoners. That Henry walked that walk was the greatest commonality this former Klansmen had with the black race he had once so hated.

Stanley Donald stood behind a thick glass window and watched as the guards strapped Henry into the chair. Stanley began to cry, and he looked down at the floor. His eyes stayed there when just after midnight 2,100 volts surged through Henry's body. Afterward, Stanley said it was bad, not as bad as his brother's death, but it was bad. "What I just witnessed was a sad sight to see a young man let his life go like that," he said.

The day after the execution, Reverend Smith said Henry had confessed to murdering Donald. Henry told the minister that James Knowles's account was correct except that it was Tiger who slashed the victim's throat, not Henry. That wrote an end to the story for most people, but not for Michael Donald's family, who would remain haunted by the lynching the rest of their lives.

In 2006, as Donald family members, local politicians, and other notables watched, Stanley Donald stood on Herndon Avenue, unveiling a sign renaming the street MICHAEL DONALD AVENUE.

Death Has No Hold

IN 2005 THE SPLC built the Civil Rights Memorial Center, a museum dedicated to the martyrs of the civil rights movement, across the street from the SPLC headquarters and next to the Civil Rights Memorial. Dees loved to visit the exhibits, and one August afternoon in 2013, he walked over to the center.

Waiting in line was a large black group enjoying a family reunion. They were originally from Alabama's Lowndes County, once one of the most dangerous places in the South for a black person to live. They were returning to visit what in some ways was a different South, and as they waited outside in line, they outdid one another with family stories. But once they entered through metal detectors, everyone from the most elderly family member in a wheelchair to small children grew quiet and solemn.

The Civil Rights Memorial Center is as dark as a cave with the illumination seeming to come out of the walls. One of the first thing visitors see is a panel featuring a large picture of Michael Donald. It is one of the most haunting images in the entire museum.

After looking at Donald's pictures, the visitors turned and stood in front of a large oval panel that completely covers the wall. The sweeping mural memorializes many of the iconic moments in the history of the civil rights movement.

Dees looked upward. The seventy-six-year-old lawyer was dressed in a gray collarless T-shirt, black shorts, and leather sandals, and except for his race was indistinguishable from the tourists who surrounded him. Dees considered himself first of all a lawyer, and he was proud that the saga of the civil rights movement portrayed here begins and ends with the law. It starts on the far left wall with Thurgood Marshall and his colleagues walking down the steps of the Supreme Court in 1954 after arguing successfully in *Brown v. Board of Education* to end school segregation. And it finishes on the far right wall in 1967 as Marshall dons his robe as the first African American justice of the Supreme Court. And between are pictures of violence, struggle, and pain.

Dees thought so much of this violence had occurred because

of George Wallace, yet there was little of him here. The four-time Alabama governor and four-time presidential candidate died in 1998 at the age of seventy-nine. There was no memorial to Wallace in Montgomery like this one for the civil rights martyrs. After his death, when the governor's family and close aides tried to raise $10 million for the George and Lurleen Wallace Center for the Study of Southern Politics, few donors contributed and the center was never built. Across the capital nothing of significance memorialized the man who was the most important governor in Alabama's history.

The same was true of Shelton, who died in 2003 at the age of seventy-three. He had always stood in the background, letting others strike the blows, and there were no pictures of him on this wall.

"We wanted to build this memorial so people would always remember," Dees said in a strong voice that carried across the space. "Folks were forgetting and it wasn't—"

"Who are you?" one of the family reunion members interrupted, startled at this man speaking out.

"I'm Morris Dees."

There were several gasps, a round of handshakes, and requests for photos. Almost everyone knew about Dees and the Southern Poverty Law Center. In the years since the 1987 legal victory in Mobile, the SPLC had grown enormously. The 225 staffers included 40 lawyers, and a 15-person investigative team called the Intelligence Project. There were SPLC satellite offices in Atlanta, Jackson, Miami, and New Orleans.

Even after a legal career spanning five decades, Dees considered *Beulah Mae Donald, as Executor of the Estate of Michael Donald, Deceased v. United Klans of America, et al.* his most important case. The verdict had put a righteous sword in his hand, a legal weapon that the SPLC used again and again in the next decades against one white supremacist group after another. The lawsuit provided a model used by SPLC lawyers to cripple and destroy a dozen racist organizations, from the White Aryan Resistance in 1990 to the Imperial Klans of America in 2008. There are still all kinds of racist hate groups in America, but for the most part, the large organizations whose leaders encourage their foot soldiers to commit acts of violence have been shut down or cowed because of the SPLC's lawsuits. As Jack Boot, the editor of Stormfront, the leading white supremacist website, put it in 2008, "Galling as it may be, no other single organization has more effectively damaged our cause."

These days Dees was so warmly welcomed all over Montgomery that when he went to local restaurants it took him forever to get to his seat as he wended his way through the many well-wishers. He still had his ranch, where he liked to go, but he spent most of his time in a house decorated in splendidly eclectic fashion by his fifth wife, Susan Starr, an Atlanta artist, in Cloverdale, the upscale neighborhood where as a farm boy he had almost never ventured.

His enemies vilified Dees as a shameless huckster whose primary function was raising money from gullible liberals. If Dees was only concerned with donations, it seemed unlikely that the SPLC would have fought so vigorously for the legal rights of undocumented immigrants, homosexuals, and LGBT children—causes that were controversial, not only to the general public but also to many donors.

Although Dees's denigrators considered his twenty-four-hour security little more than shrewd public relations, there were still people out there hoping to murder him. Over the years, more than a score of hate group members had been convicted for plots to kill Dees or to destroy SPLC property.

Dees's marketing skills had not abated, and the SPLC had amassed an endowment of close to $300 million. He felt the amount was necessary in case the economy tanked, but it created jealousy from liberal nonprofits struggling to raise money.

The past four decades had been an awesome journey, and Dees was glad he had shared most of it with Richard Cohen, who had become the president of SPLC. For all of those years

Cohen had done much of the heavy lifting, and Dees knew his friend would probably never receive the credit he deserved.

Dees had reached the age where he often found himself looking back. When he heard young black people decrying American racism, as if nothing had changed, he wanted to scream out that as bad as things sometimes were, it was a different country. It was a terrible thing to suggest that those whose names were written on the Civil Rights Memorial had died for nothing. As he looked out at the members of the family reunion, he realized that most of them were too young to remember a time in Lowndes County when if a black man saw a white man coming toward him, he got off the sidewalk and for an African American fear was never far away.

"I'm a lawyer in New Jersey," said one of the women at the family reunion. "I was a delegate to the American Bar Association convention in Chicago last year, and I was there when you received their highest honor."

"I'll be darned," Dees said. As he talked to the woman, Dees remembered that when he was a young lawyer, there were no black delegates in the ABA. He thought of the speech he had given at the annual meeting when he received the ABA Medal. He told the delegates what a lonely struggle it had been in the early years and how much this honor meant to him. As he remembered that day and the journey of his life, and reflected upon this black woman lawyer's journey, he choked back tears.

"I want you to see Michael Donald's picture here and remember his name," Dees said, turning toward the first panel. "He was a teenager, nineteen years old, when two Klansmen abducted him and lynched him.

"But the hate came first of all from Robert Shelton, the Imperial Wizard of the Klan, and the guidance came from him and other leaders of the Klan, and that's why Donald's mother agreed to have us sue the United Klans of America. We won a seven-million-dollar verdict, and it destroyed the Klan."

"Now look at this next panel," Dees said as he walked a few

steps. "Here I am with Mrs. Donald being honored by the state NAACP. I said that evening that Michael Donald would take his place in history along with others whose lives were lost in the struggle for human rights. And when the final roll is called in heaven—when they call Dr. Martin Luther King Jr., and Medgar Evers, and Viola Liuzzo—they will also call Michael Donald.

"They will not be forgotten. They have changed the world. For Michael Donald and the others, death has no hold."

Where Are They Now?

CATHY BENNETT After her involvement in the Michael Donald civil lawsuit, the jury consultant worked again with Dees and the SPLC, winning a $12.5 million judgment against the California-based White Aryan Resistance. Her last prominent case before her death, in 1992, was the successful defense of William Kennedy Smith against accusations of sexual assault.

JAMES BODMAN The FBI special agent who helped break the Michael Donald murder is retired and lives outside Mobile.

RICHARD COHEN The lawyer is the president of the SPLC.

FRANK COX Released after eleven years in prison, Cox has remarried and is back working as a truck driver.

ELLIE DEES Morris Dees's daughter gave up the idea of becoming a lawyer and studied for a master's degree in fine arts. She is married, has a young son, and works for a major real estate firm outside Alabama.

MORRIS DEES The seventy-nine-year-old lawyer is the chief trial counsel for the SPLC. He spends much of his time mentoring the SPLC's young lawyers. The lawyer still rides his 1200cc BMW bike on trips with buddies through the hairpin turns of the Appalachian Mountains and on road tours that have taken him as far as Utah. In late 2015 he filed for divorce from Susan Starr. Dees spends time with Katie Kalahar, a Michigan lawyer.

BOB EDDY   The investigator is retired and lives outside Montgomery.

MICHAEL A. FIGURES   The president pro tem of the Alabama Senate died in 1996 of an aneurysm at the age of forty-eight.

THOMAS FIGURES   The former assistant United States attorney was in private practice when he died in 2015.

MILLARD FULLER   Dees's old friend and partner founded Habitat for Humanity, an organization that has built thousands of houses for the poor. Fuller died in 2009.

CHRIS GALANOS   The former Mobile D.A. practices law in Mobile.

CYNTHIA DONALD HAMILTON   Michael Donald's sister worked for a number of years as a corrections supervisor at the Mobile County Jail. Mrs. Hamilton lives in McCalla, Alabama.

JAMES "TIGER" KNOWLES   Knowles served twenty-five years in federal prison, twenty of them in solitary confinement. Dees believed that Knowles was truly remorseful and helped him to get parole. He lives a quiet, productive life far from Mobile.

BARRY KOWALSKI   The Washington lawyer became a leading civil rights prosecutor at the Department of Justice. He convicted the police officers who beat Rodney King in Los Angeles. Kowalski, now seventy, retired in 2014.

JEFFERSON BEAUREGARD "JEFF" SESSIONS III   In 1996, the Senate Judiciary Committee voted down the former U.S. attorney's nomination for a federal judgeship. Four Justice Department lawyers, including Thomas Figures, claimed that Sessions had made racist statements. Sessions was elected to the United States Senate as a Republican in 1996 and now sits on its Judiciary Committee.

Acknowledgments

Writing *The Lynching* was a coming home to my earliest roots in journalism. When I was a graduate student in international affairs at the University of Oregon in the fall of 1967, I talked my way onto Governor George Wallace's campaign plane. I spent several days with the presidential candidate and wrote an article for *The New Republic*. It was my first foray into journalism, and I was bitten. A few months later a national magazine sent me to Montgomery to interview Wallace, and that November my professors at the Columbia University Graduate School of Journalism flew me to the Alabama capital to cover election night.

For this project, Morris Dees, the cofounder of the Southern Poverty Law Center, gave me what every nonfiction writer seeks—total access and the freedom to write whatever I wanted to write in the way I wanted to write it. Dees and Richard Cohen, the president of the SPLC, spent endless time answering all my questions and providing anything I might need to get on with my research. Dees's assistant, Judy Bruno, was unfailingly helpful as were others at the SPLC including Michelle Leland, Booth Gunter, Russell Estes, and Penny Weaver.

The time was right in getting others to talk, and I must thank the surviving convicted murderer, James Knowles, and his accomplice, Frank Cox, for their interviews. Cox's former wife, Sarah Knowles, was also helpful.

By knocking on lots of doors, I tracked down the two other living members of Klavern 900, Theodore Betancourt and Teddy Kyzar. I drove to Tuscaloosa and tapped on Betty Shelton's door, and the Imperial Wizard's widow talked extensively as did their two grandchildren, Amanda and Jason Shelton. For the Donald family, the lynching of Michael Donald is still raw, and they designated Cynthia Donald Hamilton to answer my questions. I also found it extremely useful talking to two of George Wallace's children, Peggy Wallace Kennedy and George Wallace Jr. I want to give a special note of appreciation to the late Thomas Figures. Without his deeply felt memories, this book would be less than what it is.

The other interviews included Tom Lawson, Stephan Lesher, Mrs. Charles Morgan Jr., Julian Bond, Alice Ortega, Philip R. Manuel, George Seitz, Maureene Bass, Elvin Stanton, John Mays, Beverly Belak, Joe Roy, Kenneth Mullinax, Bob Eddy, Bill Stanton, Scotty E. Kirkland, Raymond Arsenault, Gary May, Tom Turnipseed, Mark Kennedy, Randall Williams, Joe Levin, B. J. Hollars, Dan T. Carter, Thomas Harrison, Danny Welch, Jerry Keys, Nelson Malden, Morris "Scooter" Dees III, Chris Galanos, James Bodman, Barry Kowalski, Burt Glenn, James Killough, Daniel Rinzel, Eleanor Davis, Rick Kerger, John Carroll, and Gary May.

Two of my closest friends, Kristina Rebelo Anderson and Raleigh Robinson, read numerous versions of the manuscript. Other readers included Nigel Hamilton, Burton Hersh, Edward Leamer, Scotty E. Kirkland, and Diane McWhorter. Bob Ickes read the pages and provided his astute judgment. My longtime agent, Joy Harris, made crucial contributions from the conception of the idea to the marketing. Nothing she did was as important as putting these pages in the hands of Henry Ferris, my esteemed editor at William Morrow.

The SPLC provided me with the legal documents and court transcripts without which I could not have written *The Lynching*. The Mobile District Attorney's Office let me go through their extensive Michael Donald files. The Alabama State Archives are full of useful material on George Wallace and the history of the state. The public library in Mobile has a unique collection of newspaper clippings. I found helpful the Michael Donald Papers at the Doy Leale McCall Rare Book and Manuscript Library at the University of South Alabama in Mobile. I also spent several days in the Dan T. Carter research files at the Robert W. Woodruff Library at Emory University in Atlanta. The 1,500 pages of FBI documents at the National Archives about Robert Shelton opened for the first time provided crucial information on the Klan leader.

I am acknowledging my wife, Vesna Obradovic Leamer, last though by rights I should mention her first. She is used to not getting the credit she deserves, but without her this book would not exist.

Notes

Prologue

1   an elderly man went out: CID, Mobile, Alabama, Police Department investigative report relative to the murder of Michael Donald, March 27, 1981.

2   others fell to the ground: B. J. Hollars, *Thirteen Loops* (Tuscaloosa: University of Alabama Press, 2011), 126 and interview, Chris Galanos.

Part One: Night of the Burning Cross

KLAN BUSINESS

5   Thaddeus "Red" Betancourt, the Klokard: Deposition, Thaddeus Betancourt, *Beulah Mae Donald, as Executor of the Estate of Michael Donald, Deceased v. United Klans of America, et al.*, November 13, 1984, 8. Unless further noted, the depositions were taken by Morris Dees for this civil case.

6   "We serve and sacrifice": *Kloran Klan in Action Constitution*, undated publication of the United Klans of America, 7.

6   stolen Kyzar's watch: Interview, Teddy Lamar Kyzar.

6   "missionary work": Gary May, *The Informant* (New Haven, CT: Yale University Press, 2005), 9.

6   the last thing they did: Interview, Teddy Lamar Kyzar.

6   so they could not be patched: Testimony of Teddy Lamar Kyzar in *Beulah Mae Donald v. United Klans of America, et al.*, February 11, 1987, 391.

6   started slashing and puncturing away: Depositions, James Knowles, March 12, 1985, and Teddy Lamar Kyzar, March 27, 1985.

6   damaged tires on sixty-five: Deposition, Teddy Lamar Kyzar, March 27, 1985.

7   hit him with a leather: Depositions, James Knowles, March 12, 1985, and Teddy Lamar Kyzar, March 27, 1985.

7   At age sixteen, the illiterate teenager left home: *Mobile Register,* June 2, 1997

7   ridden the outlaw roads: Interview, Gail Cox.

7   In 1952, he saddled: *Mobile Register,* June 2, 1997.

8   drove to Mobile: Deposition, Bennie Jack Hays, November 13, 1984, 27.

8   a Texaco gas station: Interview, Gail Cox.

8   When Opal saw him: Ibid.

8   "half-assed Henry": *Mobile Register,* June 3, 1997.

8   caught in a hotel: *Mobile Press-Register,* June 2, 1997.

9   "No, I did," said his fourteen-year-old daughter: Interview, Gail Cox.

9   thrown out of the army: Ibid.

9   to keep his grandchildren close: *Mobile Press-Register,* June 2, 1997.

9   "We used to get in": Deposition, Denise Hays, November 12, 1984, 63.

9   in exchange for collecting rents: Deposition, Denise Hays, November 12, 1984, 37.

9   "altar boy": *Mobile Register,* June 4, 1997.

10   cut off the toes: Interviews, Frank Cox, Gail Cox, and James Knowles.

10   he weighed a whopping thirteen pounds: *Mobile Press-Register,* June 2, 1997.

11   At the convention, the teenager was given: James Knowles to Morris Dees, January 13, 1987.

11   The teenager believed that one day he would: Interview, Morris Dees.

11   cut off his hair: Deposition, Johnny Matthew Jones, July 30, 1984, 19.

A PUBLIC DISPLAY

12   had joined the Klavern: Interview, Thaddeus Betancourt.

12   Betancourt had served time for burglary: Deposition, Thaddeus Betancourt, November 13, 1984, 7.

12   the family had a full-time black maid: Ibid.

13   even made a plywood-covered scrapbook: Ibid.

13   "If a nigger can get away": Deposition, Teddy Lamar Kyzar, March 27, 1985.

13   the Klokan, a Klan state officer: Deposition, Bennie Hays, November 13, 1984, 37.

13   "Ought to be a damn": Ibid., 25.

13   "A nigger ought to be hung": Deposition, Johnny Matthew Jones, July 30, 1984.

14   Klansmen had brought pistols: Deposition, James Knowles, March 12, 1985, 8.

14   At one point Bennie: Testimony of James Knowles in *Beulah Mae Donald v. United Klans of America, et al.,* February 10, 1987, 217.

15   Henry and Knowles were convinced: Deposition, James Knowles, March 12, 1985, 38.

15   "Would the Klan": Interview, James Knowles.

THIRTEEN KNOTS

16   traitor to the cause: Deposition, James Knowles, March 12, 1985, 47, and interview, James Knowles.

16   "The goddamn nigger got off": Deposition, Denise Hays, 45.

16   "I thought I was invincible": Interview, James Knowles.

17   broken three fingers: Testimony of Crampton Harris, M.D., *The State of Alabama v. Henry F. Hays,* December 10, 1983, 772.

17   a rag, paper towels: Hollars, 98.

17   directions to the Powell Social Club: Bob Eddy interview with James Knowles, July 7, 1983.

18   taking the old truck route: Testimony of James Knowles, *The State of Alabama v. Henry F. Hays,* December 7, 1983, 143.

18   "The same thing could . . .": James Knowles testimony in *Beulah Mae Donald v. United Klans of America, et al.,* February 10, 1987, 191.

19   "I'll kill you for that": Memo: Bob Eddy to Chris Galanos, interview of James Knowles in Dallas, Texas, July 28, 1983.

19   razor knife he used: FBI investigative report of interview with James Knowles, June 14, 1983.

20   "Do you think he's dead": James Knowles testimony in *The State of Alabama v. Henry F. Hays,* December 7, 1983, 148.

"GOOD JOB, TIGER"

21 strapping the body to the tree: Deposition, James L. Knowles Jr., March 12, 1985.

21 "your shirt is soaked": Interview, Teddy Lamar Kyzar.

21 drenched in blood: Deposition, Teddy Lamar Kyzar, March 27, 1985.

21 "Had a nosebleed": Deposition, Denise Hays, November 12, 1984, 48.

22 "Next thing y'all do": Deposition, Teddy Lamar Kyzar, March 27, 1985.

22 The cross was still blazing: Ibid.

22 "Good job, Tiger": James Knowles testimony in *The State of Alabama v. Henry F. Hays*, December 7, 1983, 153.

22 newsroom at WKRG-TV: Deposition, Denise Hays, November 12, 1984, 54.

A PRECIOUS ENCLAVE

23 feared what might happen: Interview, Thomas Figures.

23 The black residents were: Shawn A. Bivens, *Mobile, Alabama People of Color: Bicentennial History, 1702–2002* (Victoria, B.C., Trafford, 2004), 8–9.

24 181,000 African Americans: "Mobile and the Boswell Amendment" by Scotty E. Kirkland, *Alabama Review*, July 2012, 210.

24 black citizens in Mobile boycotted: "The Mobile Streetcar Boycott of 1902: African American Protest or Capitulation?" by David E. Alsobrook, *Alabama Review*, April 2003, 83.

25 "So noiseless was the hanging": "Pink Sheets and Black Ballots: Politics and Civil Rights in Mobile, Alabama, 1945–1985," by Scotty E. Kirkland. A thesis for the degree of masters of arts in Department of History, University of South Alabama, 2010, 23.

25 "If the mob had": Quoted in Ibid., 24.

25 "get every one of them": Ibid., 51.

25 able to discuss: Ibid., 58.

26 African Americans did have to sit: J. Mills Thornton III. *Dividing Lines: Municipal Politics and the Struggle for Civil Rights in Montgomery, Birmingham, and Selma* (Tuscaloosa: University of Alabama Press, 2002), 64

26   FBI's most likely suspects: "Beyond the Aura of Respectability: The Civil Rights Movement in Mobile, Alabama." Unpublished essay by Scotty E. Kirkland, 14.

27   Standing there in his scarlet robe: FBI, Re: Robert Marvin Shelton, August 19, 1975. FBIFOI.

27   blue eyes: To director, FBI from SAC, Birmingham, Subject: Counterintelligence Program, February 22, 1966. FBIFOI.

27   Standing there in his scarlet robe: FBI, Re: Robert Marvin Shelton, August 19, 1975. FBIFOI

28   "Black people no longer": Quoted in Kirkland, "Beyond the Aura of Respectability: The Civil Rights Movement in Mobile, Alabama," 175.

28   a line of young black men: *Mobile Beacon*, October 1, 1977, quoted in "Beyond the Aura of Respectability: The Civil Rights Movement in Mobile, Alabama." Unpublished essay by Scotty E. Kirkland, 176.

28   "to 'write off'": Quoted in Kirkland, 17.

29   "the culmination of decades": Kirkland, "Pink Sheets and Black Ballots," 191.

29   Although African American residents made up nearly: *New York Times,* November 1, 1987.

29   he shot three white men: Interview, Thomas Figures.

THE KLAN'S SIGNATURE

30   "hysterical, weeping, wailing": Hollars, 126.

31   "See these thirteen": Ibid., and interview, Chris Galanos.

31   Diamond and a friend: *Mobile Register*, June 1, 1997. A few years later, Diamond changed his name to Casmarah Mani.

31   they put a noose around: *Mobile Register*, April 14, 1976, and June 1, 1997.

31   Just the day before: Kirkland, "Beyond the Aura of Respectability: The Civil Rights Movement in Mobile, Alabama," 166.

32   He went up to Williams: *Mobile Register*, June 1, 1997.

32   "My name's Bennie Jack Hays, and I own": Ibid.

33   "He told me if I am telling": Mobile Police Department Investigation Report, March 21, 1981.

33   "very violent people. Mr. Hays": Ibid.

33   "I'm not going to take": Ibid.

THE VALUE OF THINGS

34   "You don't need to see this": *New York Times*, November 1, 1987.

35   He also liked: *Mobile Press-Register*, June 1, 1997.

35   aunt gave him a dollar: Vanessa Wyatt testimony in *The State of Alabama v. Henry F. Hays*, 308.

36   her own sister had been murdered: Bill Stanton, *KlanWatch: Bringing the Ku Klux Klan to Justice* (New York: Grove Weidenfeld, 1991), 202.

36   "I wasn't able to get": Ibid.

36   She took her children: *New York Times,* November 1, 1987.

36   they had to be back home by 11:00 P.M.: Interview, Cynthia Donald Hamilton.

37   "I believe he might have met": *Mobile Press-Register*, June 1, 1997.

BLOODY NAILS

37   Eddy had grown up: Interview, Bob Eddy.

37   NIGGER DON'T LET: Ibid., and *New York Times*, February 26, 2010.

38   believed that four of the five: Interview, Bob Eddy.

39   "It is unknown": To Director Priority from Mobile (44A-4237), March 23, 1981. FBIFOI.

39   "There is a feeling": News release, State Senator Michael A. Figures, March 23, 1981. FBIFOI.

40   nooses hanging from highway: Kirkland, "Beyond the Aura of Respectability: The Civil Rights Movement in Mobile, Alabama," 184.

40   Donald was having an affair: *New York Times*, November 1, 1987.

AN OPEN CASKET

42   "so the world could know": Ibid.

42   Senator Michael Figures was: Interview, Cynthia Donald Hamilton.

42   "No more sorrow": *Mobile Press-Register*, June 1, 1987.

43   everywhere the Klansmen spotted: Deposition, Johnny Matthew Jones, July 30, 1984, 40.

43   to lead a protest: *Mobile Register*, June 1, 1997.

44   "conflicts in statements": *Mobile Register*, June 12, 1981.

44   "we need to give this to": Hollars, 92.

44   "Any black man with a gun": To Honorable Jeremiah Benton, from FBI Congressional Liaison Unit, July 9, 1981. FBIFOI.

45   on average more than once a week: *New York Times*, February 10, 2015.

45   his cousin Monica Jackson recalled: *Mobile Press-Register*, June 1, 1997.

46   attorneys hemmed and hawed: Interview, Cynthia Donald Hamilton.

46   "Well, you all need to get to work": Ibid.

A MAJOR INJUSTICE

47   both an M.B.A. from Indiana: *New York Times*, November 1, 1987.

48   "two *R*s, racism and redneckism": Interview, Thomas Figures.

48   he had watched: Ibid.

49   called him "boy": *Birmingham News*, May 18, 2009.

49   opened a filing cabinet: Interview, Barry Kowalski.

50   "humiliating to the South": Lou Cannon, *The Role of a Lifetime* (New York: Simon & Schuster, 1991), 520.

51   "this nation's original sin of slavery": *New York Times*, March 18, 2008.

52   shrewd bureaucrats within the agency: Interview, Barry Kowalski.

53   "What do you expect me": Interview, James Bodman.

53   "Mississippi redneck": Ibid.

54   "Why the hell do you want": *New York Times*, November 1, 1987.

MISSIONARY WORK

55   "Knowles had blood all over": FBI 302 interview with Teddy Kyzar, February 10, 1983.

PRAYERS IN THE NIGHT

56   Burt Glenn, flew down: Interview, Burt Glenn.

57   Rinzel, had heard: Interview, Daniel Rinzel.

57   The jacket fit: Interview, Barry Kowalski.

58   "It was the typical federal bullshit": Memo to Donald Investigative File from Chris Galanos, May 25, 1983.

58   "All these people": FBI 302 interview with Teddy Kyzar, February 10, 1983.

58   sent a polygraph: *Mobile Press-Register*, June 1, 1997.

59   When he drove home: Deposition, Jackie Lange, November 12, 1984, 40.

60   "The assistant attorney general": Interview, Barry Kowalski.

60   "I couldn't figure": Ibid.

60   "and Tiger Knowles had": Interview, James Bodman, and FBI 302 interview with William O'Connor by SA James Bodman Jr., May 25, 1983.

61   faced the federal grand jury twice: James Knowles testimony in *The State of Alabama v. Henry F. Hays*, December 7, 1983, 147.

61   On May 26, 1983, Kowalski: FBI 302, May 25 1983.

61   "I know this is about": Memo Francis Scarcliff to Chris Galanos, Re: James L. Knowles Jr., June 8, 1983.

A LESSER CRIME

62   Raymond could see fear: *Mobile Press-Register*, June 3, 1997.

63   "I'm not going to spend": Interview, James Bodman.

64   "Honest, Mr. Bodman, we didn't": Ibid. and FBI 302 interview with James Knowles by SA James Bodman, June 10–11, 1983.

64   "scuffle": Ibid.

64   "Tiger never told me": Interview, James Bodman.

65   The federal attorneys were afraid: Interviews Barry Kowalski and Thomas Figures.

65   "Just tell 'em what you told": Interview, James Bodman.

65   Unless the Justice Department: Interview, Barry Kowalski.

67   "Look, Tiger, here's something else.": Ibid.

68   "I would like to say": Hearing before Hon. W. B. Hand, chief judge of the United States District Court, at Mobile, Alabama, on June 16, 1983.

68   Kowalski suspected rightfully: Interview, Barry Kowalski.

BLACK SHEEP

70     $50,000 Marsal wanted: *Mobile Press-Register*, October 23, 1987.

70   set his house: *Mobile Register*, June 4, 1997.

71   "I'm learning I'm not": Henry Hays to Janet Deem July 1, 1983. These letters courtesy of the Southern Poverty Law Center.

71   spent $63,000 on the defense: Henry Hays to Janet Deem, November, 29, 1983.

71   "I'm nobody, never have been": Henry Hays to Janet Deem, August 8, 1983.

71   Henry woke up: Henry Hays to Janet Deem, September 6, 1983.

A CAPITAL OFFENSE

71   He didn't think: Interview, Chris Galanos.

72   Galanos knew he had a problem: Interview, Chris Galanos.

72   "I was afraid he'd go": Interview, James Knowles.

72   Bodman heard Galanos pacing: Interview, James Bodman.

72   "This is what you signed, Tiger": Interview, Chris Galanos.

73   Knowles told Galanos how he and Henry: Memo to file from Chris Galanos, November 22, 1983.

73   misdemeanor dismissed: *Mobile Register*, December 6, 1983.

74   D.A. got in his car: Interview, Chris Galanos.

74   had been dealing with Galanos's: Interview, Thomas Harrison.

75   The last time a white man: *Mobile Press-Register*, June 1, 1997.

75   The indictment charged: Chris Galanos testimony in *The State of Alabama v. Henry F. Hays*, December 6, 1983, 238.

76   He had heard rumors: Interview, Thomas Harrison.

76   he was happy to see: Ibid.

77   "I have a right to find": *Mobile Register*, December 6, 1983.

THE SECOND-MOST-HATED MAN

77   sensed that this: Interview, Morris Dees.

77   He loved the old: Ibid.

78   "the second most hated man": Quoted in Bill Stanton, 18.

79   He remembered hearing: Interview, Morris Dees.

79   Dees asked Figures if Mrs. Donald would: Morris Dees and Steve Fiffer, *A Lawyer's Journey: The Morris Dees Story* (New York: American Bar Association, 2001), 215.

79   ninety-eight-dollar-a-month apartment: *New York Times*, November 1, 1987.

79   "just another colored man": *New York Times*, March 8, 1987.

A MATTER OF JUSTICE

81   wore pink slacks and a: *Mobile Register,* December 7, 1983.

81   "And the defendant and myself": *The State of Alabama v. Henry F. Hays,* December 7, 1983, 146.

82   She could not believe: Interview, James Knowles.

83   "I ask the court": *The State of Alabama v. Henry F. Hays,* December 7, 1983, 155.

83   "What were you looking for": Ibid., 183.

"THE FORCES OF EVIL"

84   "I don't think I have": Ibid., 196.

85   "During that night": Ibid., 219.

85   "So, Mr. Knowles, you testify": Ibid., 247.

86   "And what did they do then?": Ibid., 265.

86   He had spent a lot of time: Interview, Morris Dees.

86   Stanton said he had been: Interview, Bill Stanton.

87   Garner and two of his associates pled: *New York Times,* February 21, 1985.

87   "Your mother, why I can": *New York Times,* November 1, 1987.

87   "come under attack by the forces": Dees and Fiffer, 49.

88   The best way: Interview, Morris Dees.

88   "Morris, I got a call from the FBI": Interview, Danny Welch.

"SIZZLING OF THE FLESH"

89   "from Bennie Hays hisself": Testimony of Teddy Kyzar in *The State of Alabama v. Henry F. Hays,* December 9, 1983, 597.

89   Dees could not wait: Interview, Morris Dees.

91   "If I had been called": Interview, James Knowles.

91   "The supreme court appointed Mr. Dees": *The State of Alabama v.. Henry F. Hays,* December 7, 1983, 612.

92   "took it that he was": Deposition, Janet Deem, November 26, 1984, 19.

92   "Tiger's car had stalled": Testimony of Henry Hays in *The State of Alabama v. Henry F. Hays,* December 9, 1983, 716.

93   "All that day": Ibid., 736.

A VERDICT

94   utterly exhausted: Interview, Thomas Harrison.

97   "Look, Bill, it would be easy to sue": Interviews Morris Dees
          and Bill Stanton.

Part Two: A Time of Judgment

"WHERE IN THE HELL . . ."

101   The previous evening: Interview, Beverly Betak.

102   As Dees watched: Interview, Morris Dees.

102   Lucy was the first black person: Diane McWhorter, *Carry Me
          Home: Birmingham, Alabama The Climactic Battle of the Civil
          Rights Revolution* (New York: Simon & Schuster, 2001), 99.

102   They drove through: Hollars, 27.

102   "exclude Autherine Lucy": : E. Culpepper Clark. *The Schoolhouse
          Door* (New York: Oxford University Press, 1993), 79.

103   when he saw *The Birth of a Nation*: Hollars, 28.

103   married . . . Betty McDaniels: To Director FBI from SAC,
          Birmingham, February 22, 1966. FBIFOI.

103   She adored her father: Interview, Betty Shelton.

104   After less than a year, however, Shelton dropped: To Director
          FBI from SAC, Birmingham, Subject: Counterintelligence
          Program, February 22, 1966. FBIFOI.

104   inexplicably to his wife: Interview, Betty Shelton.

104   she begged him: Ibid.

104   "Somebody told me": Ibid.

105   "That allowed for the leading": Howell Raines, *My Soul Is
          Rested: The Story of the Civil Rights Movement in the Deep South*
          (New York: Penguin Books, 1983), 180.

SUNDAY SCHOOL

106   "I'd like to read from First John": Interview, Morris Dees.

107   Dees liked to go: Ibid.

108   Young Dees first got: Ibid.

109   75,000 to 100,000 parade watchers: *Montgomery Advertiser*,
          January 18, 1955.

109   Coal miners and steel workers: Ibid.

110   Tampa Nugget Cigar: Seymore Trammell Unpublished
          Memoir, Alabama State Archives, 22.

110   "Bubba, Judge Wallace is going": Dees and Fiffer, 80.

111   At the annual recital: Dan T. Carter, *The Politics of Rage:*

George Wallace, the Origins of the New Conservatism, and the Transformation of American Politics (New York: Simon & Schuster, 1995), 25.

111   "I think Mozelle had more impact": Interview, Mark Kennedy.

TURNING BACK THE TIDE

112   "I think Wallace knew": Ibid.

112   "I know that my father": George Wallace Jr. and Patrick V. Cagle, *Governor George Wallace: The Man You Never Knew* (Montgomery, AL: Wallace Productions, LLC 2011), 145, 147.

112   Stephan Lesher agrees: Interview, Stephan Lesher.

112   "such conduct in my": *Montgomery Advertiser*, February 7, 1956.

112   The Justice Department was not: Carter, 84, and memo from FBI Mobile to Director, FBI, February 6, 1956. FBIFOI.

113   "rat": Memo to Mr. DeLoach from M. A. Jones, November 20, 1962. FBIFOI

113   "the judge might himself": *Montgomery Advertiser*, February 7, 1956. FBIFOI.

113   "gone soft on the nigger question": Carter, 85.

113   "courage in informing": Ibid.

"WHO IS SHELTON?"

114   soon selling 350 cakes a month: Dees and Fiffer, 79.

114   "Being around Morris Dees": Interview, Beverly Betak.

115   Dees founded a society: *Alabama Crimson*, October 1, 1957.

115   "to a huge gathering of robed Klansmen": Millard Fuller and Diane Scott, *Love in the Mortar Joints* (Association Press, 1980), 46.

116   "I'm running against": "John M. Patterson and the 1958 Alabama Gubernatorial Race" by James S. Taylor, *The Alabama Review*, July 1970, 228.

116   "a populist in the Folsom mood": Dees and Fiffer, 80.

116   "Keep Alabama Southern": *Montgomery Advertiser*, May 1, 1958.

116   WALLACE VOWS WAR ON MIXING: Ibid., May 2, 1958.

117   The Grand Dragon: Correlation Summary, Subject: Gov. George Wallace, June 9, 1964. FBIFOI.

117   Shelton took three weeks: *Montgomery Advertiser*, May 15, 1958.

117   "Not only can they nail": Raines, 305.

117   "the KKK are supporting my opposition": *Montgomery Advertiser*, May 12, 1958.

117   The article included: *Montgomery Advertiser*, May 15, 1958.

118   "Who is Shelton?": *Birmingham News*, May 15, 1958.

118   "The Klan wants": *Montgomery Advertiser*, May 17, 1958.

118   "lack of diligence": *Montgomery Advertiser*, May 23, 1958.

118   leaving it to protesters: *Montgomery Advertiser*, May 10, 1958.

118   Betty Shelton remembers: Interview, Betty Shelton.

119   defeated Wallace by 65,000 votes: *Newsweek*, June 16, 1958.

119   "Well, boys": George Wallace denied that he ever said the phrase, but Bancroft Prize–winning historian Dan T. Carter is persuasive that Wallace uttered the words. Carter, 96.

THE DAY OF RECKONING

120   "pop in": *Montgomery News*, October 11, 1959, quoted in Correlation Summary, Subject: Robert M. Shelton, April 6, 1962. FBIFOI.

120   worth $1.6 million: *Birmingham News*, November 11, 1959.

120   "much less the bunch": Correlation Summary, Subject: Robert M. Shelton, April 6, 1962. FBIFOI.

120   "were carried out, it": Ibid.

120   "if need be, citizens should take": *Montgomery Advertiser*, November 20, 1960, as quoted in ibid.

120   "Yankee lynch mob": *Montgomery Advertiser*, May 19, 1959.

121   He told his bosses: Correlation Summary, Subject: Robert M. Shelton, April 6, 1962. FBIFOI.

121   which of the professors: Patsy Sims, *The Klan* (Lexington: University Press of Kentucky, 1996), 99.

121   "We are keeping a list": Ibid., 98.

122   Most of the Alabama membership: *Montgomery Advertiser*, May 30, 1960.

123   "Zionist Jews, the money": WBAI radio interview conducted by Marsha Tompkins, December 24, 1969.

124   Birmingham his minions got on buses: Gary Thomas Rowe Jr., *My Undercover Years with the Ku Klux Klan* (New York: Bantam 1976), 20.

124   "employed in a very sensitive": To C.D. Brennan from C. C. Moore, Subject: Robert Shelton, September 17, 1970. FBIFOI. Note: The number of informants is an estimate based on 1,500 pages of FBIFOI documents on Robert Shelton open for the first time.

124   "cockroach": Eric L. Wilson report on Robert Shelton, Birmingham, April 17, 1967. FBIFOI.

125   "We want you": Rowe, 27.

FREEDOM RIDES

125   Rowe met with two: Raymond Arsenault, *Freedom Riders: 1961 and the Struggle for Racial Justice* (Oxford: Oxford University Press, 2006), 136.

125   "You've got time to beat them": Deposition, Gary Thomas Rowe, April 27, 1985, 18–19.

126   Imperial Wizard also spoke by telephone: *Montgomery Advertiser*, May 31, 1961.

126   An FBI informant said: Report of SA Pierce A. Pratt, Birmingham Re: Robert Shelton, December 11, 1963. FBIFOI.

126   A young rioter threw: Arsenault, 145.

126   a television newsman spotted: *Montgomery Advertiser*, May 31, 1961.

126   "to places where the action": May, 35.

127   "head-knockers": Rowe, 71.

127   parked near the Trailways: Thornton, 248.

127   "With the apparent connivance": Arsenault, 148.

128   "guarantee the safety of fools": Ibid., 189.

128   Shelton, wearing a silk-like: Ibid., 202.

128   "liaison aide to Shelton": Preliminary results of Investigation of United Klans of America, Knights of the Ku Klux Klan and other Klan Organizations by Richmond M. Flowers, Attorney General of Alabama, October 18, 1965, 14.

129   claw away at his face: Arsenault, 214.

129   Once the rioters knocked Barbee: Ibid.

A PERSONAL BRAWL

130   "It would be bad": Quoted in John Egerton, *Shades of Gray: Dispatches from the Modern South* (Baton Rouge: Louisiana State University Press, 1991), 216.

130   "little more than ambulance chasing": Ibid.

130   not a member: Interview, Morris Dees.

131   his name made it onto: *Montgomery Advertiser*, May 28, 1961.

132   "That's not responsive": *Montgomery Advertiser*, May 31, 1961.

133   "personal brawl": *Montgomery Advertiser*, May 30, 1961.

133   "an undue burden and restraint": *New York Times,* June 3, 1961.

133   "How can you represent": Interview, Morris Dees.

133   he stood beside Henley: *Montgomery Advertiser,* June 8, 1961.

RIDING AGAIN

134   surrounded by his security: May, 54.

134   "white trousers, red ties": Ibid.

135   run around two million copies: Deposition, Robert Shelton,
       May 17, 1985, 17.

135   he was unfailingly warm: Interview, Morris Dees.

136   drove his Mercury: Dees and Fiffer, 89.

136   Dees was also bothered: Interview, Morris Dees.

137   "I went to him": Wayne Greenhaw. *Watch Out for George
       Wallace* (Englewood Cliffs, NJ: Prentice-Hall, 1976) , 162.

137   "nigger-loving, Jew embracing Kennedys": *New York Times,*
       July 8, 1978.

138   "The UKA worked for his nomination": Correlation
       Summary, Subject: Gov. George Wallace, June 9, 1964.
       FBIFOI.

138   Carter's Klavern: McWhorter, 124–125.

138   "As far as I can remember, [Wallace]": Greenhaw, 162.

139   "scallawagging, carpetbagging liars": Quoted in Carter, 105.

139   Lurleen packed up the kids: Carter, 106.

139   On election night Shelton: Supplemental Correlation
       Summary Re: Robert Shelton, April 22, 1963. FBIFOI.

140   "This is the result": *New York Times,* September 16, 1962.

140   the 296-page official inaugural program: Official Inaugural
       Program, January 14, 1963, courtesy Mr. Thomas Lawson.

140   "Adolph Hitler must": Trammell, 61.

140   Dees had very different feelings: Interview, Morris Dees.

ETERNAL VIGILANCE

141   "a dollar-and-cents thing": Raines, 165.

142   "The Klan, they still live somewhere": McWhorter, 424.

142   "Now just let me remind you of this": Ibid., 426.

142   an FBI informant said that: Ibid., 435.

THE SCHOOLHOUSE DOOR

143   "Jesus Christ!": Quoted in Clark, 205.

144   "They will have to arrest me": *Washington Post*, February 9, 1963. FBIFOI.

144   payroll of Dixie Engineering: *New York Times*, September 12, 1964.

144   Five hundred dollars a month: Trammell, 92.

145   "I have talked to Brother": B. J. Hollars, *Opening the Doors: The Desegregation of the University of Alabama and the Fight for Civil Rights in Tuscaloosa* (Tuscaloosa: University of Alabama Press, 2013), 74.

145   Alabama state detective Ben Allen: Raines, 331.

146   "I love the people of Alabama": *New York Times*, June 6, 1963.

146   Lynne intended to spirit: Interview, Tom Lawson. (Mr. Lawson was Judge Lynne's law clerk.)

147   "Ben, do you think": Clark, 223.

148   "My father did wrong": Interview, Peggy Wallace Kennedy.

149   "to get that nigger bitch": Carter, 238.

149   "My father was so consumed": Interview, George Wallace Jr.

149   three different nights: To Director FBI from SAC, Mobile, April 7, 1963, and April 20, 1963. FBIFOI.

149   "His ambition and the bargain": George Wallace Jr. and Patrick V. Cagle, 151.

GOOD WORKING PEOPLE

150   the plane crashed on Medlin: *Greenville News*, August 28, 1963, quoted in Activities of the Ku Klu Clan, HUAC 2115-2116.

150   The Klan leader believed someone: Raines, 319.

151   Roton made copies of many: Carter, 234.

152   "sex offender": McWhorter, 493.

152   symbol taken directly: Ibid., 201.

152   Supreme Court justices: Carter, 165.

153   shut down public: Ibid, 167.

153   They ripped out the police lines: McWhorter, 495.

153   "police brutality": Carter, 172.

154   the hacks sat there: Peter Ross Range, "A Wallace is a Wallace is a Wallace," *New Times,* December 13, 1974, pp. 18–23.

154   "are not thugs; they are good": Stephan Lesher, *George Wallace: American Populist* (Reading, MA: Addison-Wesley, 1994), 248.

155   "What this country needs": *New York Times*, September 6, 1963.

155   doing it to raise: The following week Wallace participated in a

seminar on civil rights in Baltimore. The governor was already talking about running for president, and Wallace's remarks were featured on the *NBC Evening News*. "Forty-seven bombings have taken place in Birmingham since 1947 and the FBI's been in on every one of them and not a single case has been solved and not a single individual has gotten a scratch," Wallace said. "You can't bomb forty-seven times and never hurt anybody, but I will tell you what they did, they raised a million dollars": *Huntley-Brinkley Report*, September 13, 1963. FBIFOI.

"SEEDS OF HATE"

157   A witness said that: McWhorter, 654.

157   would insist to investigators: Ibid, 529.

157   "various informants advised": "Unknown Subjects Bombing of the Sixteenth Street Baptist Church, Birmingham, Alabama, September 15, 1963," quoted in Supplemental Correlation Summary, December 19, 1966.

157   "There wouldn't have": Raines, 181.

157   two of the men who had bombed: McWhorter, 529.

158   killing a sixteen-year-old: Carter, 178.

158   "for a moment": Ibid.

158   Morgan received: Interview, Camille Morgan, widow of Charles Morgan Jr.

159   "You are indeed a great": Morris Dees to Charles Morgan Jr., October 1, 1963.

159   "A substantial minority": Carter, 182.

159   "at the Alabama Highway": "Unsub: Bombing of Residence of Arthur Shores, September 4, 1963," quoted in Supplemental Correlation Summary, December 19, 1966. FBIFOI.

160   "It was established": To Director FBI from SAC, Birmingham, April 15, 1966. FBIFOI.

160   "Brothers and sisters," he began: Interview, Morris Dees.

A RACE THING

162   "There are more good people": Lesher, 271.

163   "We found our people": Greenhaw, 156–157.

164   "Why aren't you coming, Alice?": Interview, Morris Dees.

165   "It was delightful, great fun": Interview, Alice Ortega.

165   "Under a thin veneer": Fuller and Scott, 149.

166   "It was race—race, race, race": Quoted in Raines, 375.

166   "They were our family": Interview, Peggy Wallace Kennedy.

166   George Jr. learned to play guitar: Wallace Jr. and Cagle, 23.

167   The Imperial Wizard received an unsigned letter:
       Memorandum to Director FBI from SAC, Birmingham,
       Subject: Counterintelligence, November 7, 1964.

167   A letter accused: Memo F. J. Baumgardner to W. C. Sullivan,
       October 6, 1966. FBIFOI.

167   "Trying to Hide": To Director FBI from SAC, Birmingham,
       Subject: Counterintelligence Program, November 1, 1966.

167   "new counterintelligence effort [that] will take": Memorandum
       to W. C. Sullivan from F. J. Baumgardner, Subject:
       Counterintelligence Program, August 27, 1964. FBIFOI.

167   "to expose, disrupt and otherwise neutralize": Ibid.

167   "as the Communist party goes": quoted in McWhorter, 560.

168   "smear campaign": To Director FBI from SAC, Birmingham,
       Subject: Counterintelligence Program, January 5, 1967.
       FBIFOI.

168   "probably the most well-known": Counterintelligence
       Program Disruption of Hate Groups (Robert Marvin Shelton),
       September 12, 1964. FBIFOI.

168   "wear female attire for the purpose": To Director FBI from
       SAC, Charlotte, Subject: Counterintelligence Program,
       November 14, 1966. FBIFOI.

168   Beyond that, Klan attorney Matthew: To Director from SAC,
       Birmingham, November 13, 1965. FBIFOI.

168   "Operation Nancy": To Director FBI from SAC, Cleveland,
       May 31, 1966. FBIFOI.

168   a special phone: Report of Eric L. Wilson on Robert Shelton,
       Birmingham, April 17, 1967. FBIFOI.

168   he did not like grits: To Director FBI from SAC, Birmingham,
       Subject: Counterintelligence Program, February 22, 1966.
       FBIFOI.

168   "a report that Shelton has some": To SAC, Birmingham, from
       Director FBI, Subject: Counterintelligence Program, February
       4, 1966. FBIFOI.

168   "to secure information that Shelton": To Director FBI from
       SAC, Birmingham, Subject: Counterintelligence Program,
       November 13, 1964. FBIFOI.

SCRAWNY PINE

169   twenty-one state police squad cars: Thornton III, 486.

169   The police rushed forward: Carter, 242.

169   It was not until 2010: *New York Times*, November 15, 2010.

169   "career and professional": Thornton, 486

170   overwhelmingly black marchers: Discussion, Julian Bond.

170   noxious C-4 tear gas: Carter, 247.

170   a line of fifteen men: Thornton III, 488.

171   "You was attacking me, George": Lesher, 332.

172   "mobs, employing the street-warfare": *New York Times*, March 8, 1965.

172   Dees and Fuller led: Interview, Morris Dees.

173   "Morris is going to lose his": Ibid.

173   "requested that a severe beating": Quoted in Supplemental Correlation Summary, December 19, 1966. FBIFOI.

174   "Damn it, we have to go down": Deposition, Rowe, 31.

174   Shelton met with Wallace: Quoted in Supplemental Correlation Summary, December 19, 1966. FBIFOI.

174   A white minister in one of the advance: *New York Times,* March 22, 1965.

174   returned in the next two days: Deposition, Rowe, 29.

175   A black flag of mourning: Lesher, 337.

175   "Tears of patriotic pride": Interview, Morris Dees.

175   "Don't say that": Bill Jones, *The Wallace Story* (Northport, AL: American Southern Publishing Company, 1966), 432.

176   "Millard, get away from him": Interview, Morris Dees.

176   Wallace had gone back: Jones, 432.

A FOLLOWER OF CHRIST

179   Rowe was an FBI informant: Arsenault, 136.

179   "very close to the Negro": Mary Stanton, *From Selma to Sorrow: The Life and Death of Viola Liuzzo* (Athens: University of Georgia Press, 1998), 54.

179   "had been dying of cancer": *New York Times*, March 28, 1965. Duncan Howlett's 1993 biography of Reverend Reeb, *No Greater Love: The James Reeb Story*, does not even mention the cancer allegation but describes a man in full health.

180   "liberated relationship": Mary Stanton, 55.

180   "Nobody in this section of the country believes": Ida B.
       Wells-Barnett, *On Lynchings* (Amherst, MA: Humanity Books,
       2002), 29.

181   "it will be the duty of those": Ibid., 30.

181   "Why else do you see": *Playboy Interviews* (Chicago: Playboy
       Press, 1967), 230.

182   included an examination: Memo, Paul E. Shoffeitt, March 29, 1965.

182   The results showed: Memo, Paul E. Shoffeitt, April 5, 1965.

182   "You remember what that nigger": Stanton, 120.

183   "I don't believe you would": Quoted in Lesher, 344.

183   "Our polar star is Christ": Memorandum to Director, FBI
       from SAC, Boston, Subject: Counterintelligence Program,
       December 27, 1965. FBIFOI.

A PAIN IN THE STOMACH

184   Dees challenged him:Interviews, Morris Dees and Beverly Betak.

186   When one rich Cloverdale: Ibid.

A POLITICAL PRISONER

184   "hooded bigots": *New York Times*, March 27, 1965.

186   "before it is too late": Ibid.

188   to take the robe: To W. C. Sullivan from F. J. Baumgardner,
       Subject: HUAC investigation, October 25, 1965. FBIFOI.

188   more than a hundred times: *New York Times,* December 5, 1965.

188   "as small-time con men": Ibid.

189   "a lack of criminal": Intelligence Division Internal Revenue
       Service, Birmingham, Re: Robert Shelton, July 3, 1967.
       FBIFOI.

189   "We were out to destroy": Interview, Philip R. Manuel.

190   "a patent violation of the First": *New York Times*, September 16,
       1966.

190    $75,168.12 in gross revenues: Intelligence Division, Internal
       Revenue Service, Re: Robert Shelton, July 3, 1967. FBIFOI.

190   "had been a guest": To Director FBI from SAC, Jackson,
       November 17, 1966. FBIFOI.

191   "In return for Shelton's" : Supplemental Correlation Summary,
       Subject: Robert M. Shelton, April 29, 1969. FBIFOI.

191   Shelton initiated 644: Report of Eric L. Wilson on Robert
       Shelton, Birmingham, April 17, 1967. FBIFOI.

191   120,000 miles by automobile: Intelligence Division, Internal Revenue Service, Re: Robert Shelton, July 3, 1967. FBIFOI.

NEVER

193   Shelton and his Klansmen handed out: Carter, 281.

193   "Morris, they're just controlling me": Interview, Morris Dees.

194   "Well, Bill, you're a good Christian": Ibid.

194   Fuller & Dees held a company picnic: Interviews, Morris Dees and George Seitz.

CENSORED

196   "Tell Bobby what I'm doing": Interview, Morris Dees.

197   "We had done enough": Interview, George Seitz.

198   A LAMENT FOR DR. ROSE: *Tropolitan*, April 17, 2014.

199   Beverly watched her husband's: Interview, Beverly Betak.

200   "has won the fight": Carter, 319.

201   ABC had been filming: *New York Times,* June 28, 1968.

201   pelted with everything: Carter, 363.

201   It was as empty: The author was there that evening.

LOWERING THE BOOM

202   "We are chained to the infested": *New York Times*, November 18, 1969.

202   "No individual has a basic knowledge": WBAI interview, December 24, 1969.

202   estimated 14,000 members: *New York Times*, November 28, 1970.

202   "the anti-Christ conspiracy": Ibid.

202   "were taking all the gold": Report of Eric L. Wilson on Robert Shelton, Birmingham, April 17, 1967. FBIFOI.

202   90 percent of American Jews: Federal Bureau of Investigation, Birmingham, Re: Robert Marvin Shelton, April 19, 1975. FBIFOI.

202   "held all the key positions": Federal Bureau of Investigation, Birmingham, Re: Robert Marvin Shelton, February 20, 1976. FBIFOI.

203   "Textbooks are controlled": Ibid.

203   "Jewish conspiracy to take": Ibid.

203   "due to a lack of funds": Supplemental Correlation Summary, Subject: Robert Marvin Shelton, May 14, 1975. FBIFOI.

203 "out-in-the-open": Secret to the Attorney General from Director FBI, Re: Robert Shelton, December 11, 1969.

203 "fear put in them": Supplemental Correlation Summary, Subject: Robert Marvin Shelton, May 14, 1975. FBIFOI.

203 told an informant: Ibid.

204 "Hoover is a 'queer'": To Director, FBI from SAC, Columbia, January 25, 1971, and to Mr. C. D. Brennan from A. W. Gray, January 29, 1971. FBIFOI.

204 "almost handsome": *New York Times*, November 28, 1970.

PRIVATE MATTERS

204 bought a paperback copy: Interview, Morris Dees, and Dees and Fiffer, 96.

207 Maureene helped Morris: Interview, Maureene Bass.

207 "He asked me to marry him": Interviews Eleanor Davis and Maureene Bass.

207 "There's nothing you can do": Interview, Beverly Betak.

210 "I think it's only a slight exaggeration": Dees and Fiffer, 113.

212 "If your father were alive": Interview, Morris Dees.

212 "Connie, I am for you" Ibid.

212 the court ruled: http://law.justia.com/cases/federal/district-courts/FSupp/380/1244/1457873/.

FIGHTING THE FIGHT

216 Dr. Watkins runs: http://www.leagle.com/decision/19781658451FSupp1207_11479.xml/CRAIG%20 v.%20ALABAMA%20STATE%20UNIVERSITY.

A WANNABE

217 "promise them the moon": Quoted in Carter, 392.

217 "got folks believing now that": *New York Times*, May 7, 1972.

217 Edward W. Brooke as a "nigger": Ibid.

218 "Well, I guess I'm gonna die": Interview, Elvin Stanton.

219 The lawyer even suggested: Interview, Morris Dees, and discussion, Richard Viguerie.

219 "We had plenty of money": Interview, Elvin Stanton.

220 Dees helped to arrange: Interview, Morris Dees.

221 "It's unfortunate, really, that there": Sims, 95.

Part Three: Roll Call of Justice

"NOVEL, BUT UNLIKELY"

225   called the SPLC lawyers: Interview, Morris Dees.

226   "Can't be done": Dees and Fiffer, 220.

227   "Three of the four goals are not relevant": Memo, Re: Proposed "Klanwatch," October 10, 1980.

227   Even Carroll received a death threat: Interview, John Carroll.

AN EYE FOR AN EYE

228   "Darling, I'm really serious": Henry Hays to Janet Deem, January 14, 1984, SPLC Archives

228   the nightmares: Henry Hays to Janet Deem, January 24, 1984, SPLC Archive.

229   "outbursts in the courtroom": Henry Hays to Janet Deem, Wednesday night 11:10 P.M., SPLC Archives.

229   "To get me, they got my son": *Mobile Register*, June 3, 1997.

229   He had a recurring dream." Henry Hays to Janet Deem, February 24, 1984.

230   Bennie said there was no way: Deposition, Janet Deem, November 26, 1984, 18.

230   an evil man: Henry Hays to Janet Deem, February 27, 1984.

230   "dreading more than anything": Henry Hays to Janet Deem, February 15, 1974, SPLC Archives.

230   "You said I was afraid": Henry Hays to Janet Deem, March 22, 1984.

231   "when things started to look": Henry Hays to Janet Deem, April 10, 1984, SPLC Archives.

231   "He's really a devil in disguise": Henry Hays to Janet Deem, April 12, 1984, SPLC Archives.

A CLEAR AND POWERFUL MESSAGE

232   killing as many as twenty: Associated Press, April 8, 1996, and *New York Times*, June 3, 1982.

232   "This was the missing": Interview, Morris Dees.

NATURAL CONSEQUENCES

235   Mays said later: Interview, John Mays.

235   "We were all mad": Deposition, Teddy Kyzar, 31.

236   "It's a pretty well-known policy": Ibid., 64.
236   "When Morris Dees got to": Interview, Cynthia Donald Hamilton.

A BOOK OF PROPHECY

238   "We've gathered good intelligence on him": Thomas Martinez and John Guinther, *Brotherhood of Murder: How One Man's Journey through Fear Brought The Order—the Most Dangerous Racist Gang in America—to Justice* (New York: ToExcel, 1999), 158.
238   "was a type of guy": Deposition, Bennie Hays, 41.
239   Dees had asked his help: Dees and Fiffer, 215.
239   "I don't know where you got": Interview, Morris Dees.
240   Gail and Frank Cox were also stunned: Interviews, Frank Cox and Gail Cox Knowles.
240   "I'm sorry about your son": Interview, Morris Dees.
240   would be a conflict of interest: Interview, John Mays.
240   "Bennie was one of the most": Ibid.

"AS YOU LIE, YOU FORGET"

241   twenty-five-foot tall iron cross: Bill Stanton, 210.
241   diesel fuel–soaked rags: Deposition, Denise Hays, 33.
242   "Mr. Hays, you know I have no control": Interview, Morris Dees.
243   "As you lie, you forget": Interview, E. T. Rolison, and *Mobile Press-Register,* June 4, 1997.
243   took his cane with both hands: *Mobile Press-Register*, October 23, 1984.
243   three years in prison: *Mobile Press-Register*, November 29, 1984.
244   "What do you mean by that?": Deposition, Henry Hays, 8.
244   Stanton had knocked on Opal's door: Deposition, Opal Hays, 22.
245   "For what reason did you get": Deposition, Thaddeus Betancourt, 9.
246   founded by six: Wyn Wade, *The Fiery Cross: The Klux Klan in America* (New York: Simon & Schuster, 1987), 33.

INTRUDERS IN THE NIGHT

247   He appeared not to give a damn what people thought: Egerton, 226.

248 *"Two men in camouflage":* Interview, Morris Dees.

248 "First, they burn down: Ibid.

"BLOOD WILL FLOW"

249 "Blood will flow and it grieves me": *New York Times,* February 7, 1986.

250 "And it wasn't a discussion": Deposition, James Knowles, March 12, 1985, 28.

252 Stanton had flown up to New York: Interview, Bill Stanton.

252 "I learned my lesson": Deposition, Robert Shelton, April 17, 1985, 59.

253 "I think we may have a little": Ibid., 68.

SHOTS IN THE NIGHT

253 "You'll be the star of the show": Interview, Morris Dees.

254 "I won't sit in the same": Ibid.

255 "The building design establishes": Egerton, 231.

257 trying to get black men appointed to the police: *Wilmington Morning Star,* April 5, 1979.

257 He was about to give up: Interview, Joe Roy.

258 "No, you didn't redeem": Ibid.

258 Roy looked at those: Ibid.

259 Dees loosened his tie: Interview, Morris Dees.

259 Dees offered to rent him: Dees and Fiffer, 309.

260 "of some sort of settlement": James Morris to Morris Dees, January 12, 1987.

260 study for his B.A.: James L. Knowles Jr. to Morris Dees, February 17, 1987.

261 On May 15, 1985, Opal: *Mobile Register,* June 4, 1997.

THE END OF AN ERA

262 "For weeks now he has been": *Montgomery Advertiser,* March 22, 1983.

262 Wallace took 100 milligrams: Associated Press, January 23, 1985.

262 Wallace spent fifty-one days: Ibid.

263 25 percent of the black: *New York Times,* January 27, 1983.

263 "Forgiveness is in our Christian upbringing": *Ebony,* September 1983.

264   "I have a lot of regrets": Interview, Kenneth Mullinax.

264   "a person's profession described as that of 'hereditary
       bagman'": *New York Times*, June 3, 1990.

264   "that legal action is appropriate": Elvin Stanton to Maury D.
       Smith, July 16, 1990. Wallace Papers, Alabama State Archives.

265   Wallace preferred to sit: Carter, 464.

SENDING A SIGNAL

266   His grandchildren were taunted: Interviews, Beverly, Jason,
       and Angela Shelton.

266   neighbors liked to be around: Interview, Cynthia Donald
       Hamilton.

268   "Now if you want to cite": *Beulah Mae Donald v. United Klans
       of America, et al.*, February 10, 1987, 4.

269   His job was to watch: Interview, Richard Cohen.

270   Dees had named: Interview, Morris Dees.

270   Cohen had a different: Interview, Richard Cohen.

270   "I do want to object": *Beulah Mae Donald v. United Klans of
       America, et al.*, February 10, 1987, 176.

CURVEBALLS

272   "We have a piece of": Ibid., p. 66.

273   "Everything that happened": Ibid., 73.

"NICE JOB, DADDY"

276   "Nice job, Daddy": Interview, Morris Dees.

278   "And finally Donald just fell": *Beulah Mae Donald v. United
       Klans of America, et al.*, February 10, 1987, 192.

280   "Well, that's between you": Ibid., 248.

281   "I plead my right": Ibid., 263.

PURITY OF THE RACE

282   she saw Kyzar standing: Interview, Morris Dees.

282   When Ellie got back: Ibid.

283   "It was a pretty sight": *Beulah Mae Donald v. United Klans of
       America, et al.*, February 11, 1987, 302.

284   "Worse than that": Ibid., 333.

285   "Shelton was totally in charge": Deposition, Gary Thomas
       Rowe, April 27, 1985, 20.

285   "Damn it, we had": Ibid., 31.

286   "Yeah, he talked about during": *Beulah Mae Donald v. United Klans of America,* February 11, 1987, 455.

A JURY OF ONE'S PEERS

289   Dees was convinced: Interview, Morris Dees.

TRADING PLACES

291   "I want to make it real clear": *Beulah Mae Donald v. United Klans of America, et al.,* February 12, 1987, 559.

291   "I hope at the end of this case": Ibid., February 13, 1987, 586.

293   Knowles did not want: Interview, James Knowles.

294   "I forgive you": *New York Times,* November 1, 1987.

"THAT'S MY MOM"

295   "I could not help but be": *Beulah Mae Donald v. United Klans of America, et al.* February 12, 1987, 612.

298   Cohen busied himself preparing: Interview, Richard Cohen.

298   he worried that the judge: Interview, Morris Dees.

300   "The strongest thing. . . .": Kirkland, "Beyond the Aura of Respectability: The Civil Rights Movement in Mobile, Alabama," "190.

300   "He would say": Ibid.

300   Betancourt had despised: Interview, Thaddeus Betancourt.

300   "I just hope it helps": *New York Times,* March 12, 1987.

300   "I don't need it": *New York Times,* November 1, 1987.

REMEMBRANCE

302   Dees lamented how: Interview, Morris Dees.

302   Flying down to Montgomery: Interview, Richard Cohen.

302   "one of the most notorious characters": *Atlanta Journal* and *Atlanta Constitution,* October 26, 1987.

303   "That this white southerner": Ibid.

303   sold for a net amount: Contract of Sale, Pritchett-Moore, Inc., January 27, 1988.

304   granddaughter Amanda talked: Interview, Amanda Shelton.

304   "The Klan is my belief, my religion": Quoted in *New York Times,* March 20, 2003.

304   Shelton's sixteen-year-old grandson: Interview, Jason Shelton.

305   "Morris, I'm not going to be able": Dees and Fiffer, 334.

305   "Now the world will remember": Ibid.

A QUESTION OF JUSTICE

306   three newly elected black council: Kirkland, "Beyond the Aura of Respectability: The Civil Rights Movement in Mobile, Alabama," 193.

306   "Nothing was good for him": Interview, Cynthia Donald Hamilton.

306   "Go to hell": Undated clipping, *Mobile Press-Register.*

307   looked like Jesus: Interview, Frank Cox.

307   no murderer: Ibid.

308   The DA decided that he would: Interview, Chris Galanos.

308   "It was Frank Cox . . .": Interview, Frank Cox.

308   "Punishing a person": *Mobile Press-Register*, June 23, 1989.

309   "If I had been charged": *Mobile Register,* August 9, 1993.

309   diagnosed with cardiac artery disease: Admission Record, Mary Rutan Hospital, July 29, 1992.

310   taken off the plane wearing: *Mobile Register*, May 8, 1993.

310   favorite book, *Wild Freedom*: *Mobile Register*, June 5, 1997.

310   It is the story of Tom: Max Brand, *Wild Freedom* (London: Pearl Necklace Books, 2014).

311   "You'll remember a smile": *Mobile Register,* June 5, 1997.

311   seemingly stoned much of the time: Rick Kerger, "Hatred Wins," unpublished manuscript, 16.

312   executed 118 black prisoners: These figures are from the research of the Equal Justice Initiative in Montgomery and http://en.wikipedia.org/wiki/Yellow_Mama.

312   Stanley said it was bad: *Mobile Register*, June 10, 1997.

312   "What I just witnessed": *Orlando Sentinel*, June 7, 1997.

DEATH HAS NO HOLD

314   George and Lurleen Wallace Center for the Study of Southern Politics: Proposal for George and Lurleen Wallace Center for the Study of Southern Politics, Wallace Papers at Alabama State Archives.

314   "I'm Morris Dees": The author was present.

315   As Jack Boot, the editor of : https://www.stormfront.org/forum/t511719-2/.

Bibliography

Arsenault, Raymond. *Freedom Riders: 1961 and the Struggle for Racial Justice.* Oxford: Oxford UP, 2006. Print.

Ball, Edward. *Slaves in the Family.* New York: Farrar, Straus and Giroux, 1998. Print.

Bass, Jack. *Taming the Storm: The Life and Times of Judge Frank M. Johnson and the South's Fight over Civil Rights.* New York: Doubleday, 1993. Print.

Bivens, Shawn A. *Mobile Alabama's People of Color: A Tricentennial History, 1702-2002.* Victoria, B.C.: Trafford, 2004. Print.

Boyle, Kevin. *Arc of Justice: A Saga of Race, Civil Rights, and Murder in the Jazz Age.* New York: Henry Holt, 2004. Print.

Bragg, Rick. *Ava's Man.* New York: Alfred A. Knopf, 2001. Print.

Branch, Taylor. *Parting the Waters: America in the King Years, 1954–63.* New York: Simon & Schuster, 1988. Print.

Cannon, Lou. *President Reagan: The Role of a Lifetime.* New York: Simon & Schuster, 1991. Print.

Carter, Dan T. *The Politics of Rage: George Wallace, the Origins of the New Conservatism, and the Transformation of American Politics.* New York: Simon & Schuster, 1995. Print.

Chestnut, J. L., and Julia Cass. *Black in Selma: The Uncommon Life of J. L. Chestnut, Jr.* New York: Farrar, Straus and Giroux, 1990. Print.

Clark, E. Culpepper. *The Schoolhouse Door: Segregation's Last Stand at the University of Alabama.* New York: Oxford University Press, 1993. Print.

Dattel, Eugene R. *Cotton and Race in the Making of America: The Human Costs of Economic Power.* Chicago: Ivan R. Dee, 2009. Print.

Dees, Morris, and James Corcoran. *Gathering Storm: America's Militia Threat.* New York: HarperCollins, 1996. Print.

Dees, Morris, and Steve Fiffer. *A Lawyer's Journey: The Morris Dees Story.* Chicago: American Bar Association, 2001. Print.

Dixon, Thomas, with an introduction by Cary D. Wintz. *The Clansman: An Historical Romance of the Ku Klux Klan*. Armonk, NY: M. E. Sharpe, 2001. Print.

Dray, Philip. *At the Hands of Persons Unknown: The Lynching of Black America*. New York: Random House, 2002. Kindle.

DuBois, W. E. B. *The Souls of Black Folk*. New York: Dodd, Mead and Company, 1961. Print.

Egerton, John. *Shades of Gray: Dispatches from the Modern South*. Baton Rouge: Louisiana State University Press, 1991. Print.

Ford, Lacy K. *Deliver Us from Evil: The Slavery Question in the Old South*. New York: Oxford University Press, 2009. Print.

Frady, Marshall. *Southerners: A Journalist's Odyssey*. New York: New American Library, 1980. Print.

Fuller, Millard. *Beyond the American Dream*. Macon, GA: Smyth & Helwys, 2010. Print.

Fuller, Millard, and Diane Scott, *Love in the Mortar Joints: The Story of Habitat for Humanity*. Association Press, 1980.

Greenhaw, Wayne. *Fighting the Devil in Dixie: How Civil Rights Activists Took on the Ku Klux Klan in Alabama*. Chicago: Lawrence Hill, 2011. Print.

———. *Watch out for George Wallace*. Englewood Cliffs, NJ: Prentice-Hall, 1976. Print.

Hart, Gary. *Right from the Start: A Chronicle of the McGovern Campaign*. New York: Quadrangle, 1973. Print.

Hollars, B. J. *Opening the Doors: The Desegregation of the University of Alabama and the Fight for Civil Rights in Tuscaloosa*. Tuscaloosa: University of Alabama Press, 2013. Print.

———. *Thirteen Loops: Race, Violence, and the Last Lynching in America*. Tuscaloosa: University of Alabama Press, 2011. Print.

Johnson, Walter. *River of Dark Dreams: Slavery and Empire in the Cotton Kingdom*. Cambridge, MA: Harvard University Press, 2013. Print.

Jones, Bill. *The Wallace Story*. Northport, AL: American Southern Publishing Company, 1966. Print.

King, Gilbert. *Devil in the Grove: Thurgood Marshall, the Groveland Boys, and the Dawn of a New America*. New York: Harper, 2012. Print.

Lemann, Nicholas. *The Promised Land: The Great Black Migration and How It Changed America*. New York: Alfred A. Knopf, 1991. Print.

Lesher, Stephan. *George Wallace: American Populist*. Reading, MA: Addison-Wesley, 1994. Print.

Levine, Bruce C. *The Fall of the House of Dixie: The Civil War and the Social Revolution That Transformed the South*. New York: Random House, 2013. Print.

Lewis, John, with Michael D'Orso. *Walking with the Wind: A Memoir of the Movement*. New York: Simon & Schuster, 1998. Print.

Martinez, Thomas, with John Guinther. *Brotherhood of Murder*. New York: McGraw-Hill, 1988. Print.

May, Gary. *The Informant: The FBI, the Ku Klux Klan, and the Murder of Viola Liuzzo*. New Haven, CT: Yale University Press, 2005. Print.

McWhorter, Diane. *Carry Me Home: Birmingham, Alabama: The Climactic Battle of the Civil Rights Revolution*. New York: Simon & Schuster, 2001. Print.

Raines, Howell. *My Soul Is Rested: Movement Days in the Deep South Remembered*. New York: Putnam, 1977. Print.

Rowe, Gary Thomas. *My Undercover Years with the Ku Klux Klan*. New York: Bantam, 1976. Print.

Seay, Solomon S., with Delores R. Boyd. *Jim Crow and Me: Stories from My Life as a Civil Rights Lawyer*. Montgomery, AL: NewSouth Books, 2008. Print.

Sikora, Frank. *Until Justice Rolls Down: The Birmingham Church Bombing Case*. Tuscaloosa: University of Alabama Press, 1991. Print.

Sims, Patsy. *The Klan*. Lexington: University Press of Kentucky: 1996. Print.

Singular, Stephen. *Talked to Death: The Life and Murder of Alan Berg*. New York: Beech Tree, 1987. Print.

Slavery in America: The Montgomery Slave Trade. Montgomery, AL: Equal Justice Initiative, 2013. Print.

Stanton, Mary. *From Selma to Sorrow: The Life and Death of Viola Liuzzo*. Athens: University of Georgia Press, 1998. Print.

Thorne, T. K. *Last Chance for Justice: How Relentless Investigators Uncovered New Evidence Convicting the Birmingham Church Bombers*. Chicago: Lawrence Hill, 2013. Print.

Thornton, J. Mills. *Dividing Lines: Municipal Politics and the Struggle for Civil Rights in Montgomery, Birmingham, and Selma*. Tuscaloosa: University of Alabama Press, 2002. Print.

Twitty, W. Bradley. *Y'all Come*. Nashville, TN: Hermitage, 1962. Print.

Wade, Wyn Craig. *The Fiery Cross: The Ku Klux Klan in America*. New York: Simon & Schuster, 1987. Print.

Wallace, George, Jr., and Patrick V. Cagle. *Governor George Wallace: The Man You Never Knew*. Montgomery, AL: Wallace Productions, LLC, 2011. Print.

Wells-Barnett, Ida B. *On Lynchings*. Amherst, NY: Humanity, 2002. Print.

Wilkerson, Isabel. *The Warmth of Other Suns: The Epic Story of America's Great Migration*. New York: Random House, 2010. Print.

Williamson, Joel. *A Rage for Order: Black-White Relations in the American South since Emancipation*. New York: Oxford University Press, 1986. Print.

Woodward, C. Vann. *The Strange Career of Jim Crow*. New York: Oxford University Press, 1974. Print.

———. *Tom Watson: Agrarian Rebel*. New York: Oxford University Press, 1963. Print.

Index

ALSO BY LAURENCE LEAMER

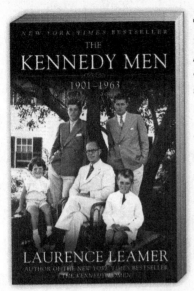

THE KENNEDY MEN
1901–1963
Available in eBook and Digital Audio

"If there is only one book about the Kennedys to read, this must be it."

— Myer Feldman,
Deputy Special Counsel to President Kennedy

"Engaging and fast-moving...a stirring narrative."

— *Publishers Weekly*

The renowned biographer and *New York Times* bestselling author of *The Kennedy Women* returns with this first volume in a multigenerational history that will forever change the way America views its most famous family...

SONS OF CAMELOT
The Fate of an American Dynasty
Available in eBook and Digital Audio

"Leamer's interviews with his friends and associates provide the fullest portrait of [JFK Jr.'s] adult life to date."

— *New York Times Book Review*

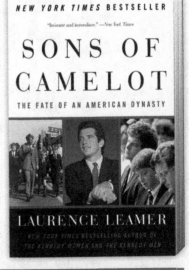

Sons of Camelot is the compelling story of that message and how it shaped each Kennedy son and grandson in the aftermath of President John F. Kennedy's death. Based on five years of rigorous research and unprecedented cooperation from both the Kennedys and the Shrivers, *Sons of Camelot* examines the lives characterized by overwhelming drama—from the most spectacular mishaps, excesses, and tragedies to the remarkable accomplishments that have led to better lives for Americans and others around the world.